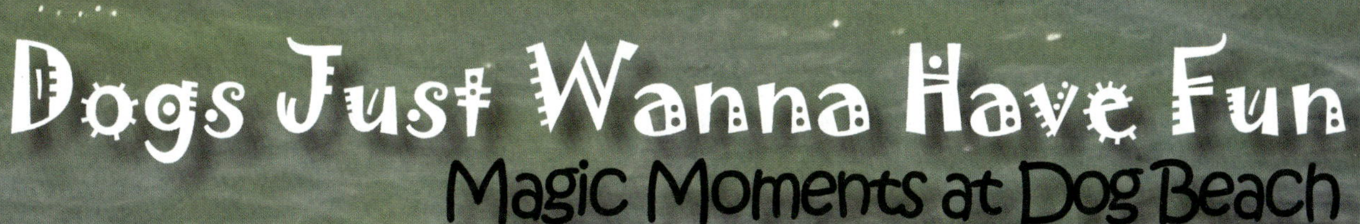

# Dogs Just Wanna Have Fun

## Magic Moments at Dog Beach

Elisabeth Haug

Sharing Magic Moments
2129 Sand Crest Way,
San Marcos, CA 92078

ISBN: 9780982606407

Library of Congress number

First edition

Photography Elisabeth Haug
Editor Lars Perner

**More info and photographs at http://SharingMagicMoments.com**

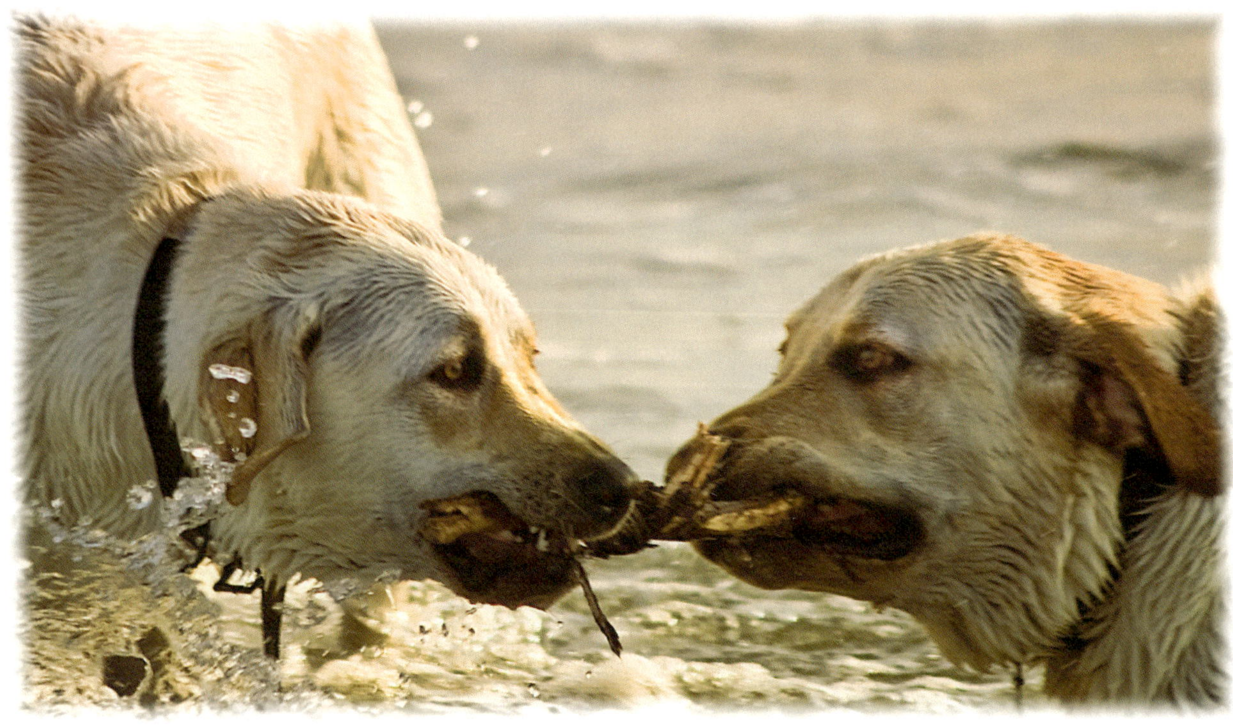

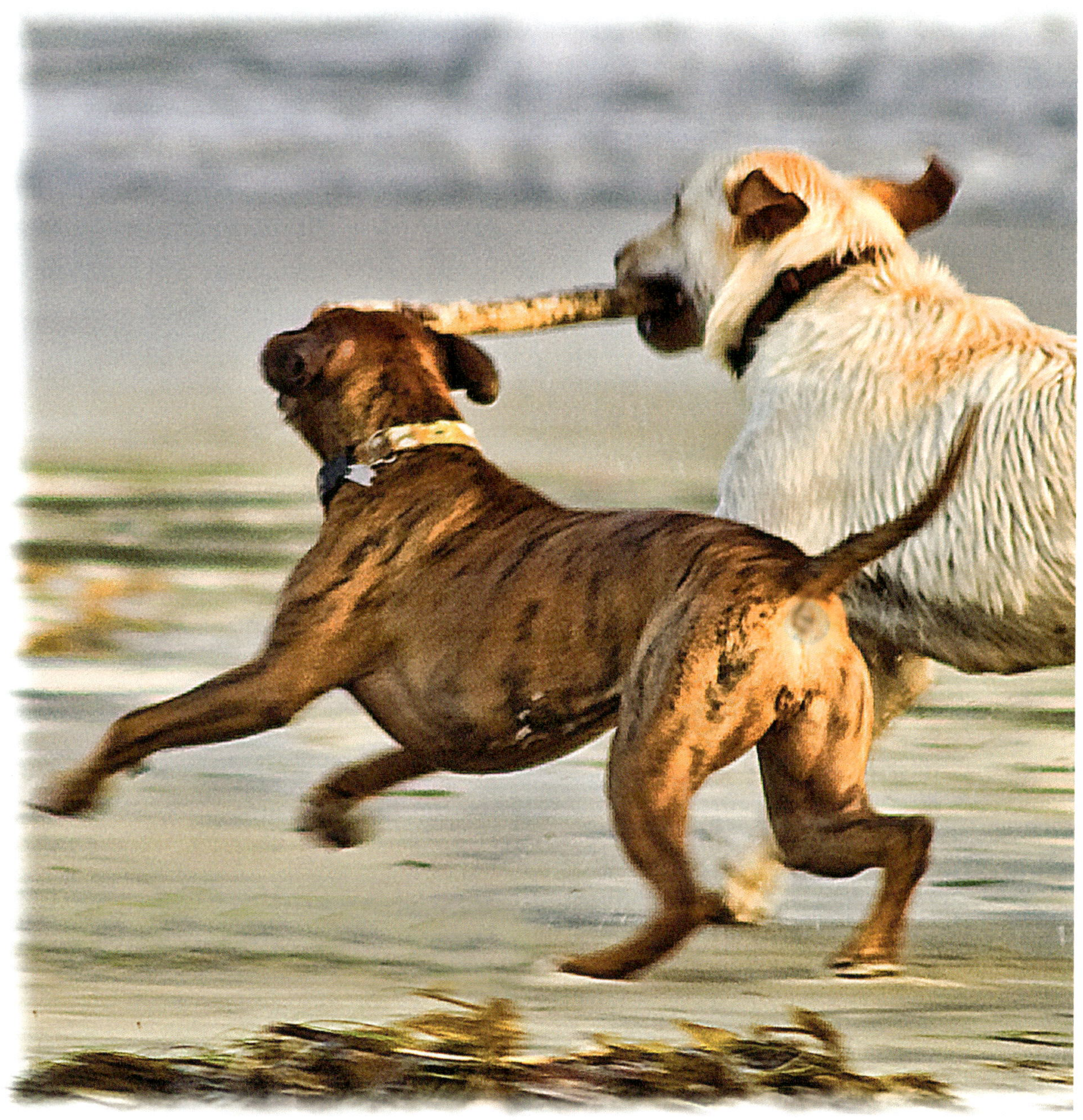

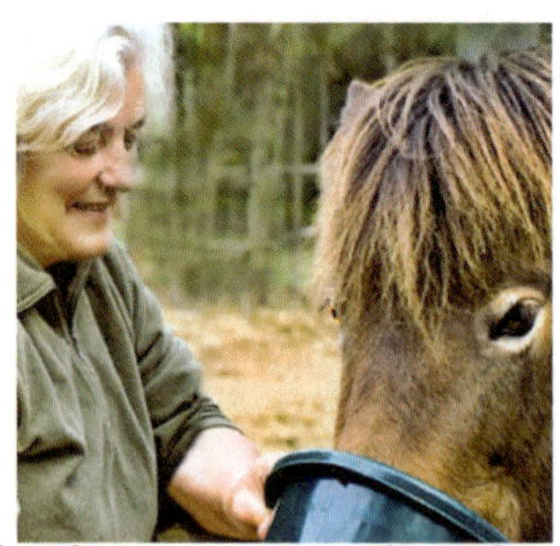

# About the Photographer:

"Looking back", says author and photographer, Elisabeth Haug, "I realize that my life has always been about preserving magic moments and sharing them. It's amazing how great life is when you focus on the positive.

"I've had a fantastic life filled with opportunities. There have been trials and tribulations, of course, but we all need those in order for growth. The main thing is for us to keep learning—not by berating ourselves for perceived failures, but by constantly envisioning ways to improve our results—all the time getting a tad closer to the life we truly desire.

"My many adventures have all been fulfilling, yet—beyond a doubt—the most rewarding has been my children and my grand kids."

"I am an American citizen now and live close to San Diego in California, but I was born in Denmark at the tail end of World War II. Some might imagine that's why world peace and happiness for all has become my biggest dream. But I believe there is more. The universal dream of peace is one we all share. It's a part of the human spirit. When we tend to label it as unrealistic, it is just that the magnitude of the project makes it difficult for us to envision.

"I believe that we can at least make a dent, if we all join in sharing our magic moments rather than our gripes. Just click away! Everybody has cameras these days and there are millions of Internet uploading sites to choose from.

"My parents had gypsy blood. We moved continually. Apart from Denmark—our home base—we lived in Barbados, Canada, Switzerland, Italy, and Spain. I attended fourteen schools before I was admitted to engineering school in Copenhagen—one of three girls in a class of three hundred freshmen.

"As time went by, I realized that nature, animals, and communication were closer to my heart than engineering. I became involved with Icelandic Horses and have been surrounded by them ever since.

"On Thanksgiving Day in 1978, my family and I landed in Los Angeles with a plane load of Icelandic Horses. We settled in Paso Robles, California and began the challenging somewhat challenging job of pioneering an unknown pony breed in a totally Quarter

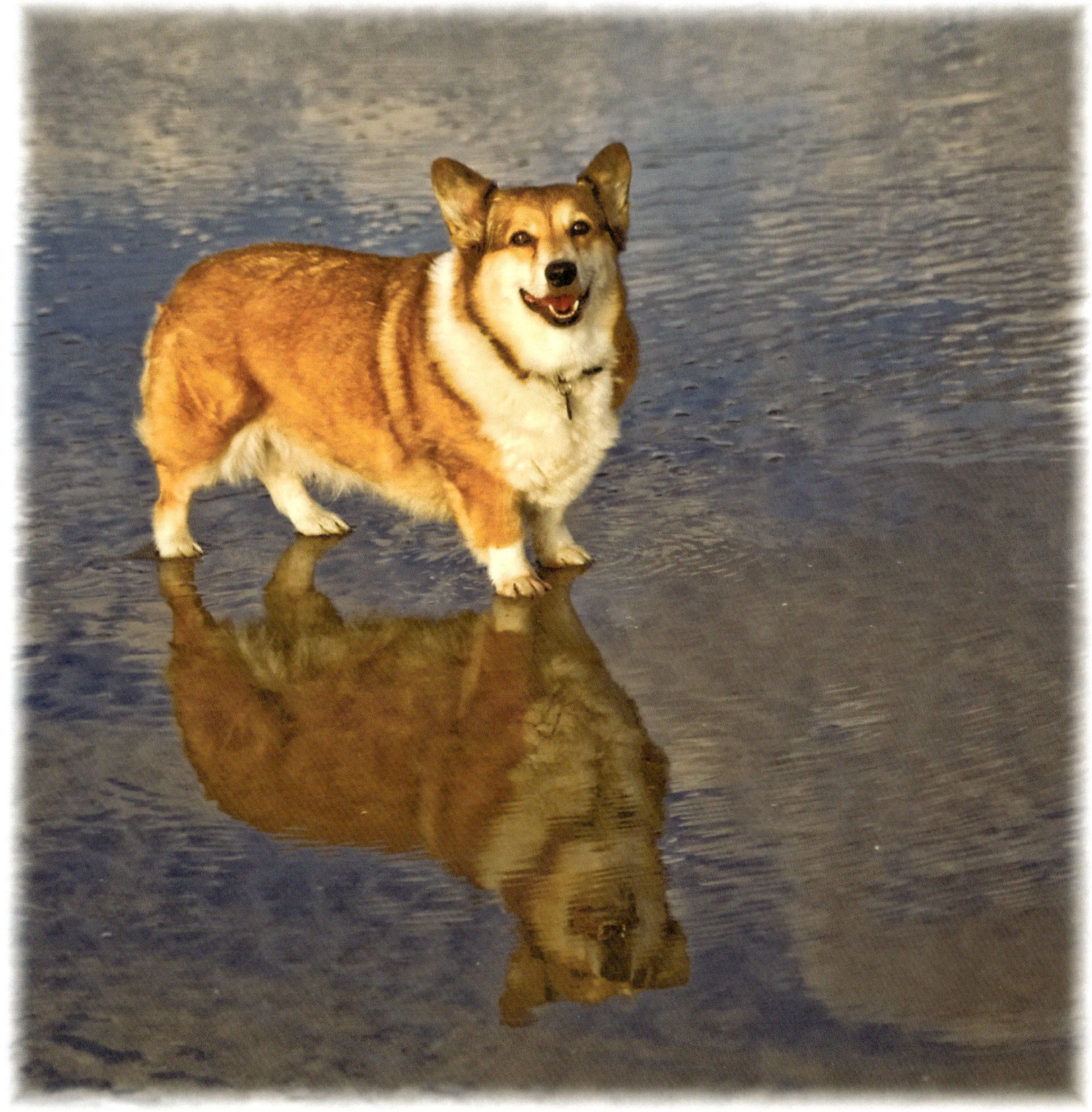

*Elisabeth's companion, Bucky*

Horse, cowboy territory. I was dubbed the "Pony Lady" and serious horse people thought I was funny. What saved the day, and made the project possible, was the charisma of the breed. Their unpretentious, natural beauty slowly but surely won people's hearts.

"Some years ago, when I retired from active horse business, I decided to focus my next career on some of the other things I have always loved—books, photography, and video.  The result—so far—is the following books:

ISBN:  9780982606407     *Dogs Just Wanna have Fun—Magic Moments at Dog Beach*
ISBN:  9780966271584  *The Legend of God and Pegasus*
ISBN:  9780966271553  *New Age Vikings—Volume One The Icelandic Horse*
ISBN:  9780966271522  *New Age Vikings—Volume Two Horsegathering in Iceland*
ISBN:  9780966271508  *In the Hoofprints of the Vikings*
ISBN:  9780966271515  *A Finger on the Shutter—A sharpshooter's guide to action Photography.*

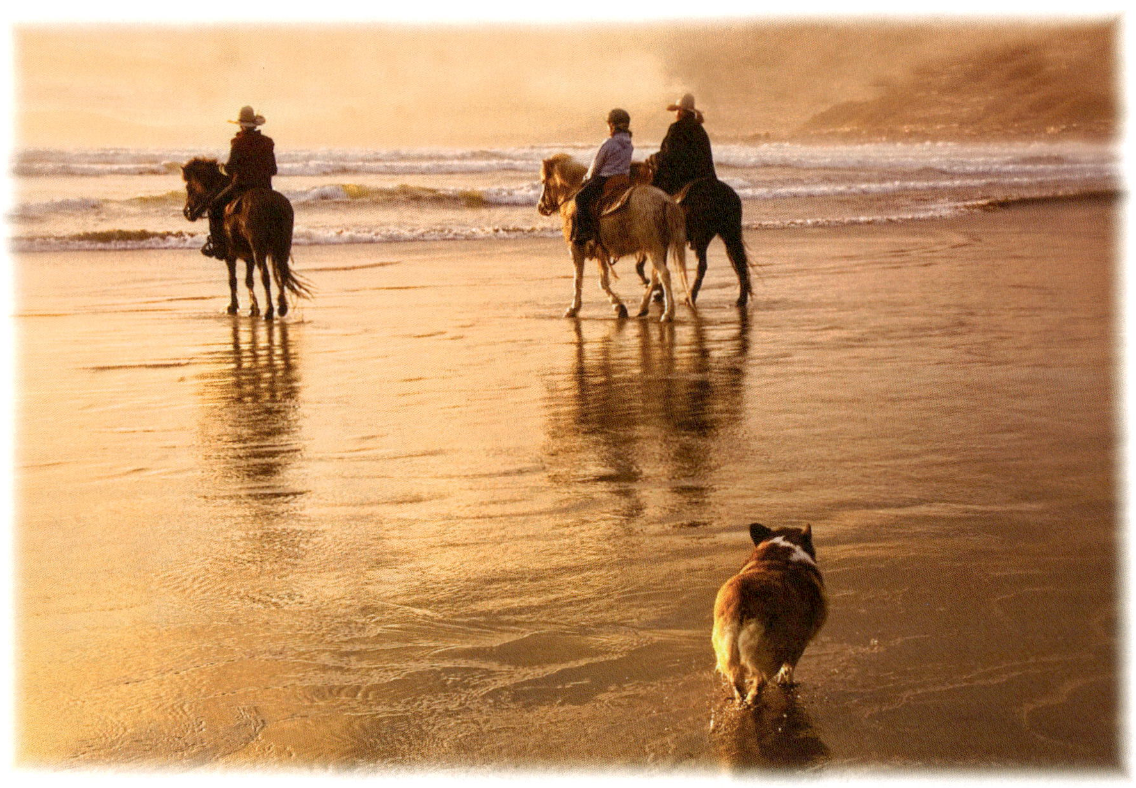

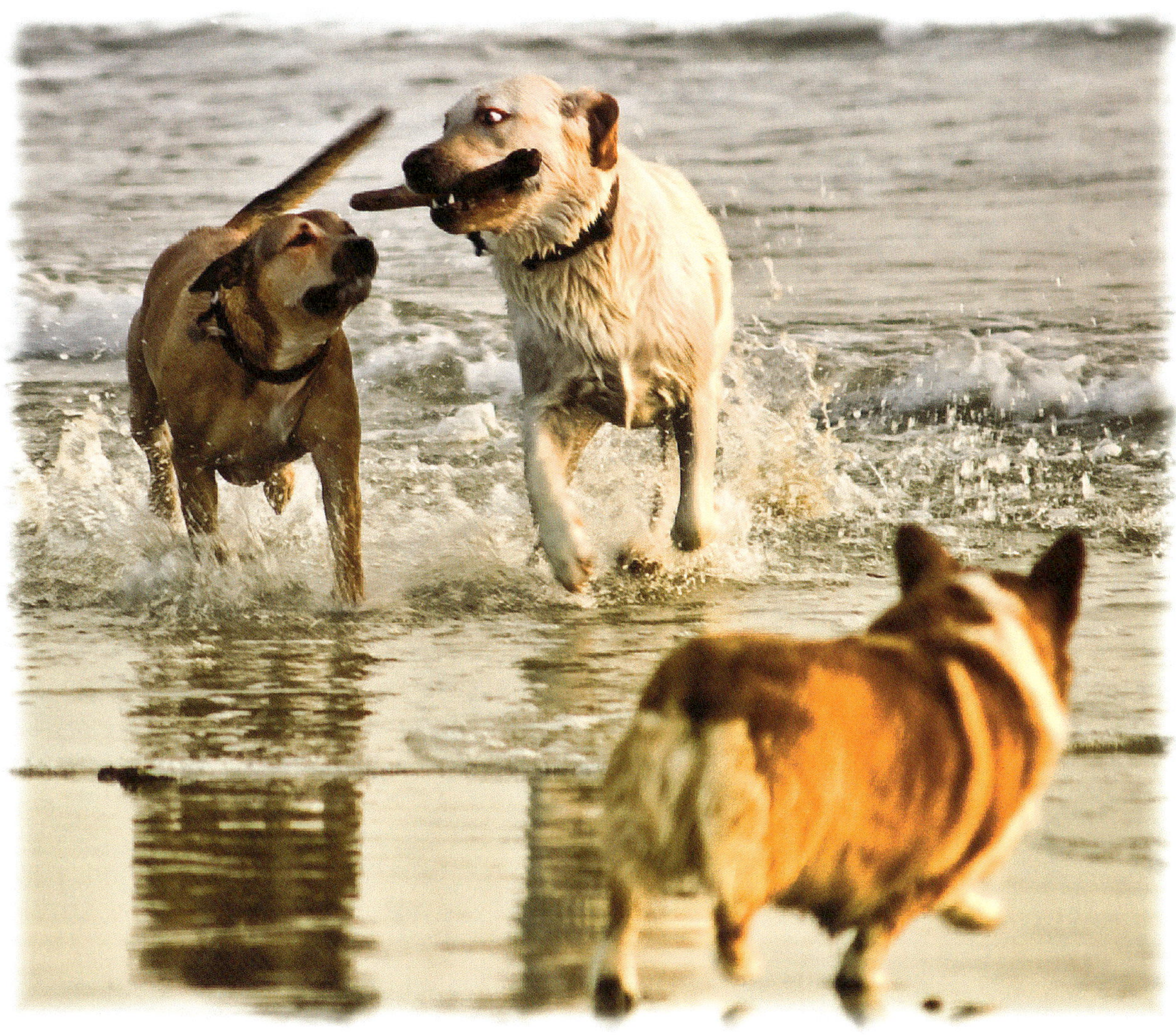

"You  can get read excerpts from the books, view countless photos and videos, and  get more information on my website: **http://SharingMagicMoments.com**

# About Dog Beach

Join me in a celebration of Dog Beach in Del Mar. Regardless of whether you are a frequent visitor or live too far away to have had the pleasure of being there, I guarantee you will enjoy the adventure. The atmosphere is uplifting—fun, happy, and active. It supplies you with all the vitamins and minerals of the soul you need as a supplement in our busy, complicated, modern environment. Sun, surf, sea, and beach! What better tools could one employ  in connecting to the universe?

Dog Beach is the happening place in Del Mar, a small, friendly coastal community close to San Diego in Southern California. Here's always commotion and a party atmosphere.  It's one of the few beaches in Southern California that most of the year allow dogs to run free.

People come from near and far as often as they can to enjoy the heartening energy. That's understandable. I'd go myself just for the merriment even if I didn't have Bucky, my little Welsh Corgi, to please!

Dog Beach is like a community in itself. Here people easily connect and get to know one another. It's a perfect setting. Everybody shares common interests—a love of action, fun, nature, and animals. Nothing breaks the ice as easily as somebody else's dog approaching you to socialize with yours. It inspiring to see so many different types of people and dogs getting along like one big, happy family.

Dog Beach is especially popular around sunset. Seeing the dogs and their owners romp at the end of a busy day reminds one of a group kids celebrating the end of a long school day.

The first few times I experienced Dog Beach, I was amazed at the harmony. So many loose dogs and no sign whatsoever of aggression. Bands of strange dogs cavorting through the waves and sharing each other's toys without rancor. Now—after years of visiting—I take the laid back atmosphere for granted. My perception of dog behavior has changed.

Another thing about Dog Beach that has altered my concept of dogs is an incredibly popular event—the dog surf-a-thon—that is hosted yearly by the Helen Woodward Animal Center. Who would have imagined dogs riding the waves and even enjoying it? Peruse the photos in the book for yourself, if you can't believe it. Surely, only Californians could have come up with an idea like this!

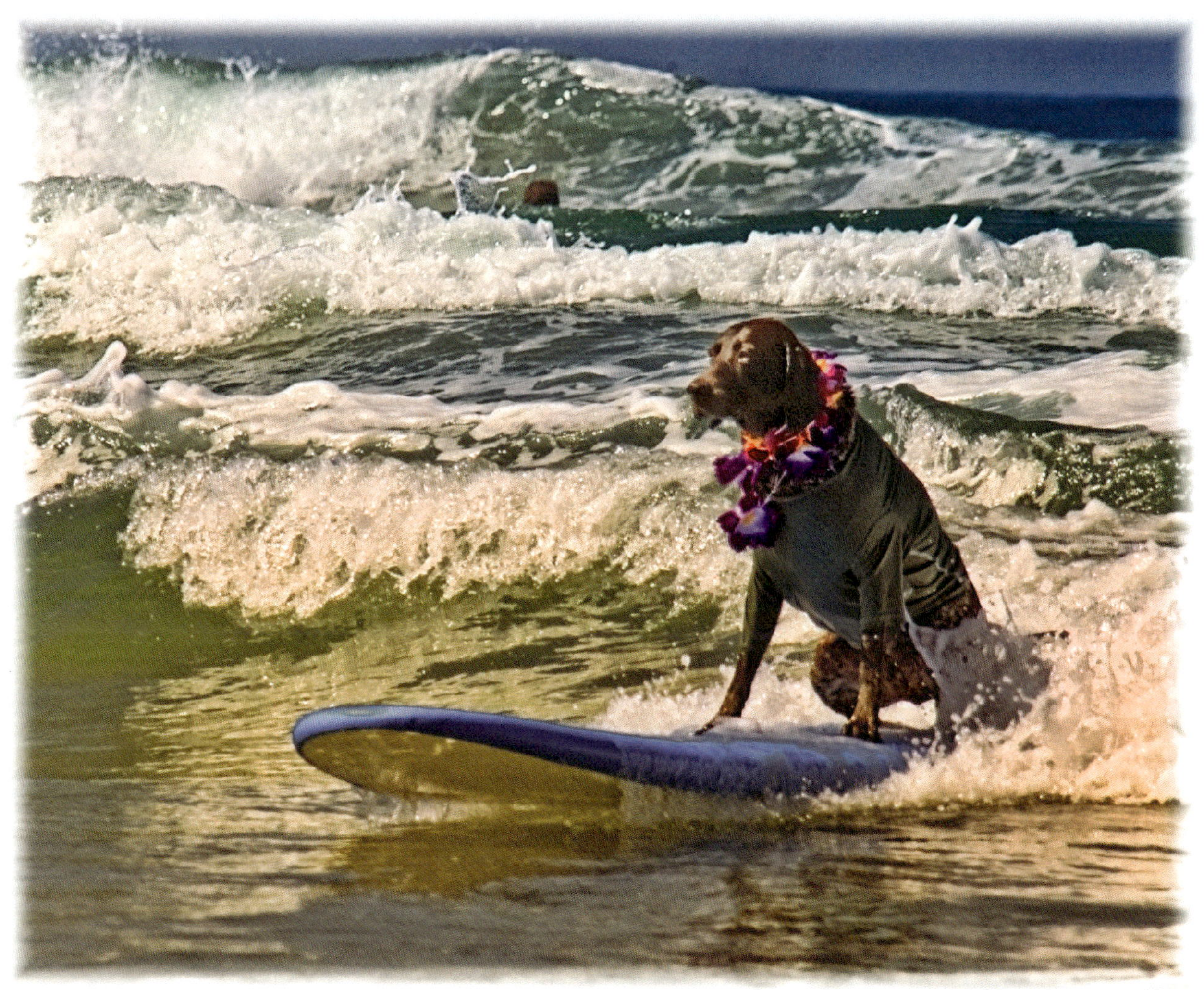

**A few bits of advice if you a planning a visit to Dog Beach:**

- Plan way more time than you expect to spend. Once you are there, you won't want to go home.
- For the optimal experience, check the tide tables for low tide timing.
- Rule of thumb: Dogs must be leashed between Memorial Day and Labor Day. Dates may be subject to change.
- Plastic sleeves (bags) are supplied for emergency cleanup.
- Coming from Interstate 5, exit at Via de la Valle and go west. When the road intersects with Highway 101, after a mile or so, turn left (south). Parking begins almost straight away, but most of the time you can find parking closer.
- Be sure to feed your parking meter abundantly. The meter maids are very zealous at this location.

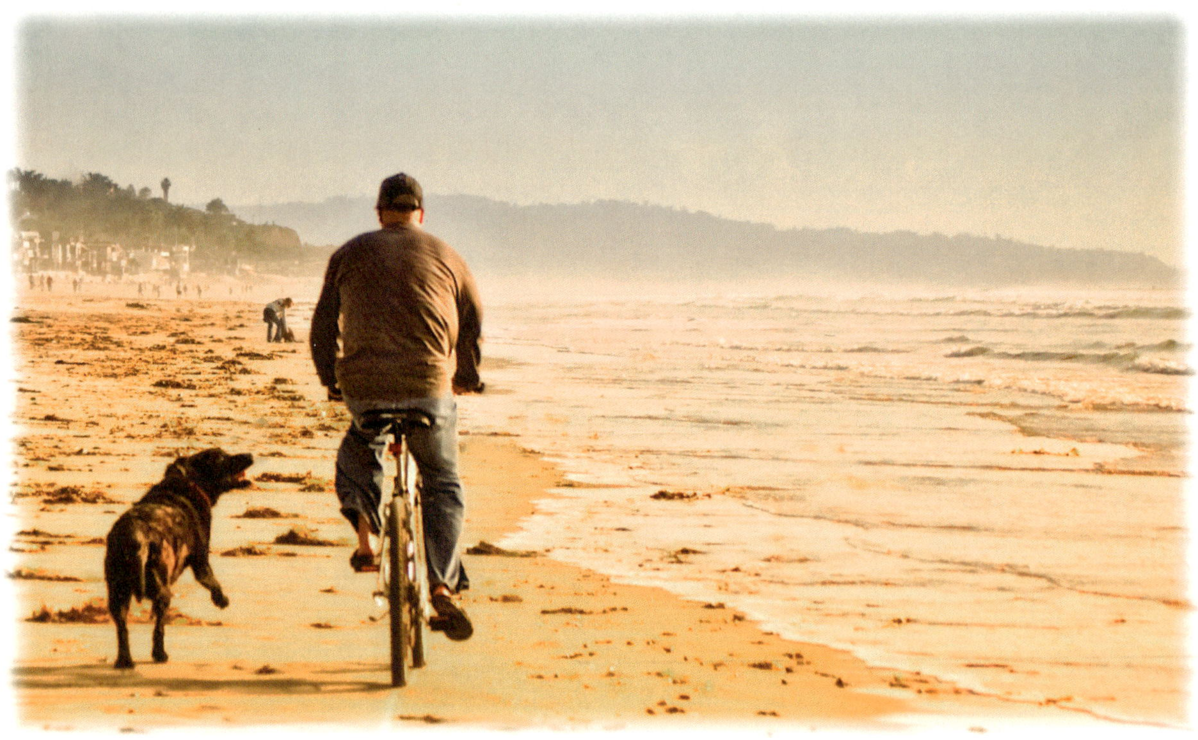

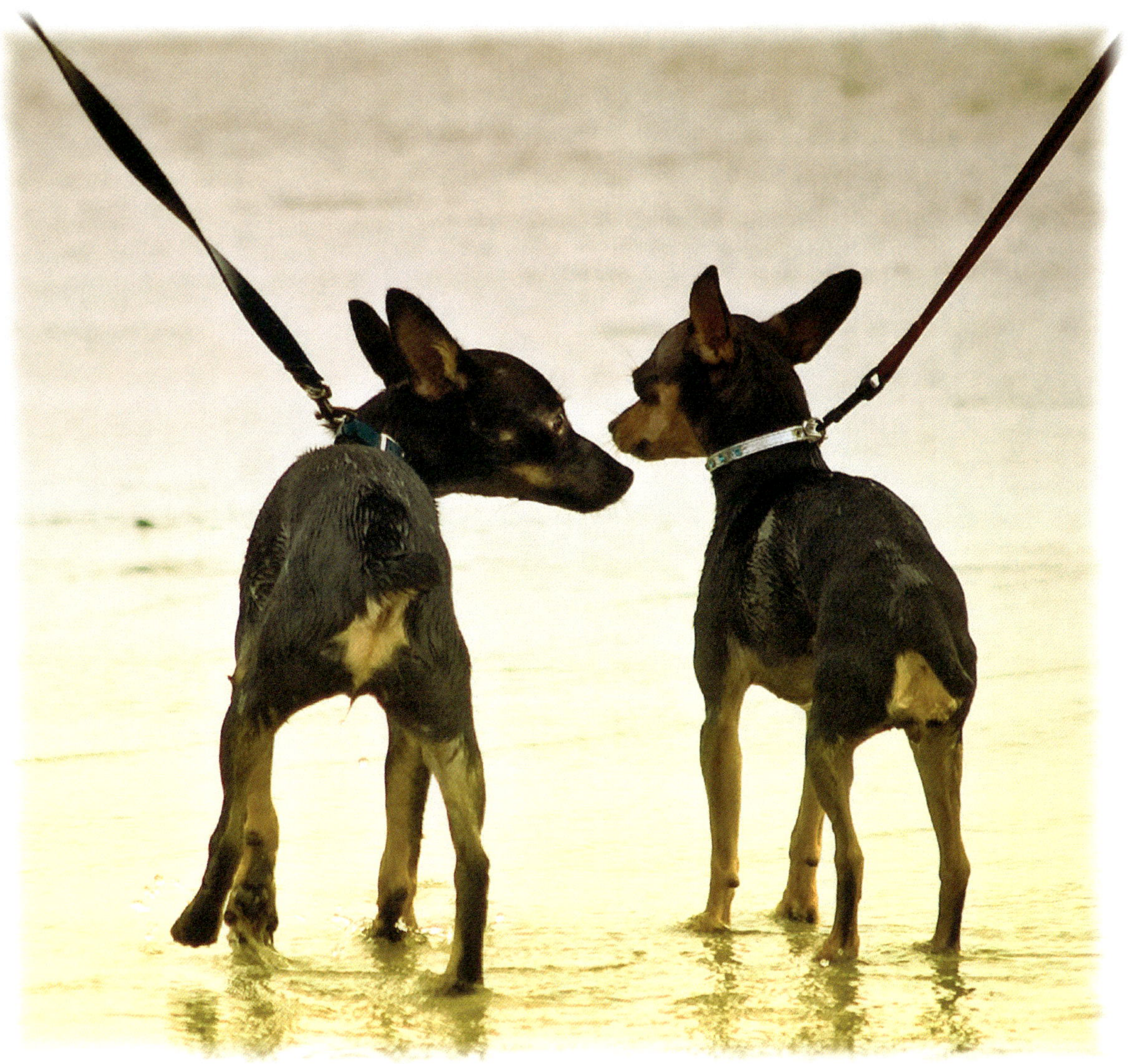

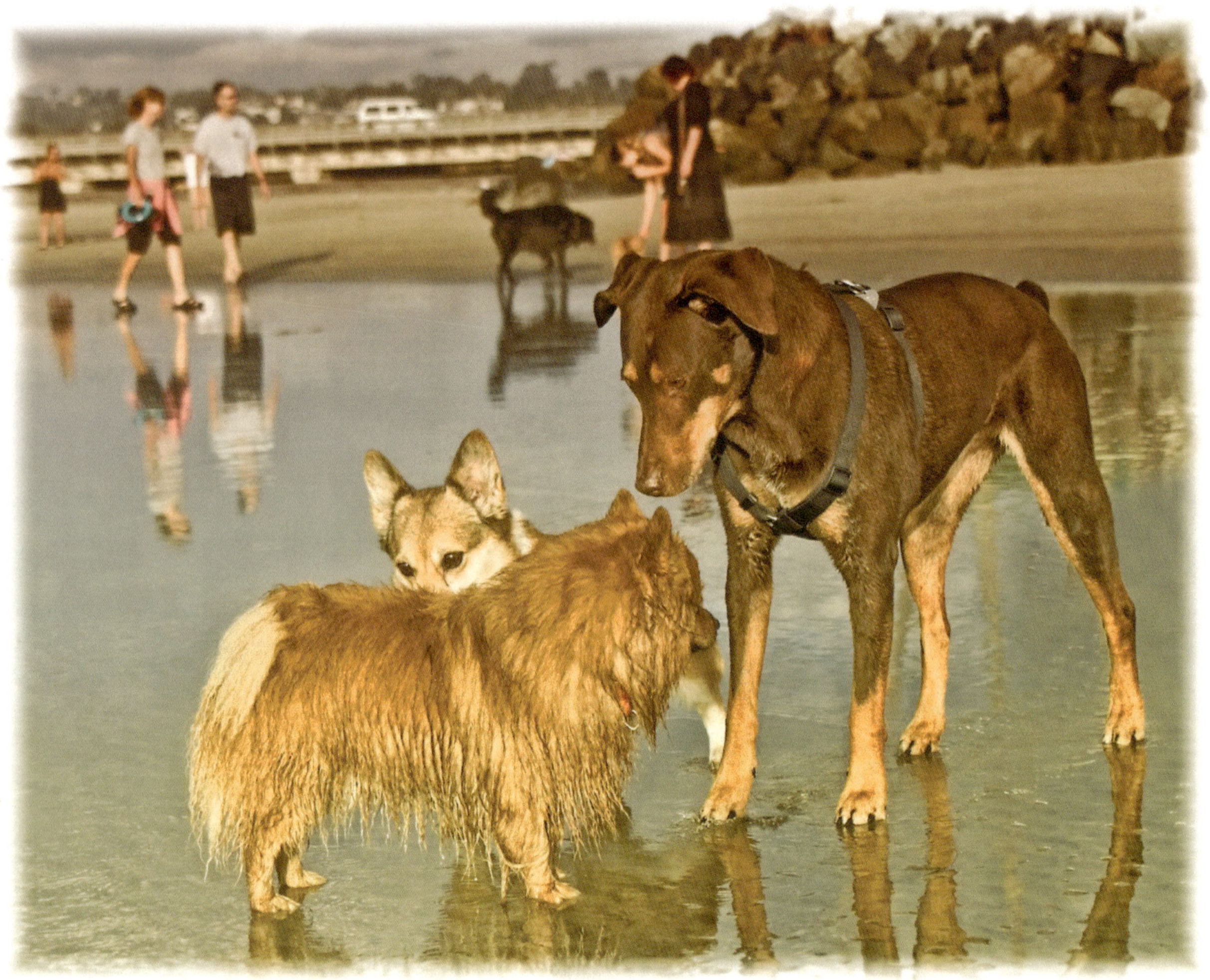

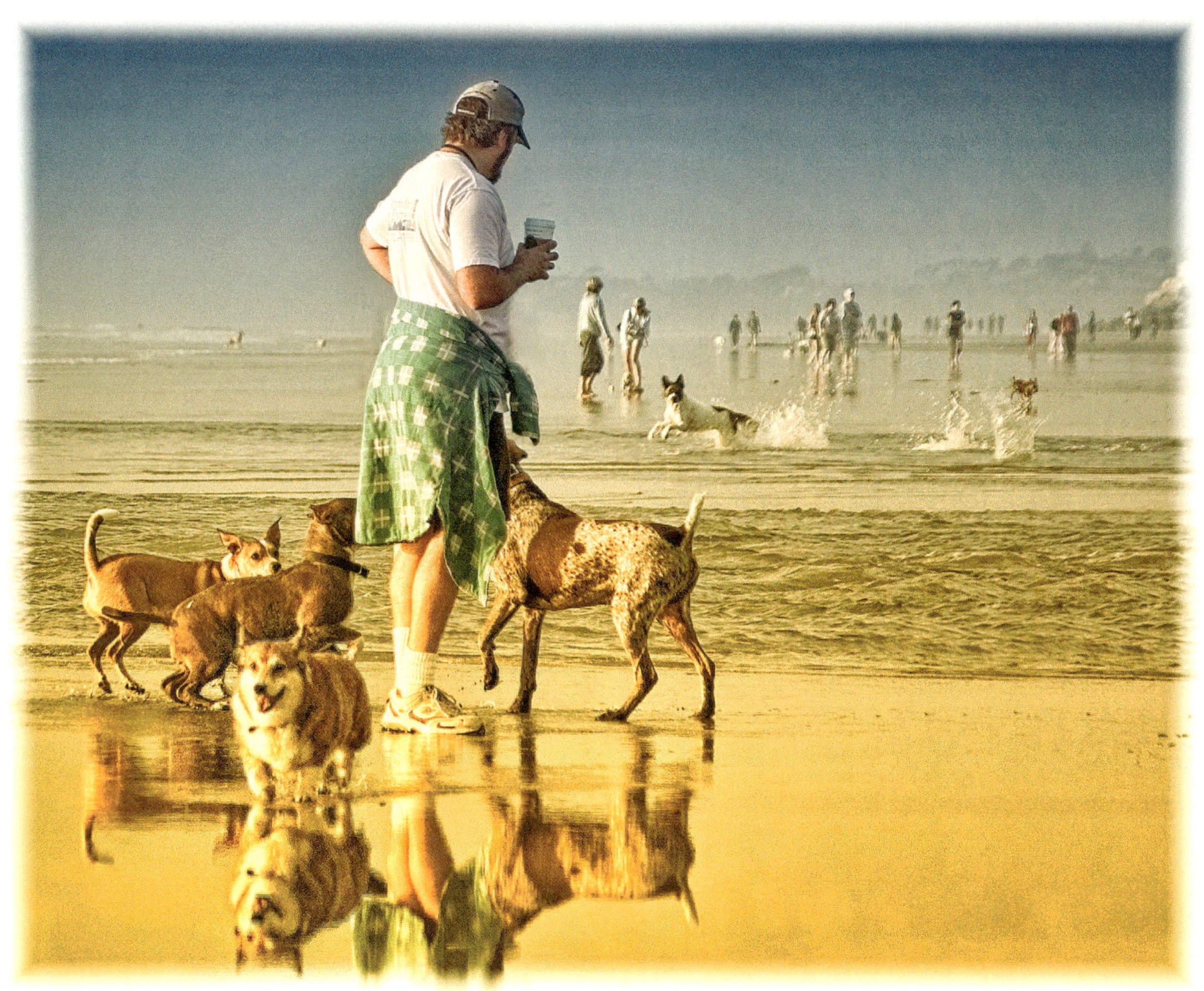

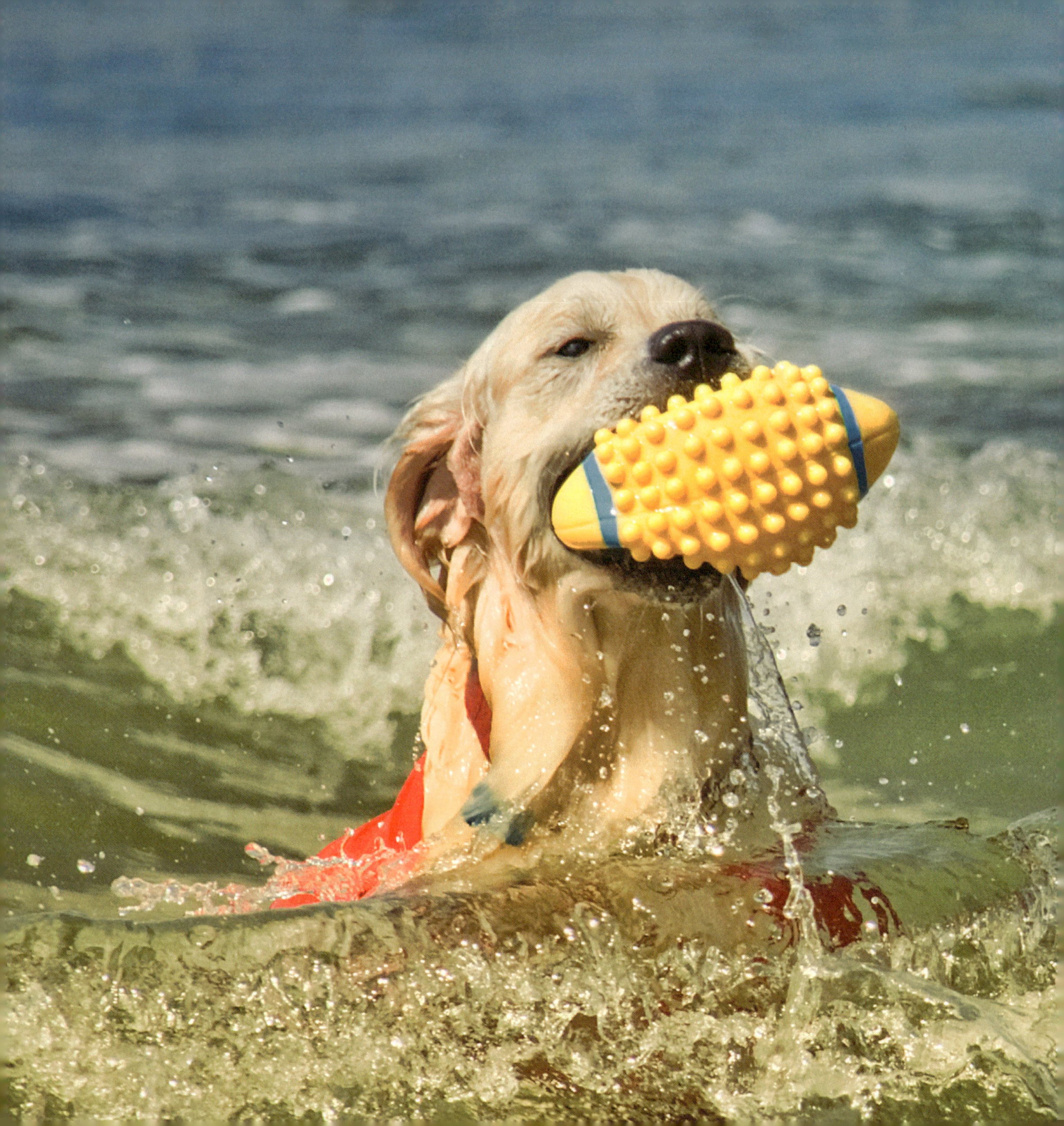

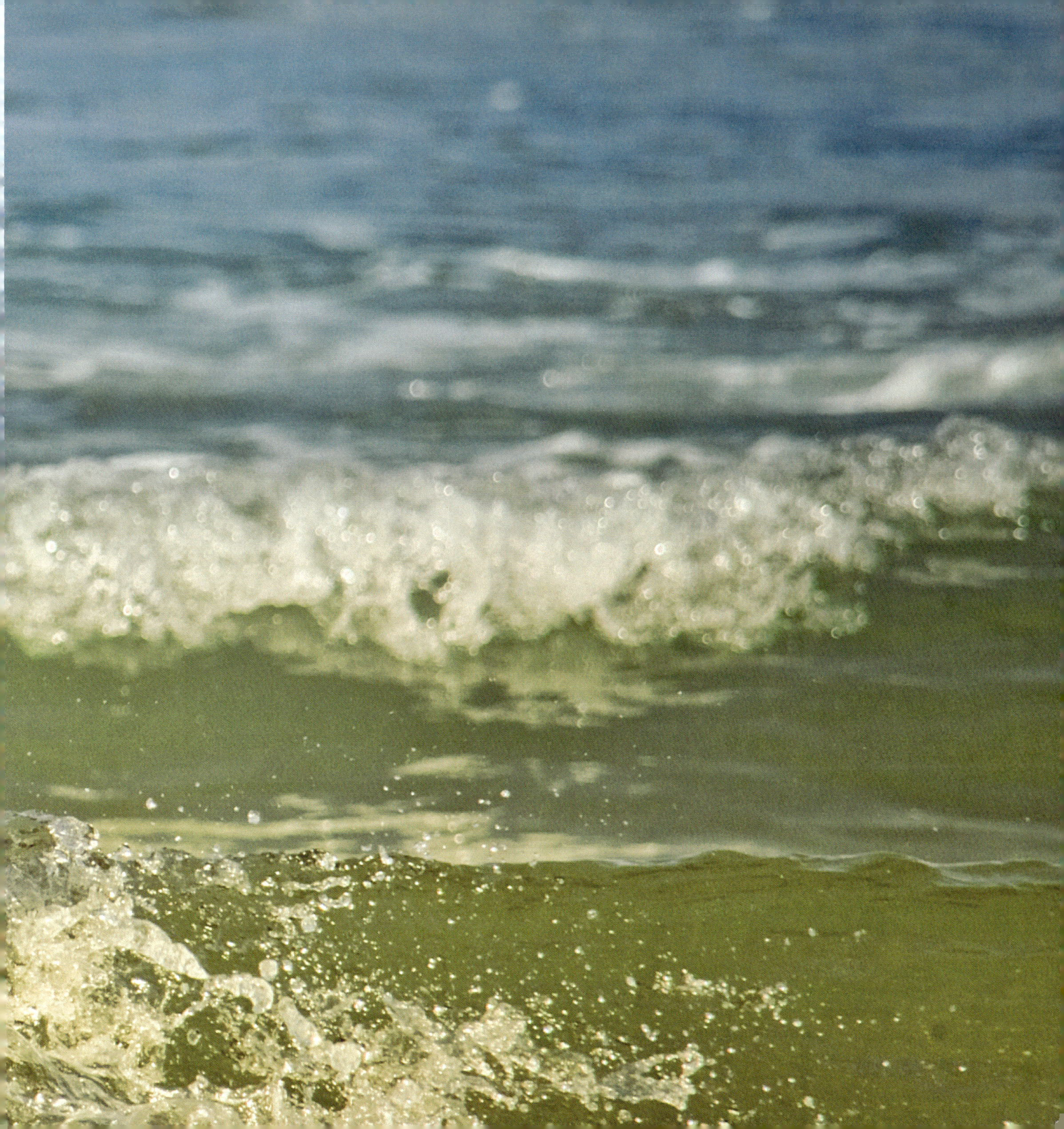

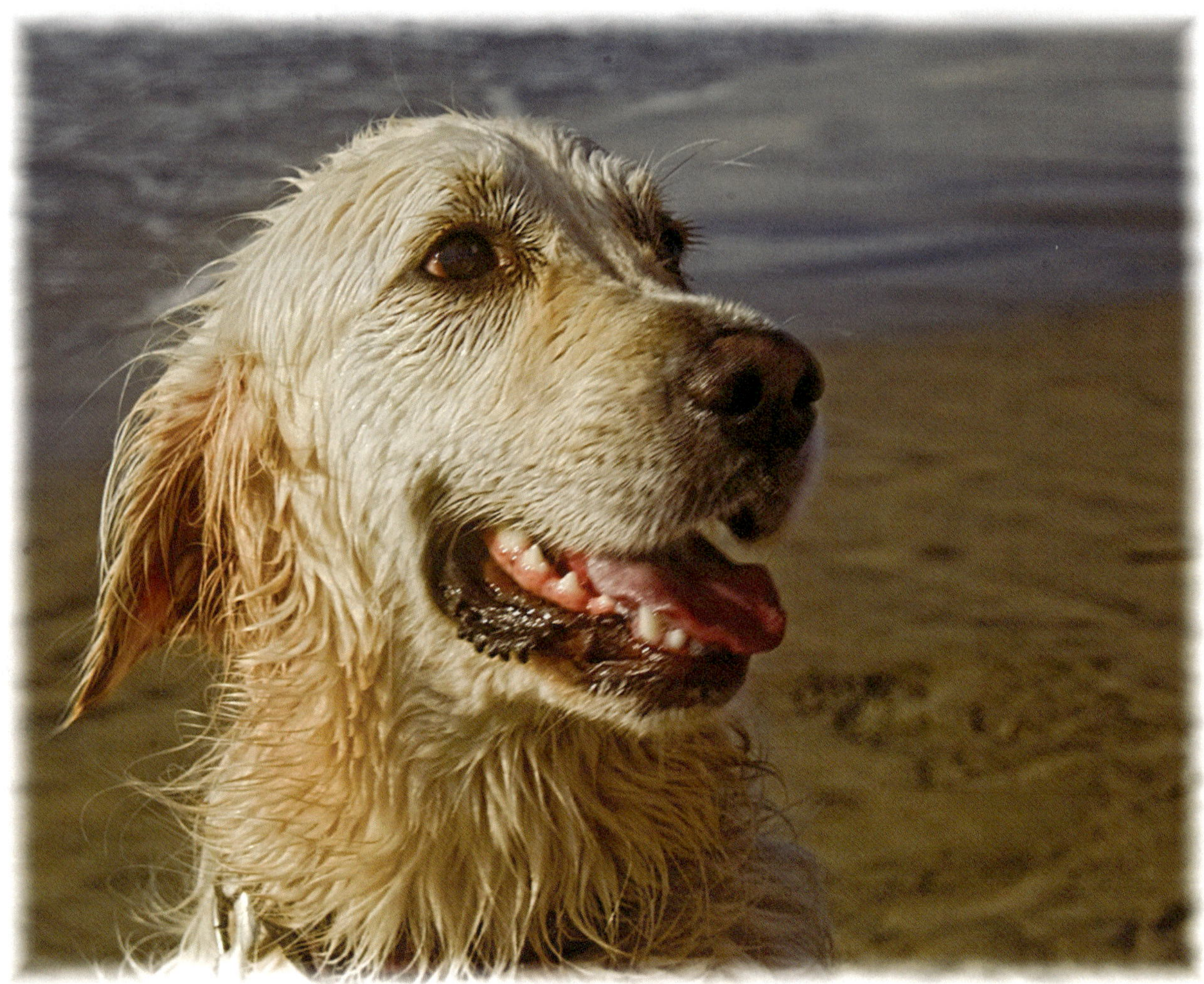

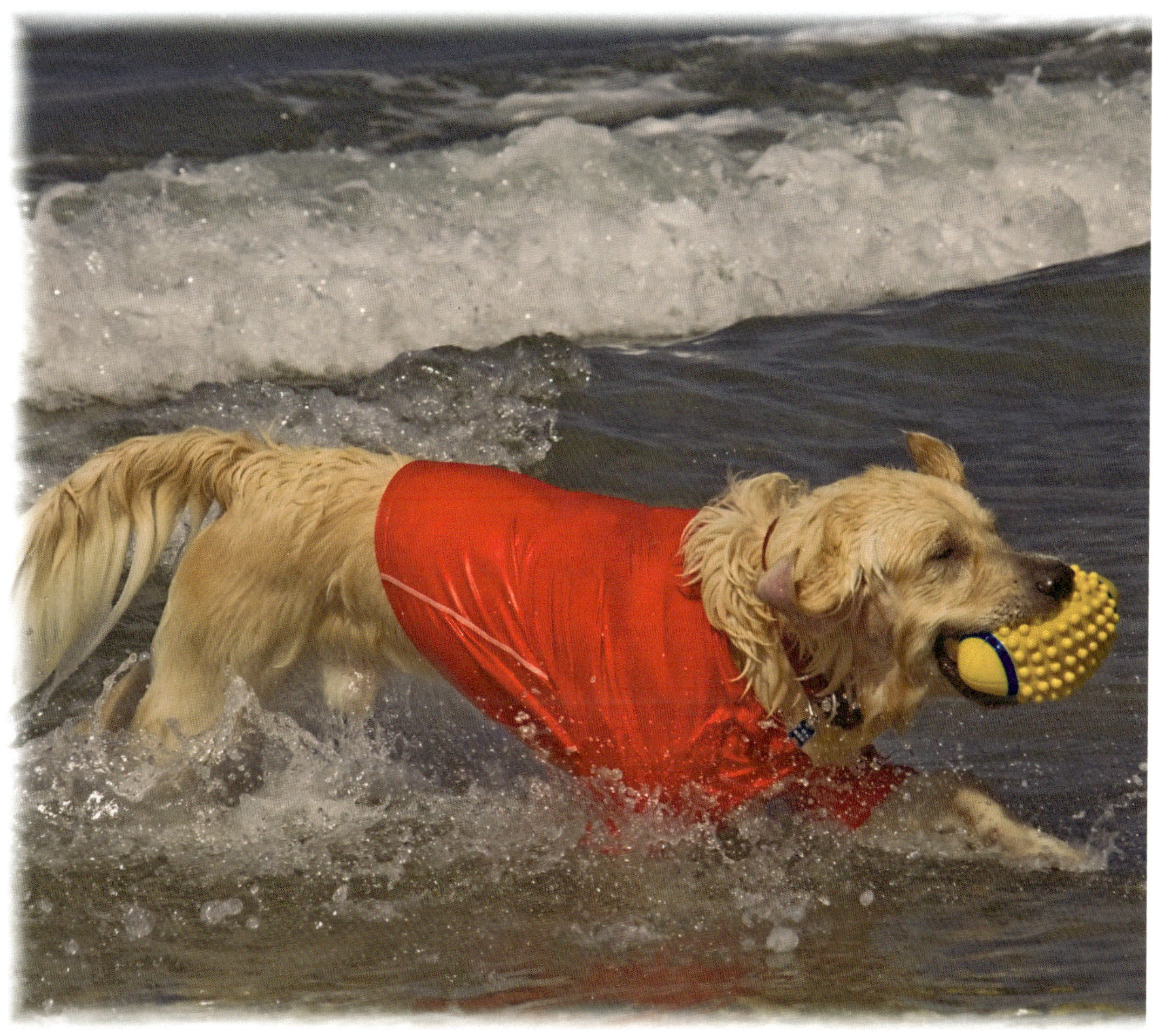

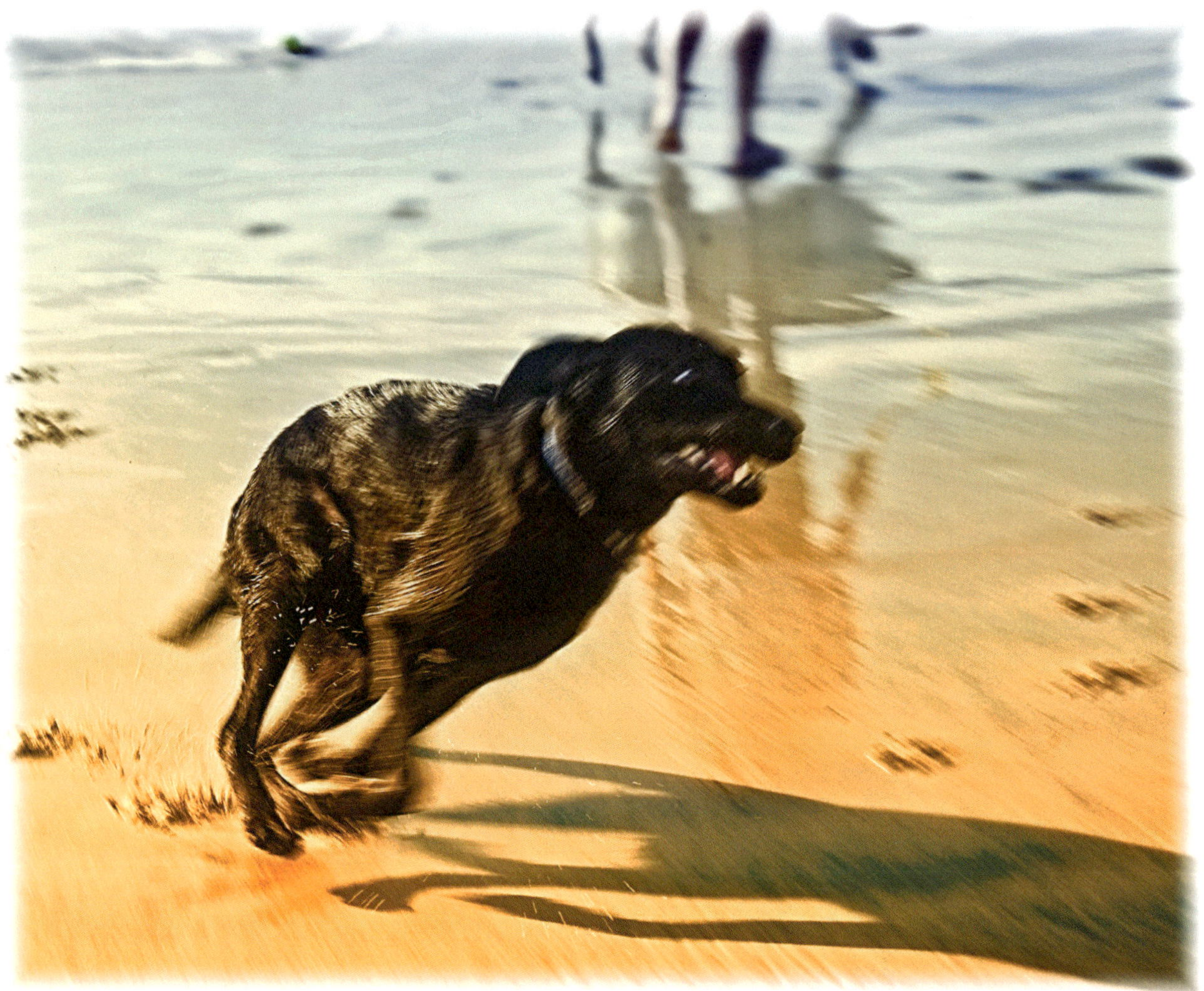

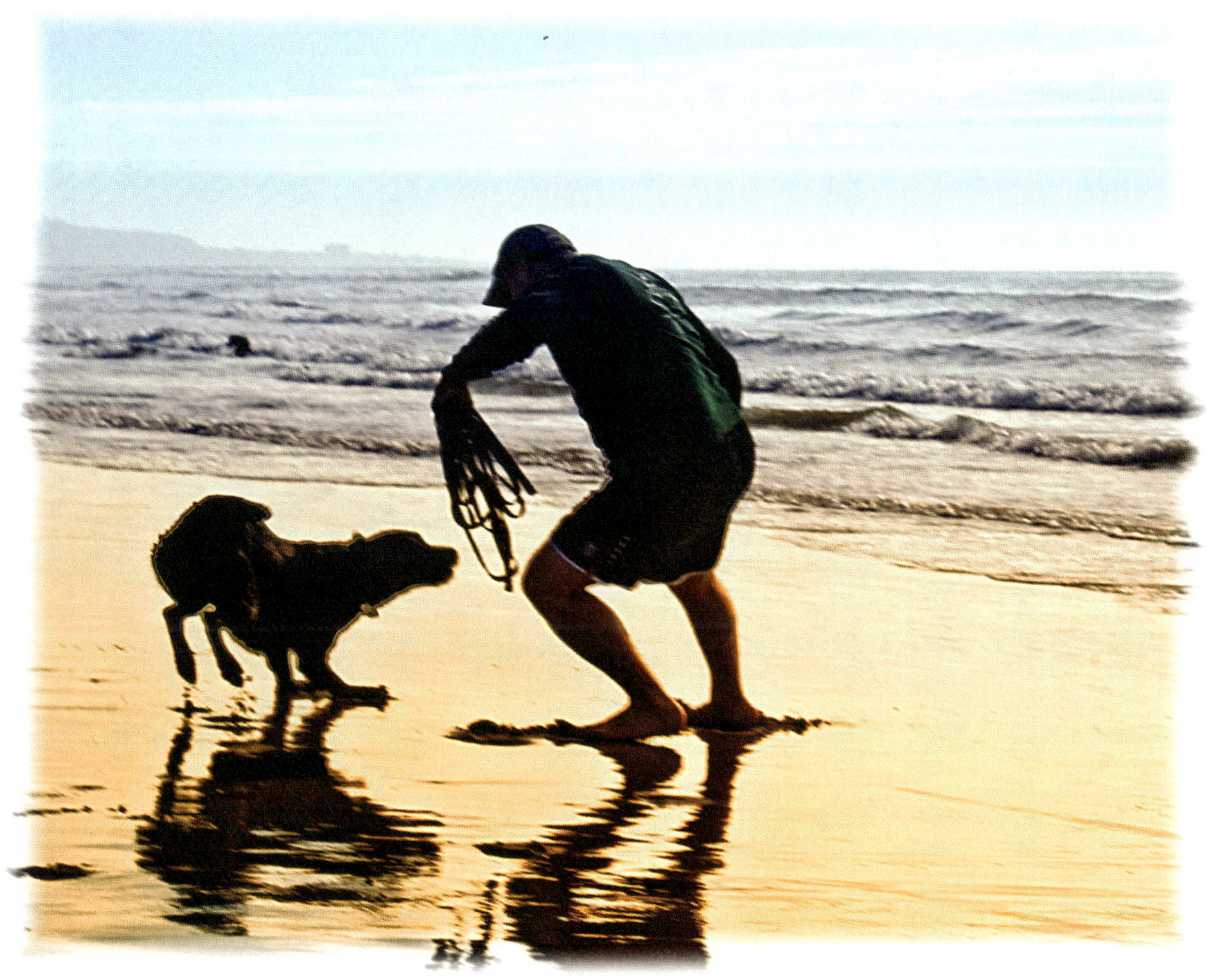

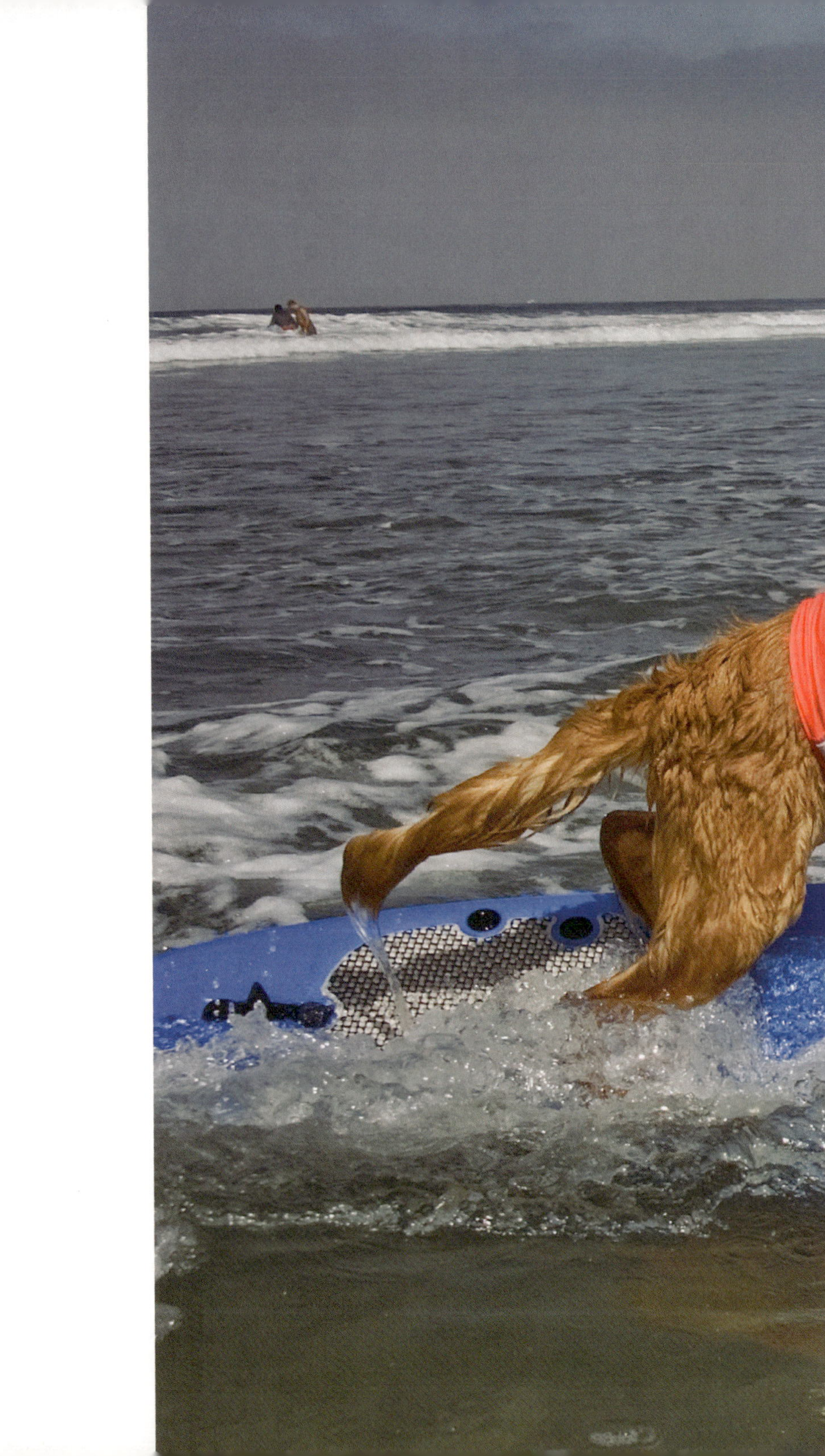

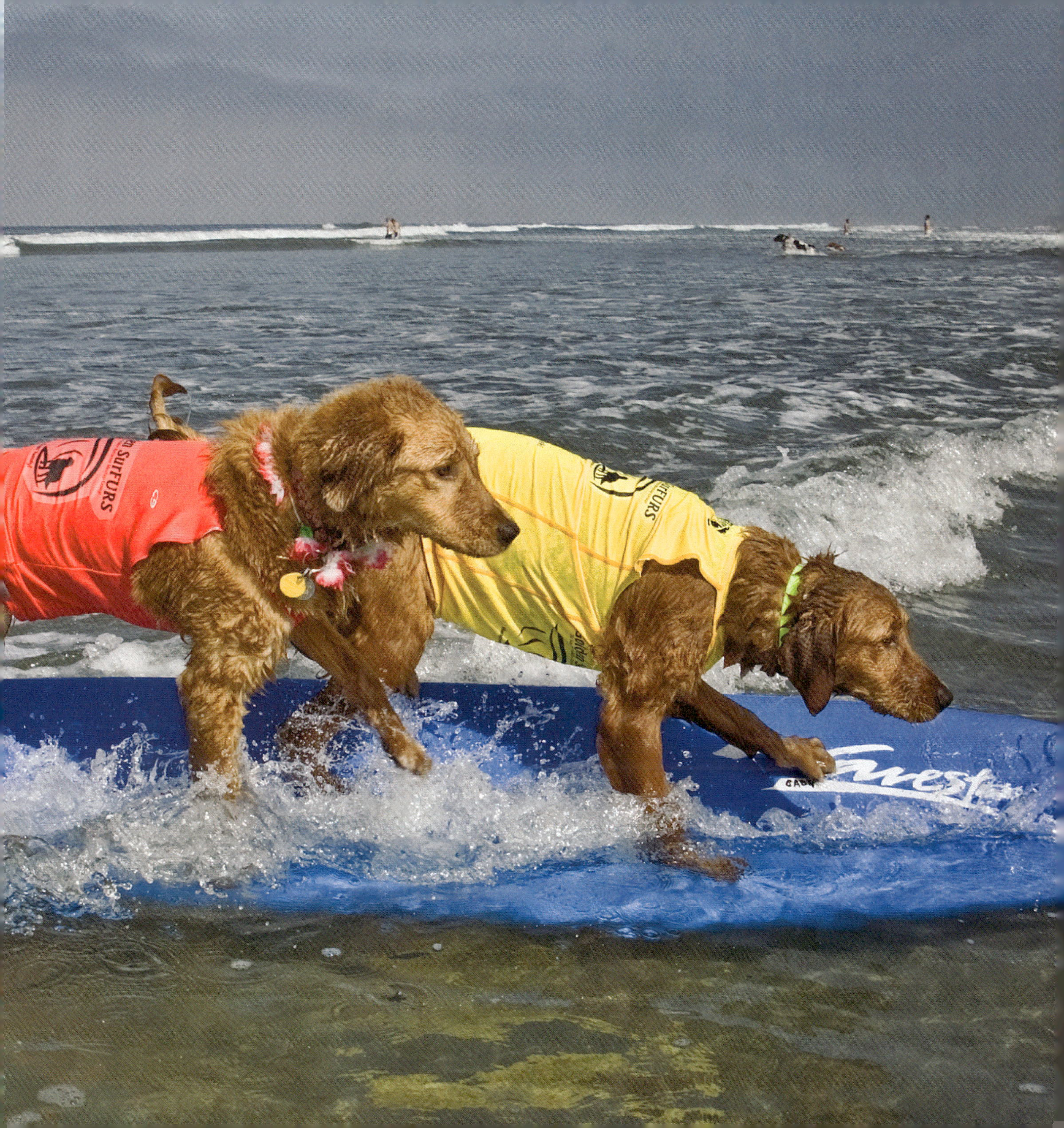

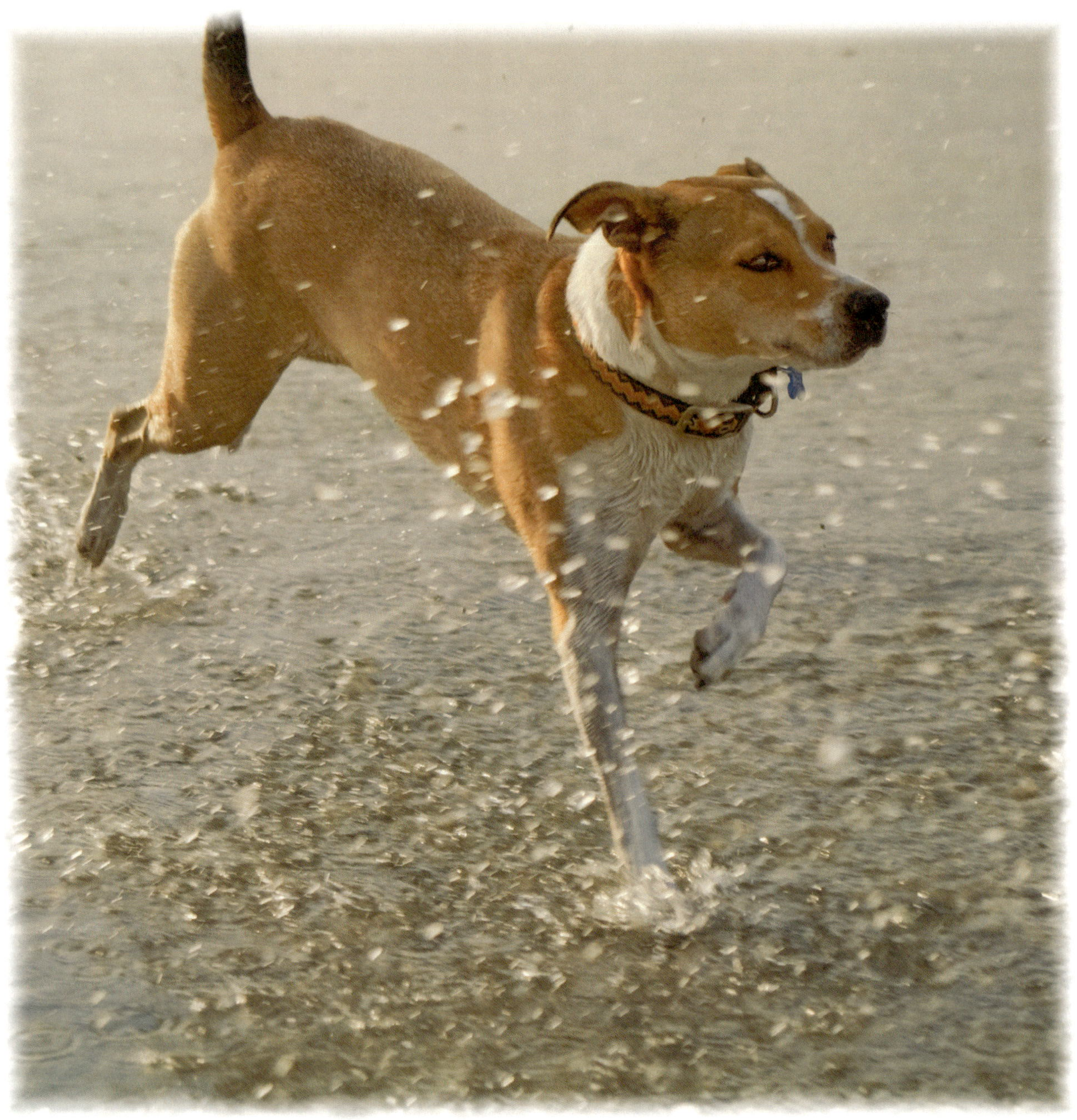

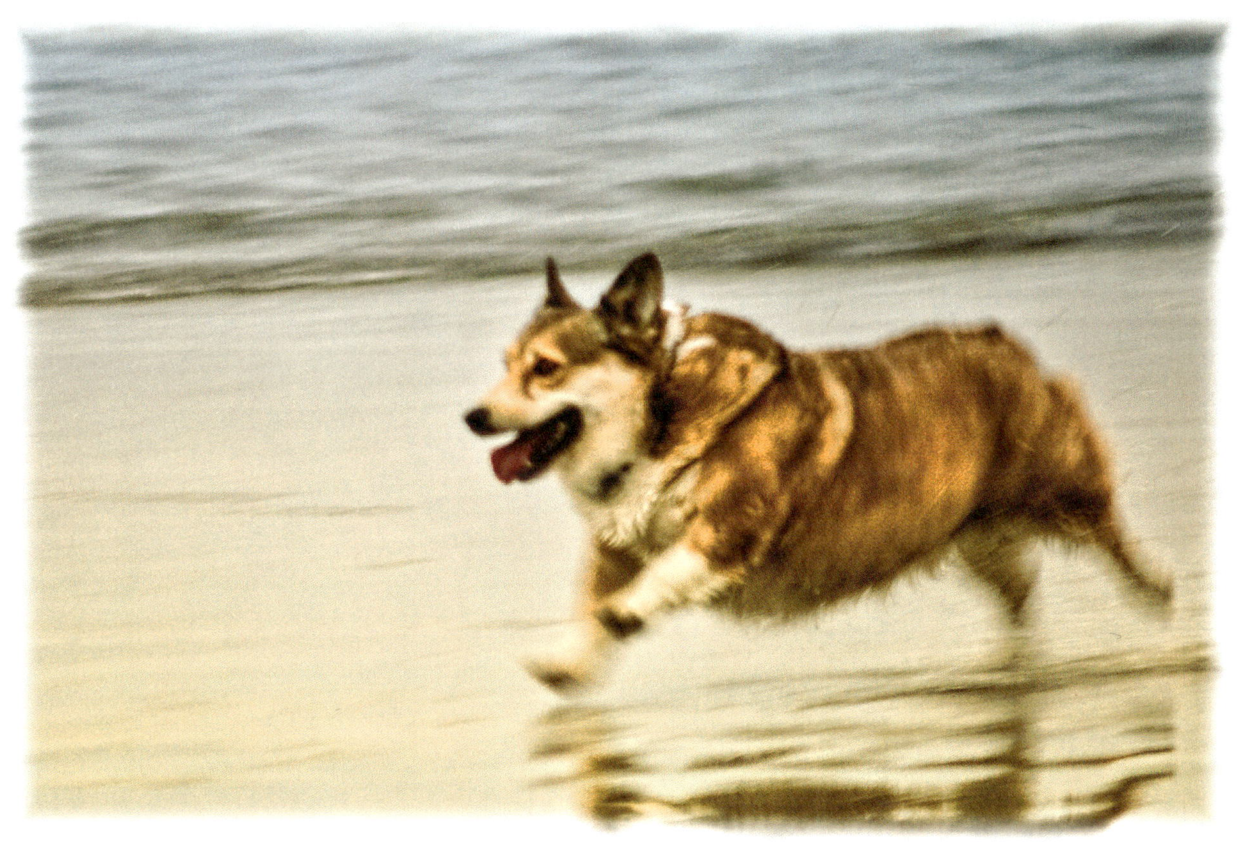

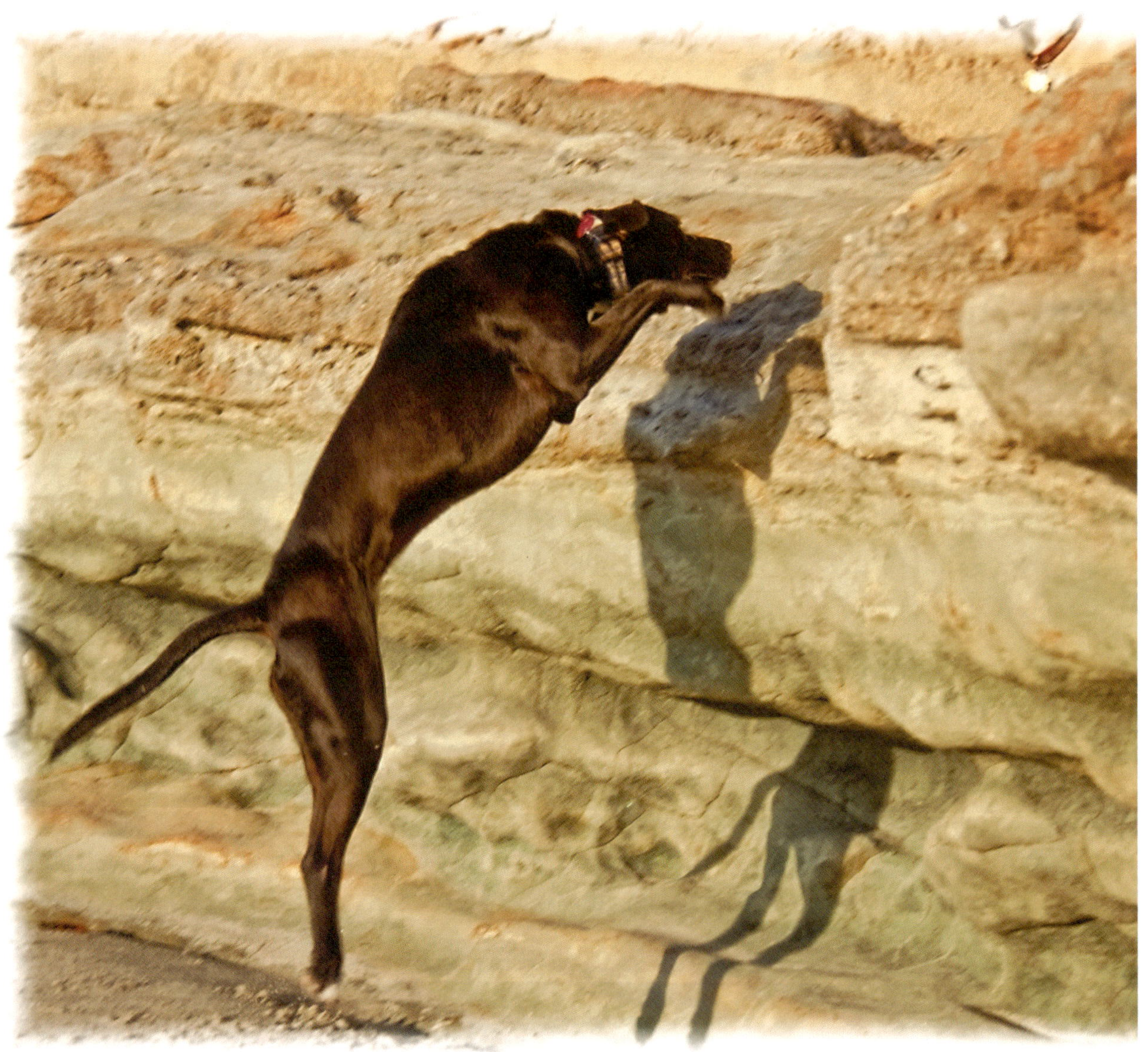

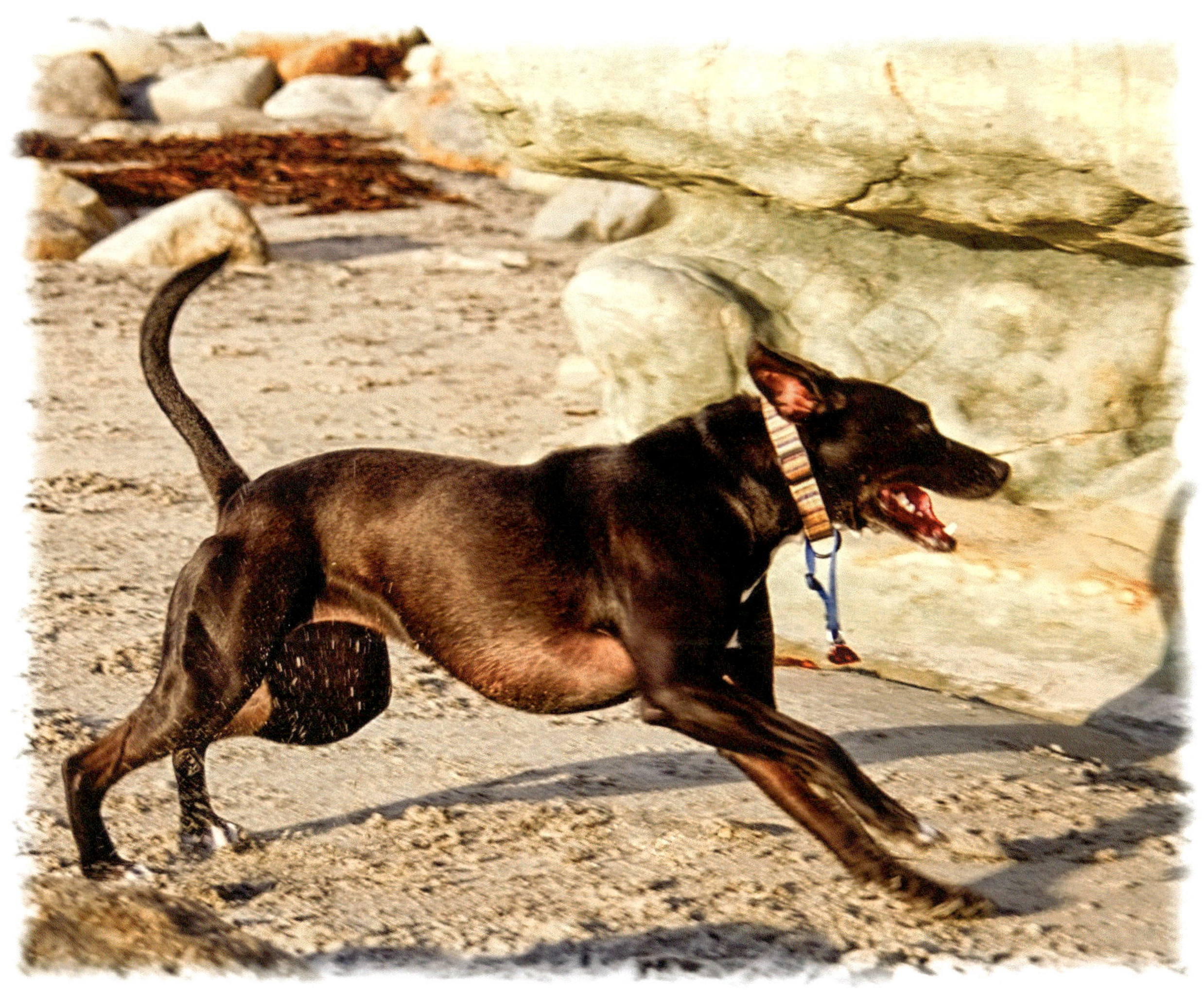

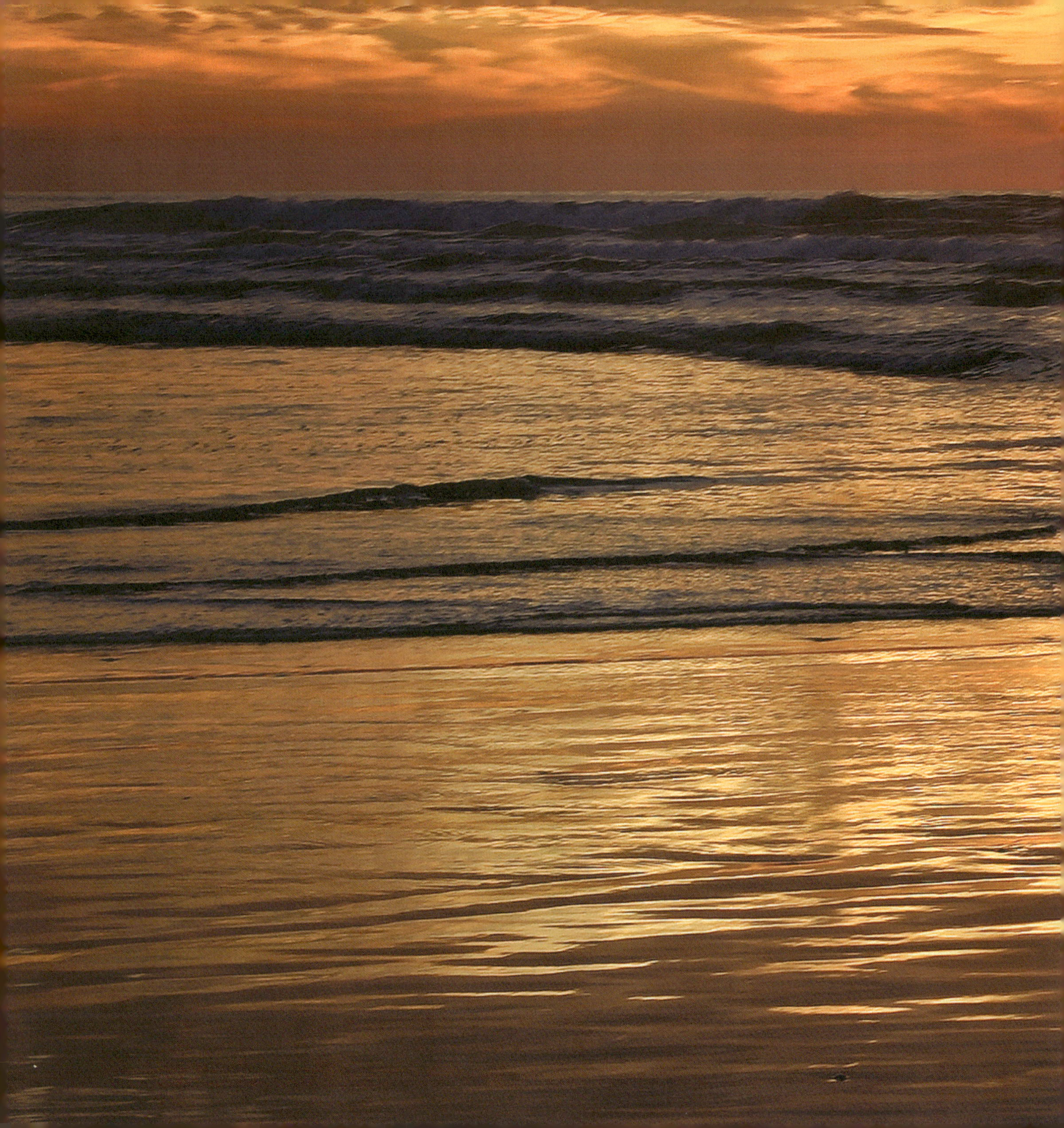

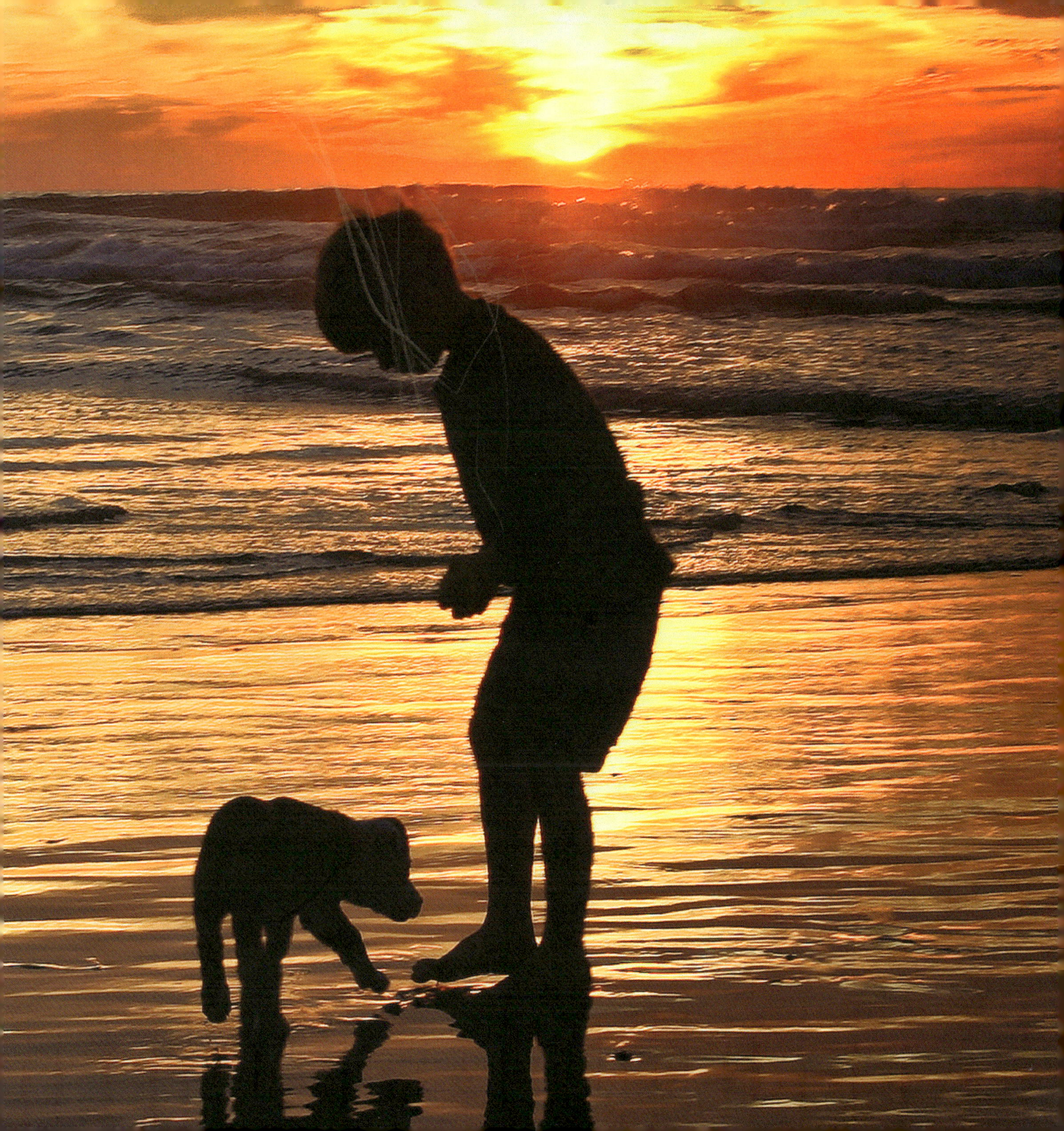

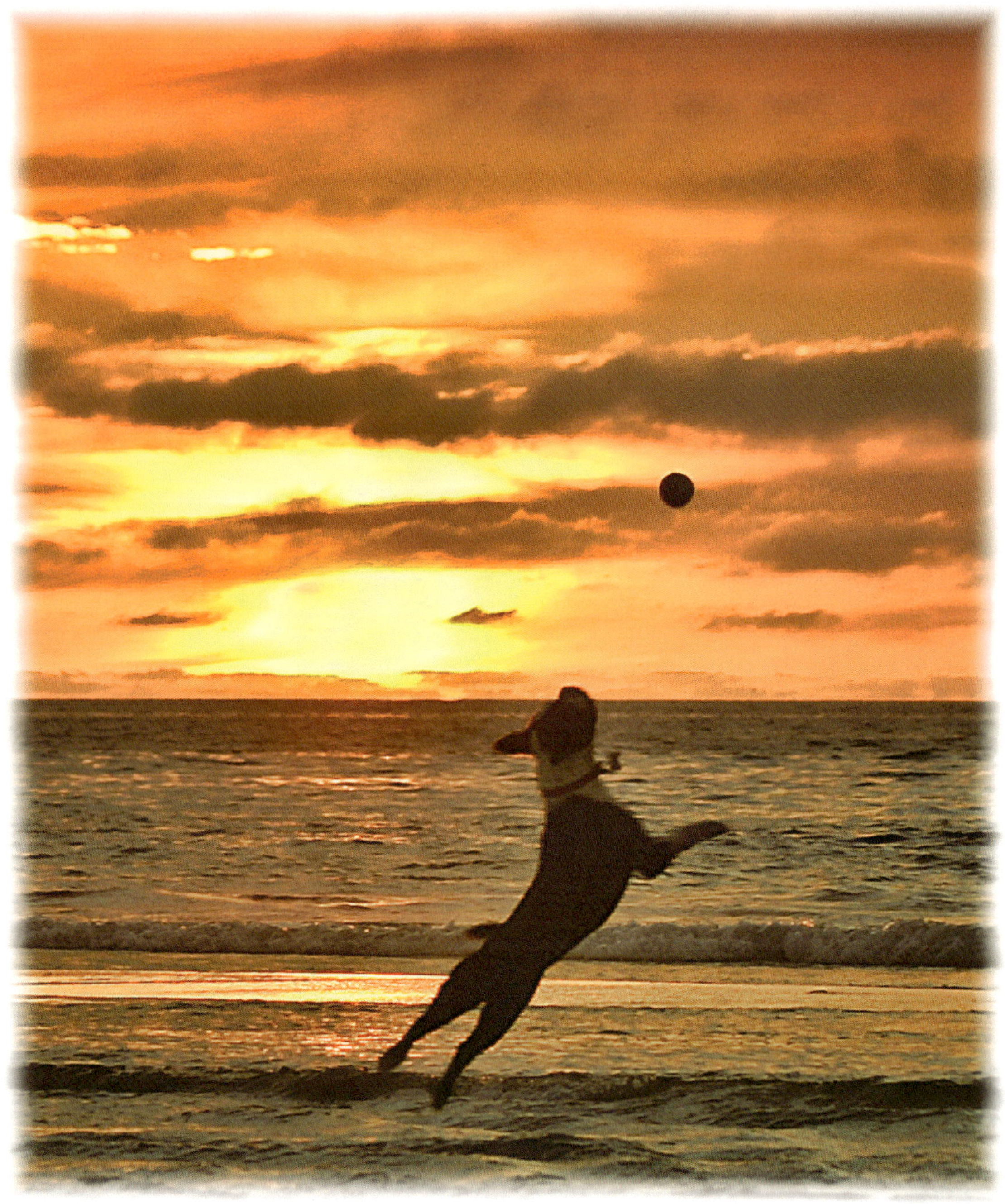

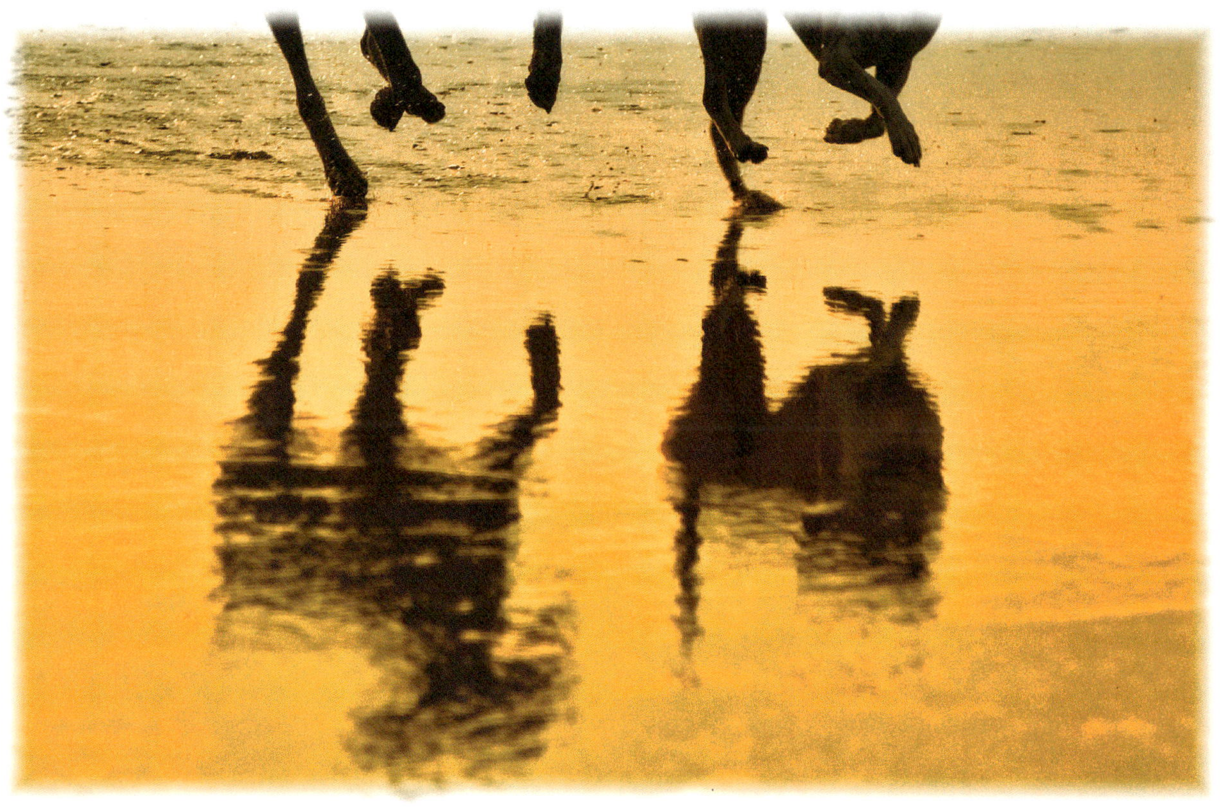

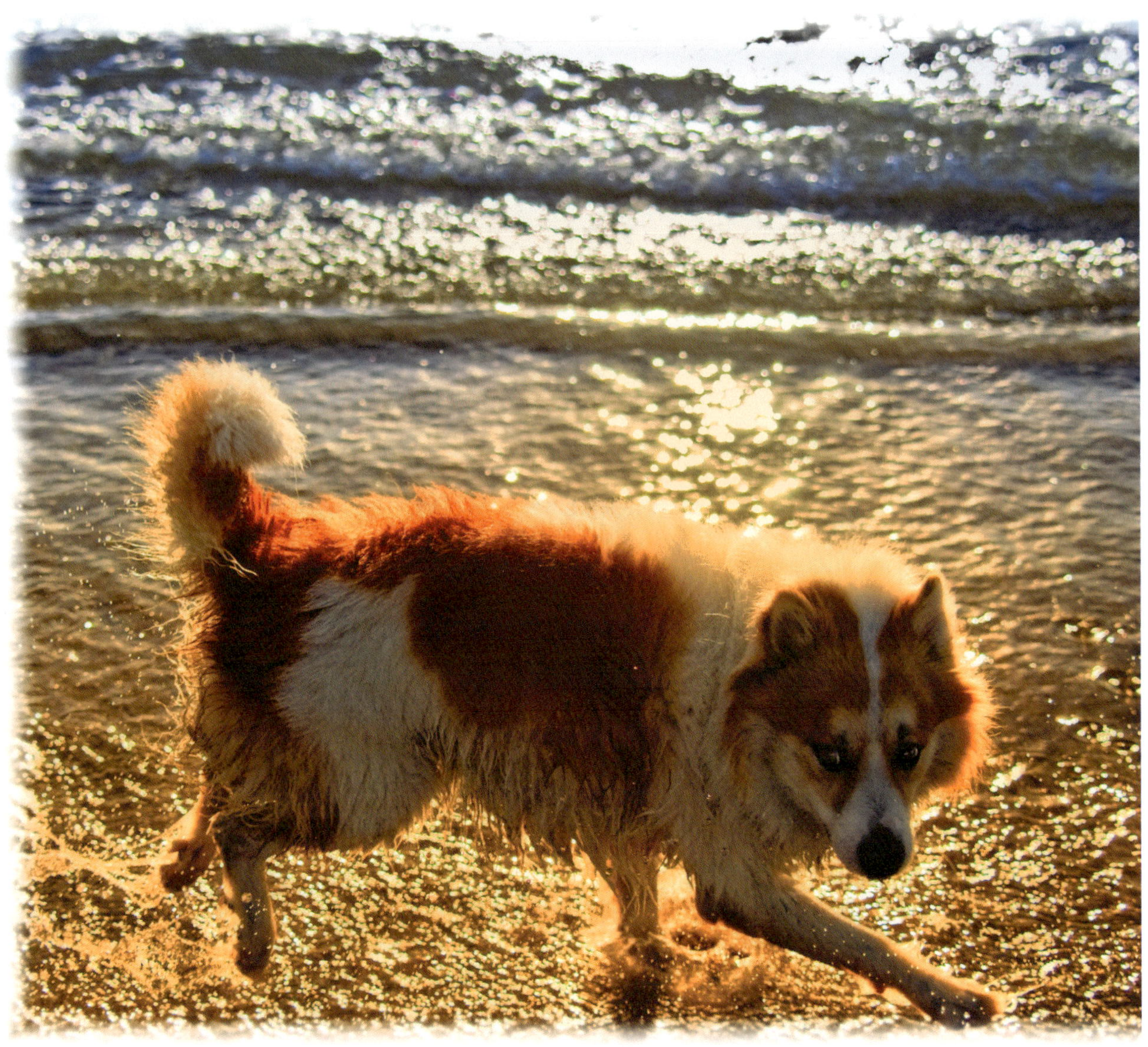

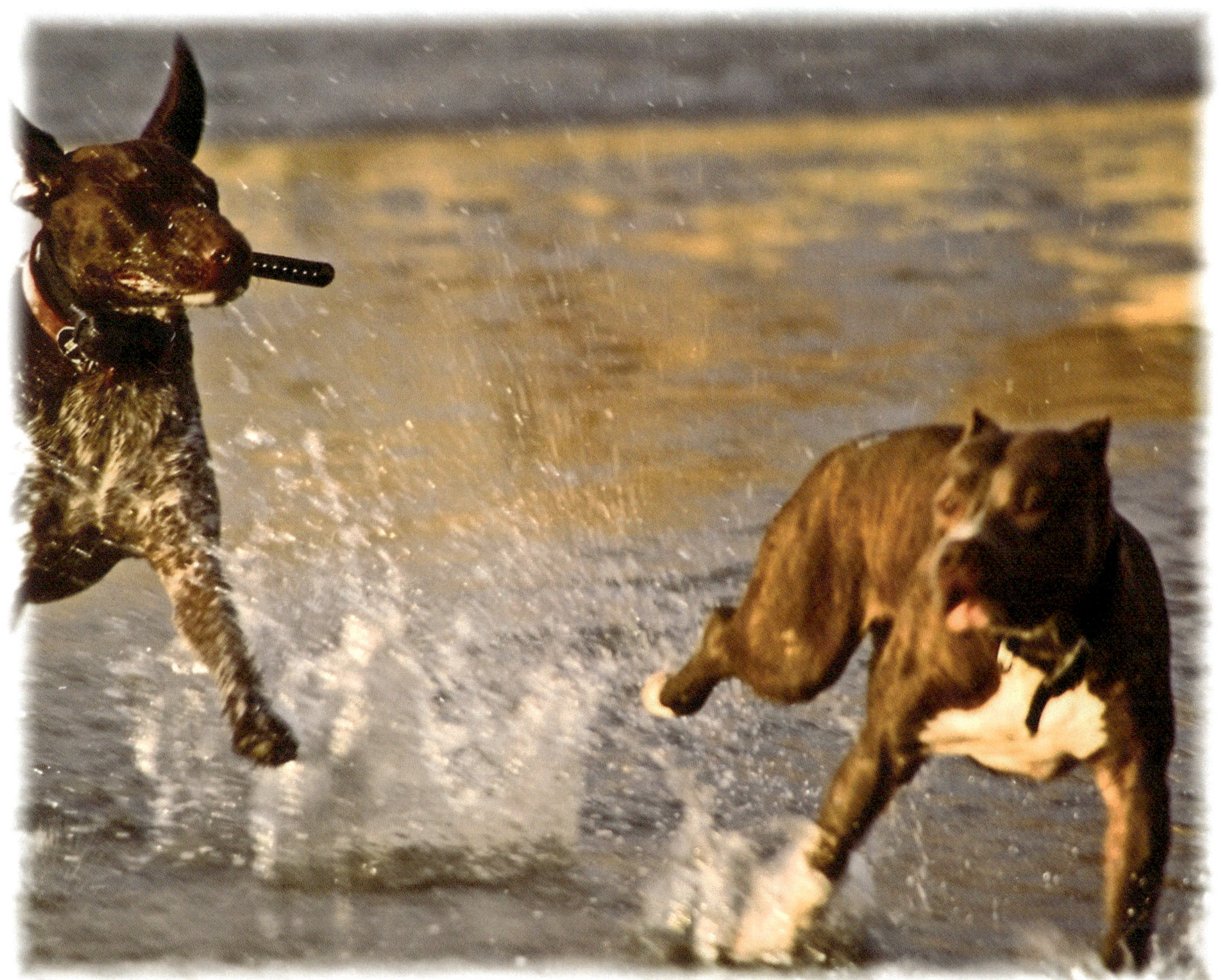

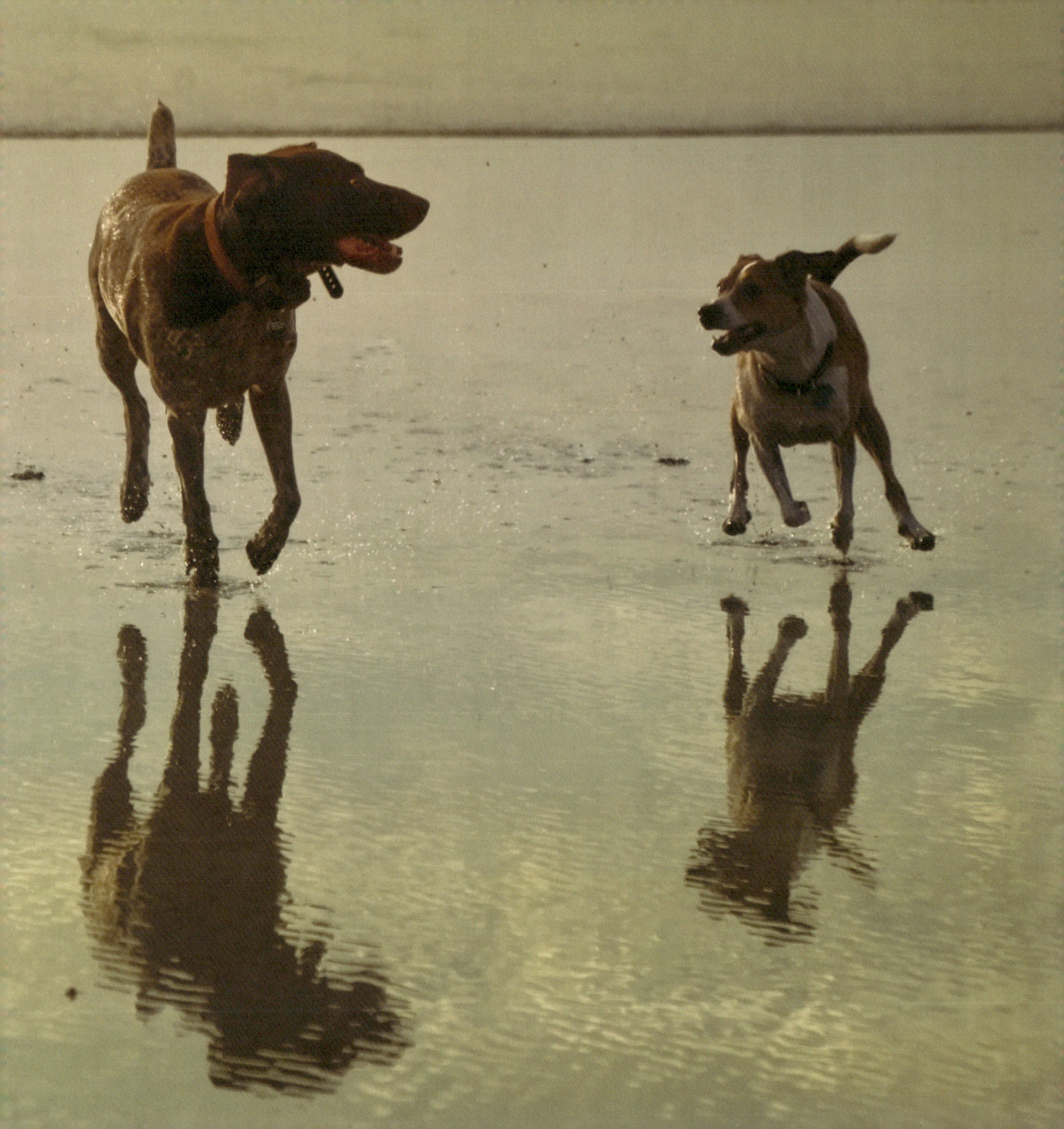

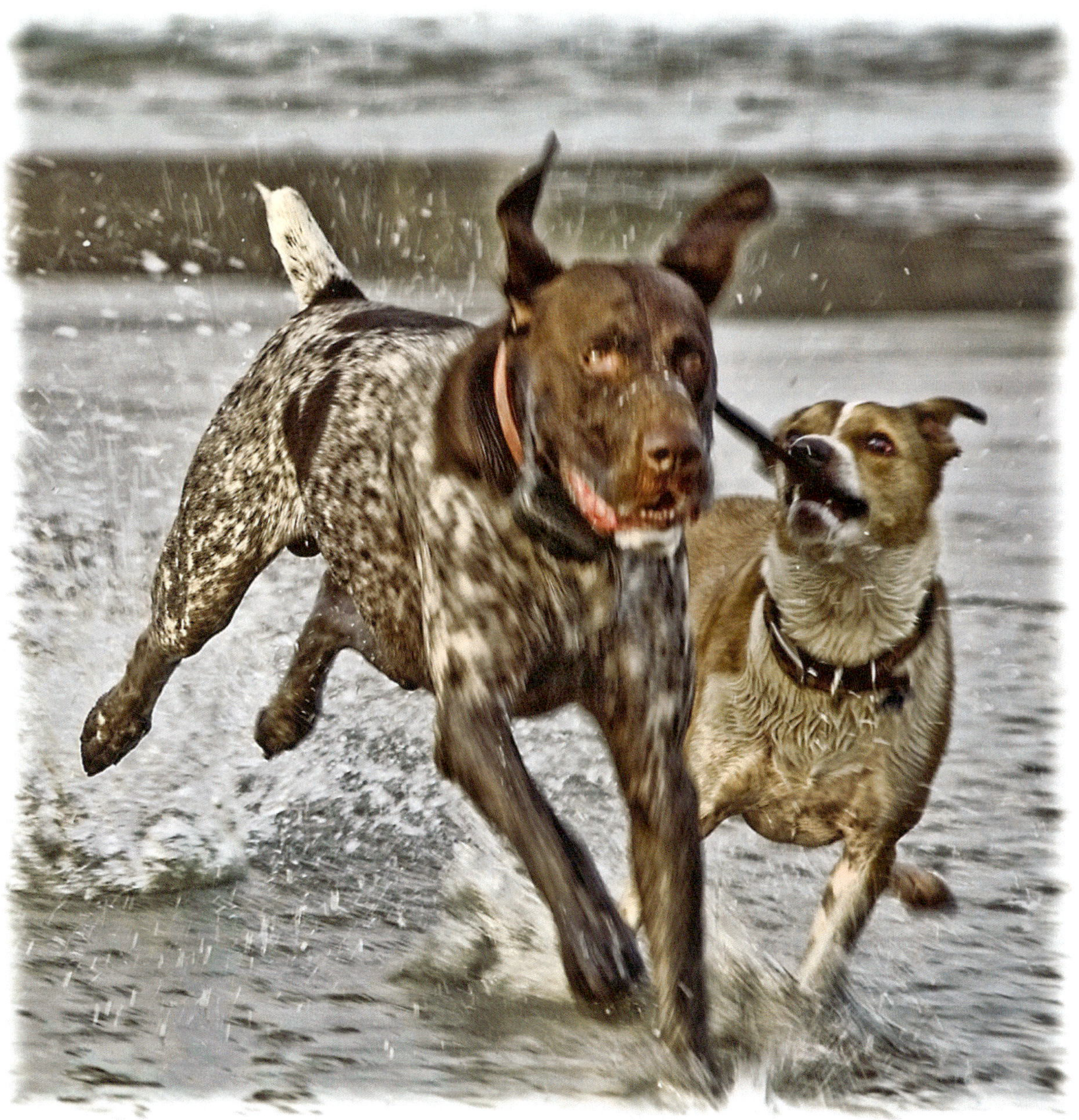

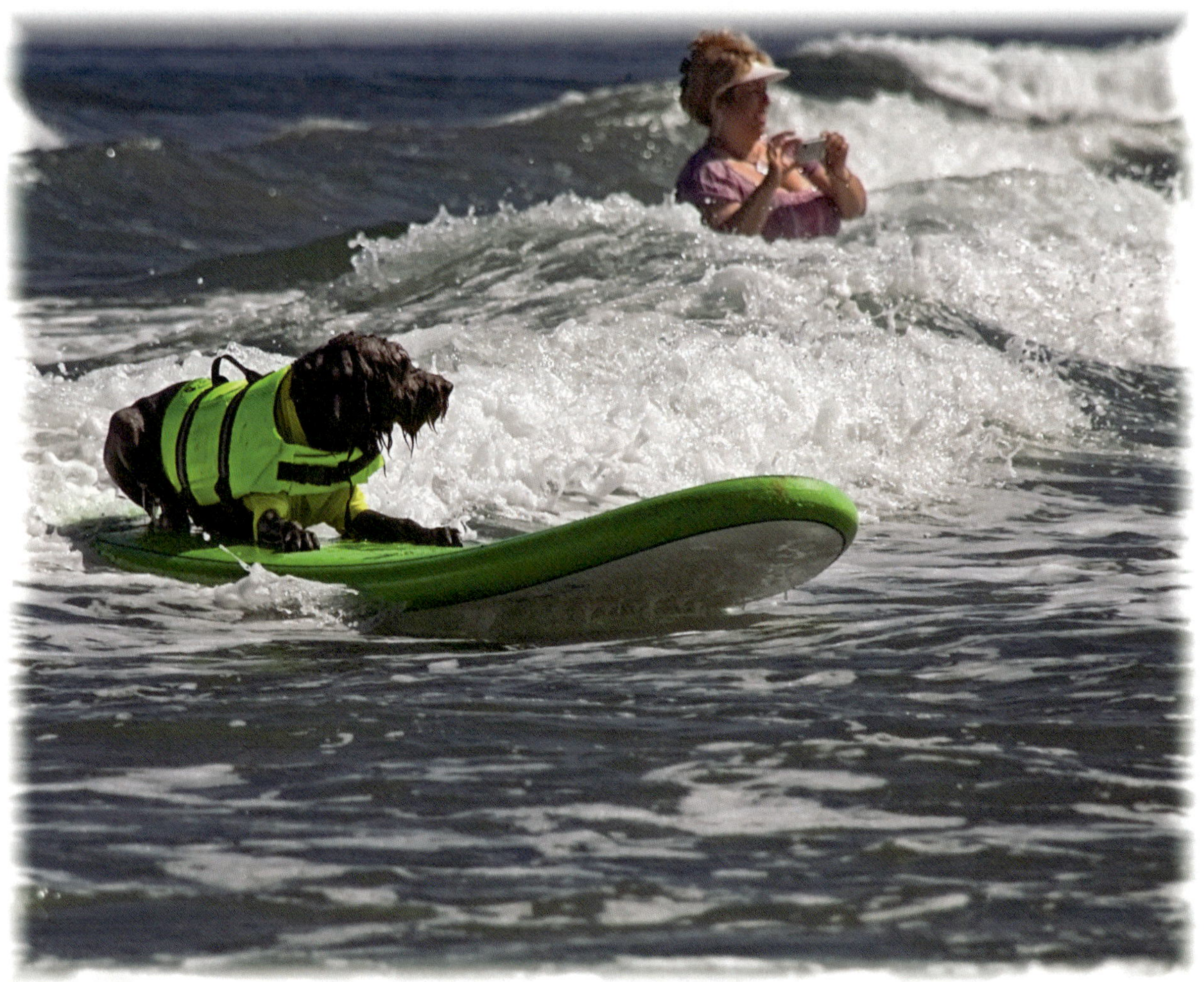

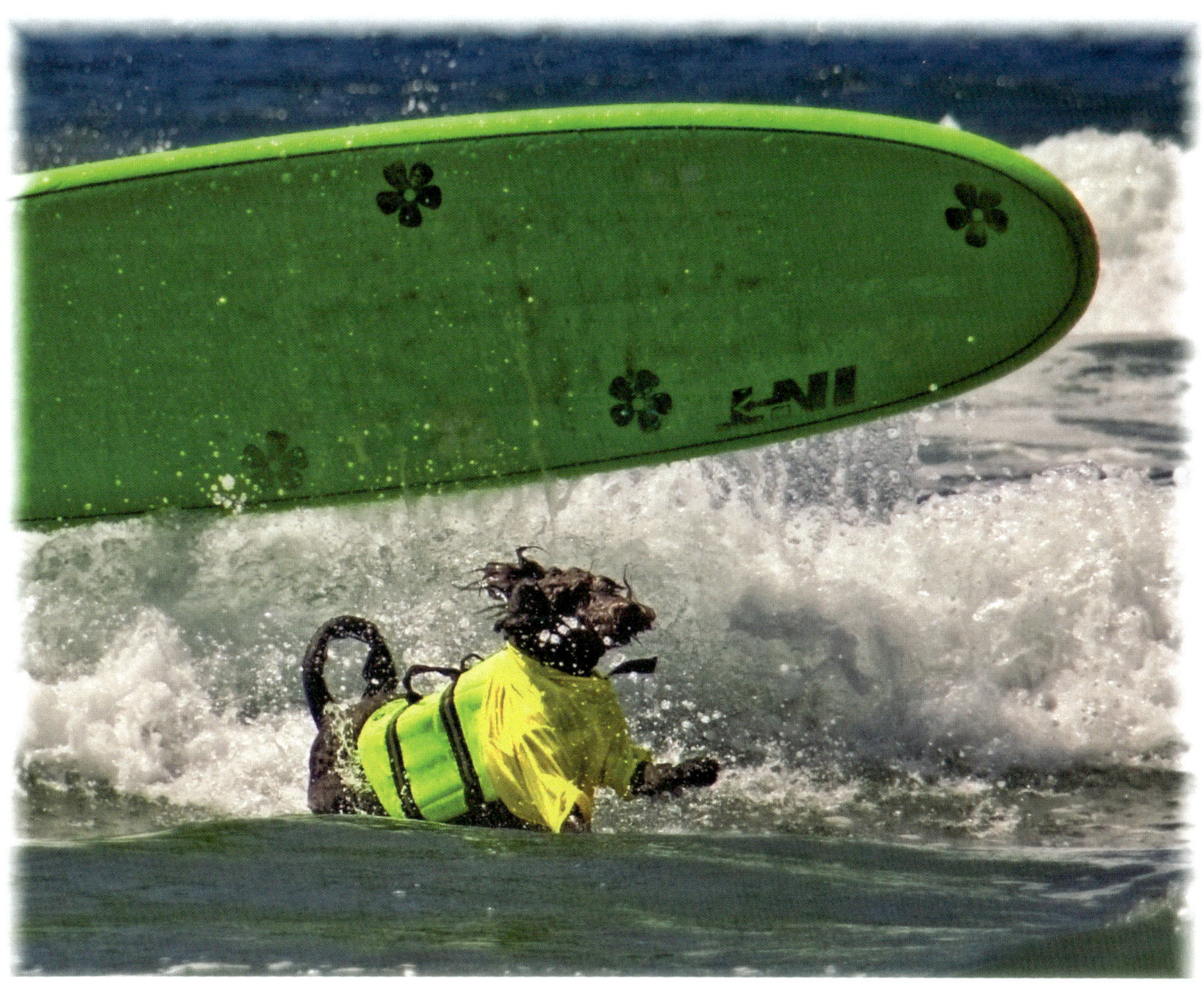

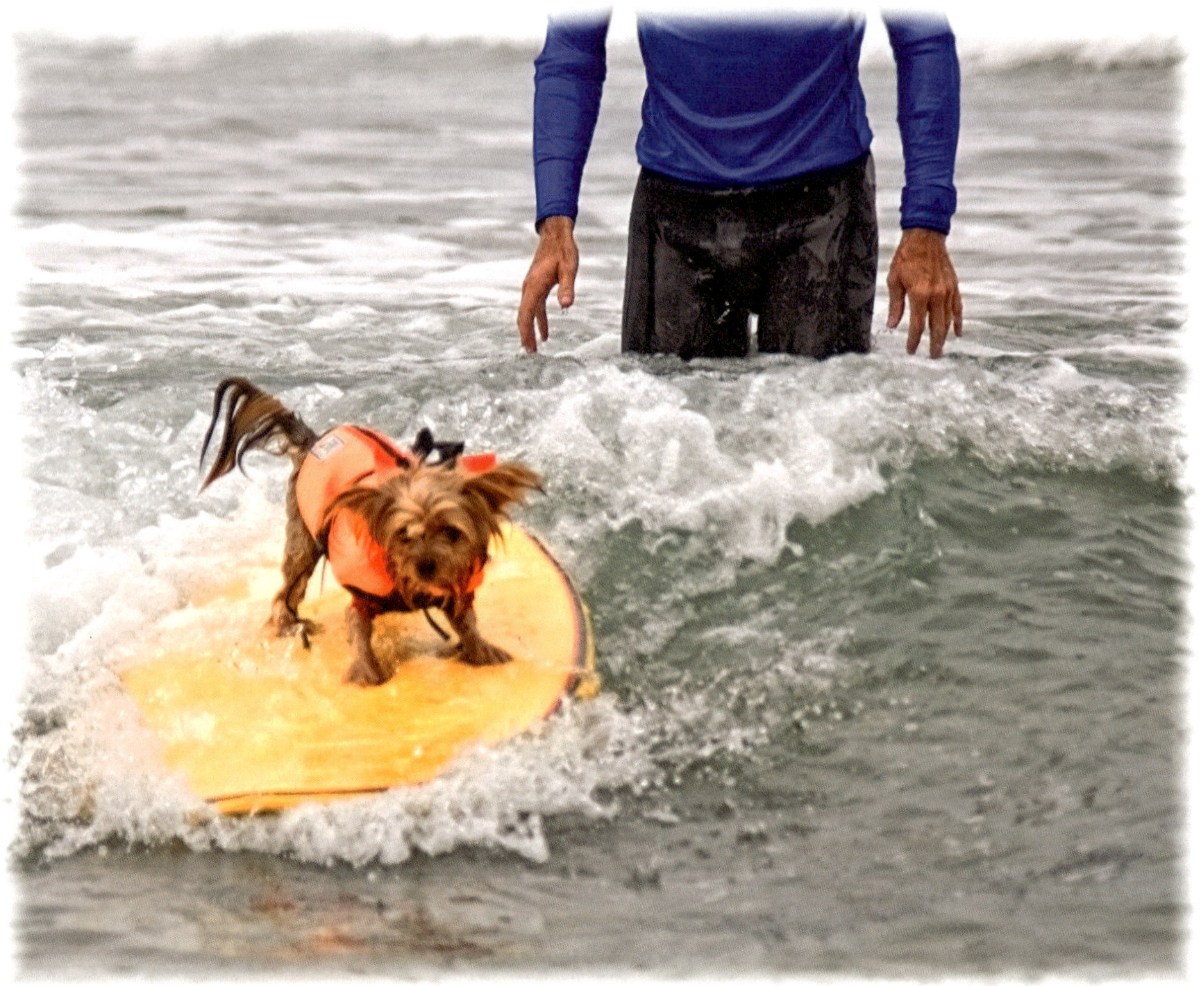

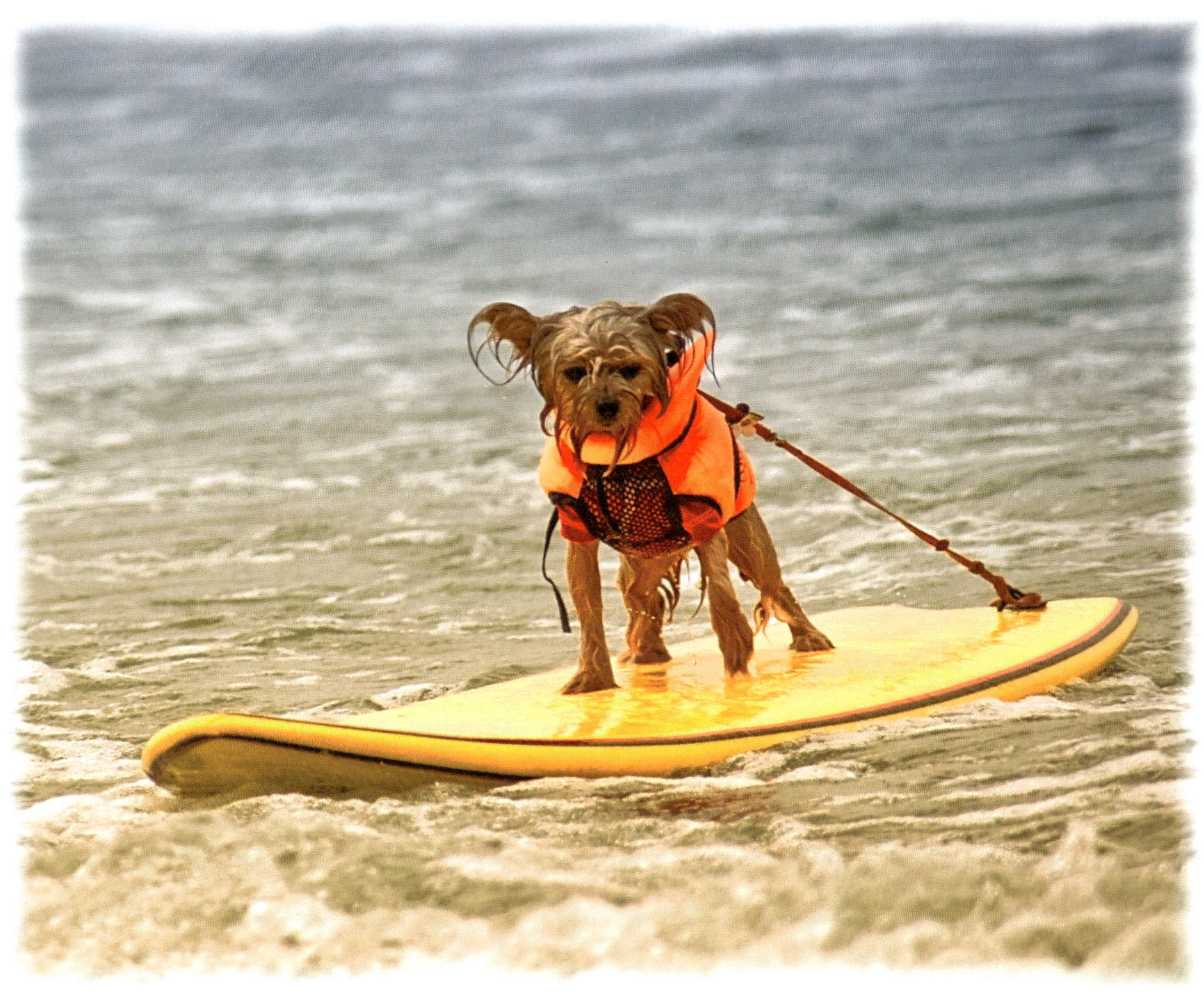

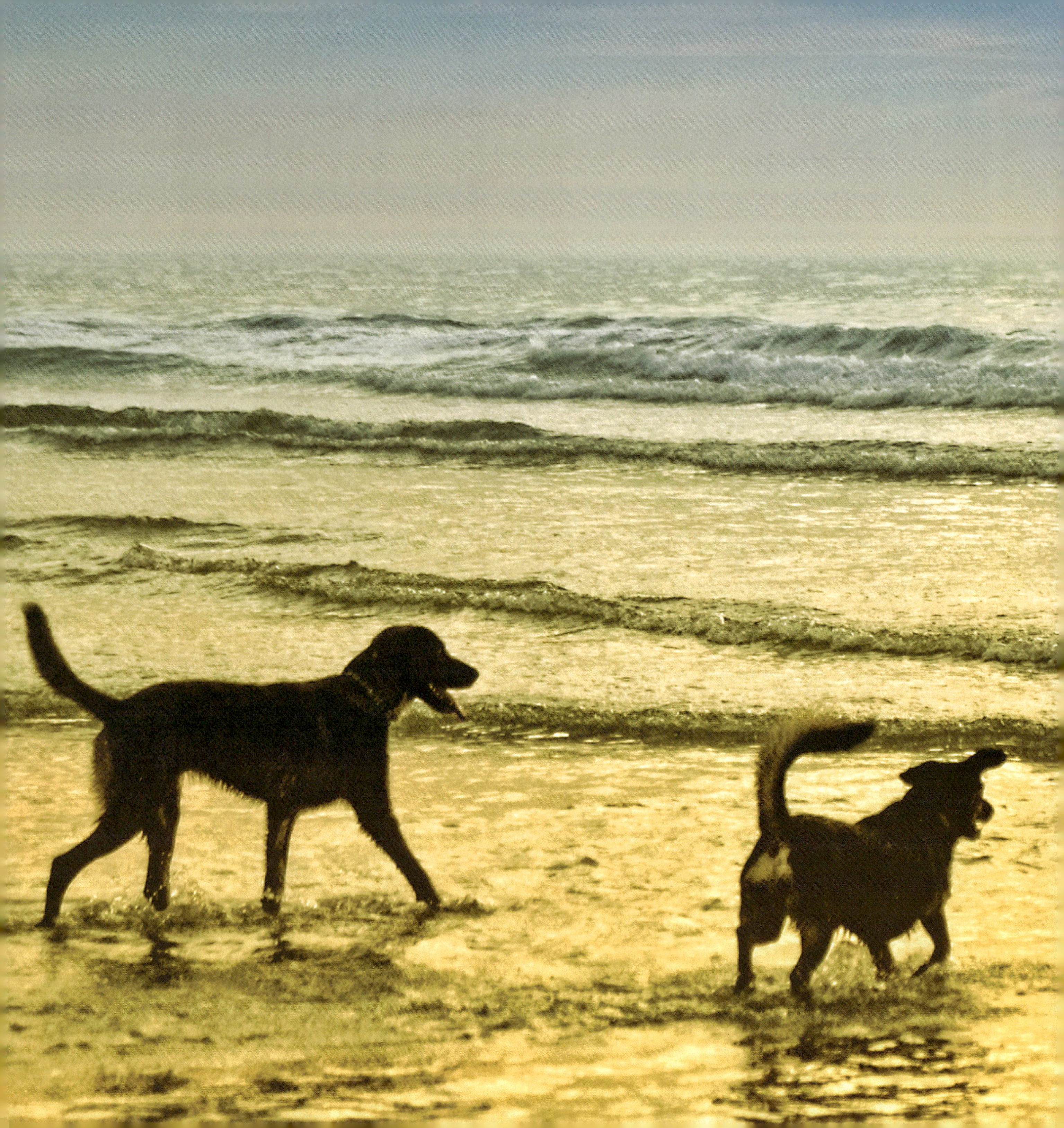

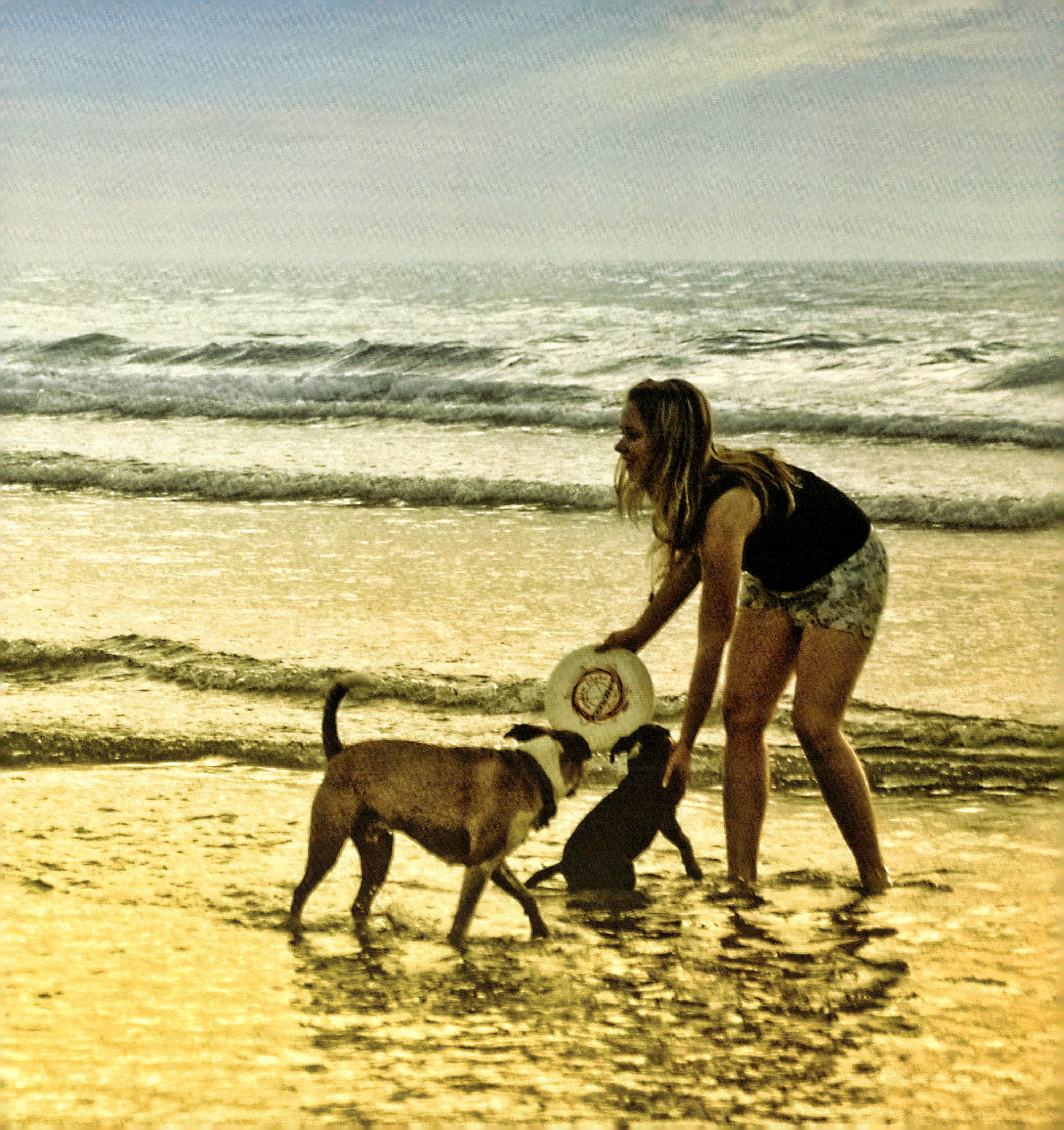

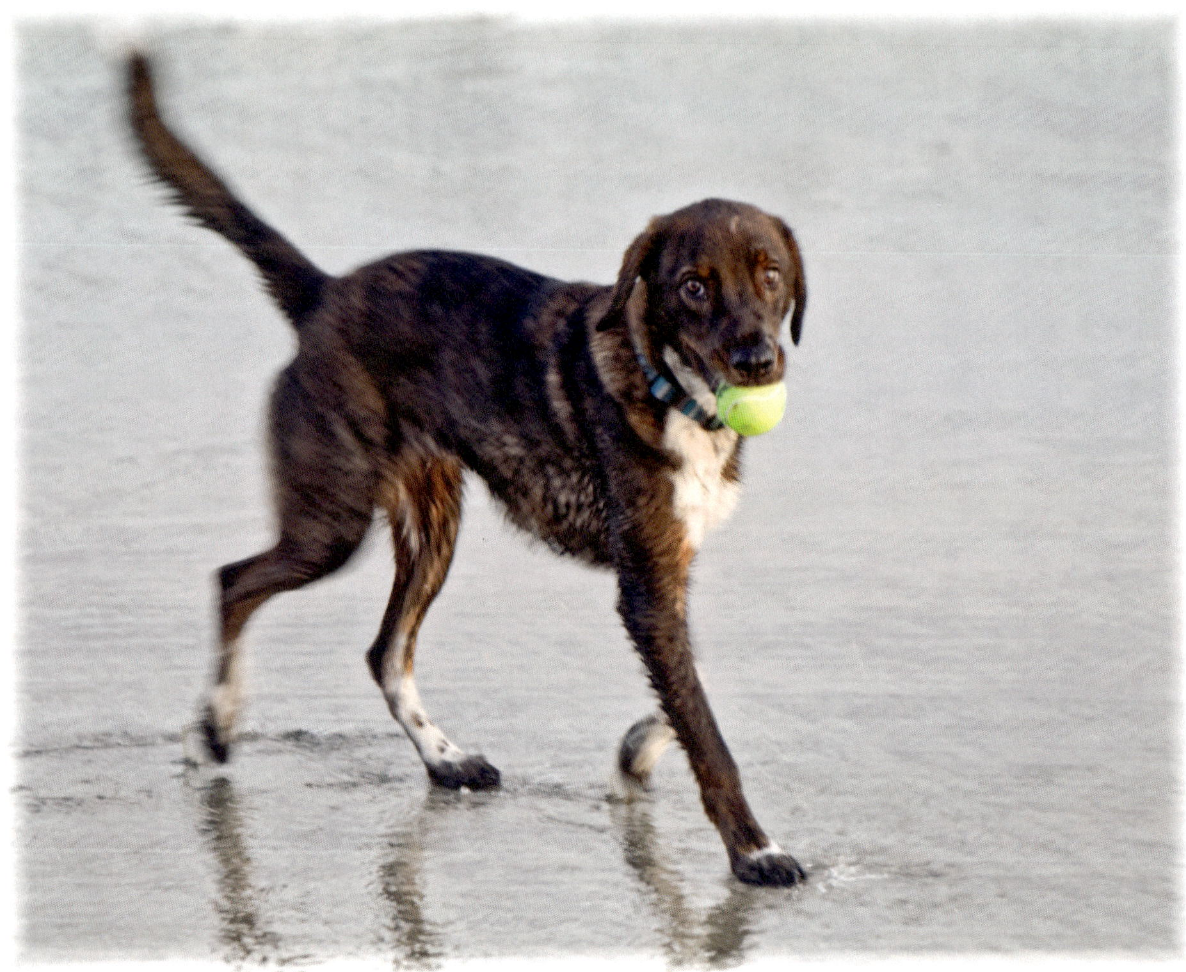

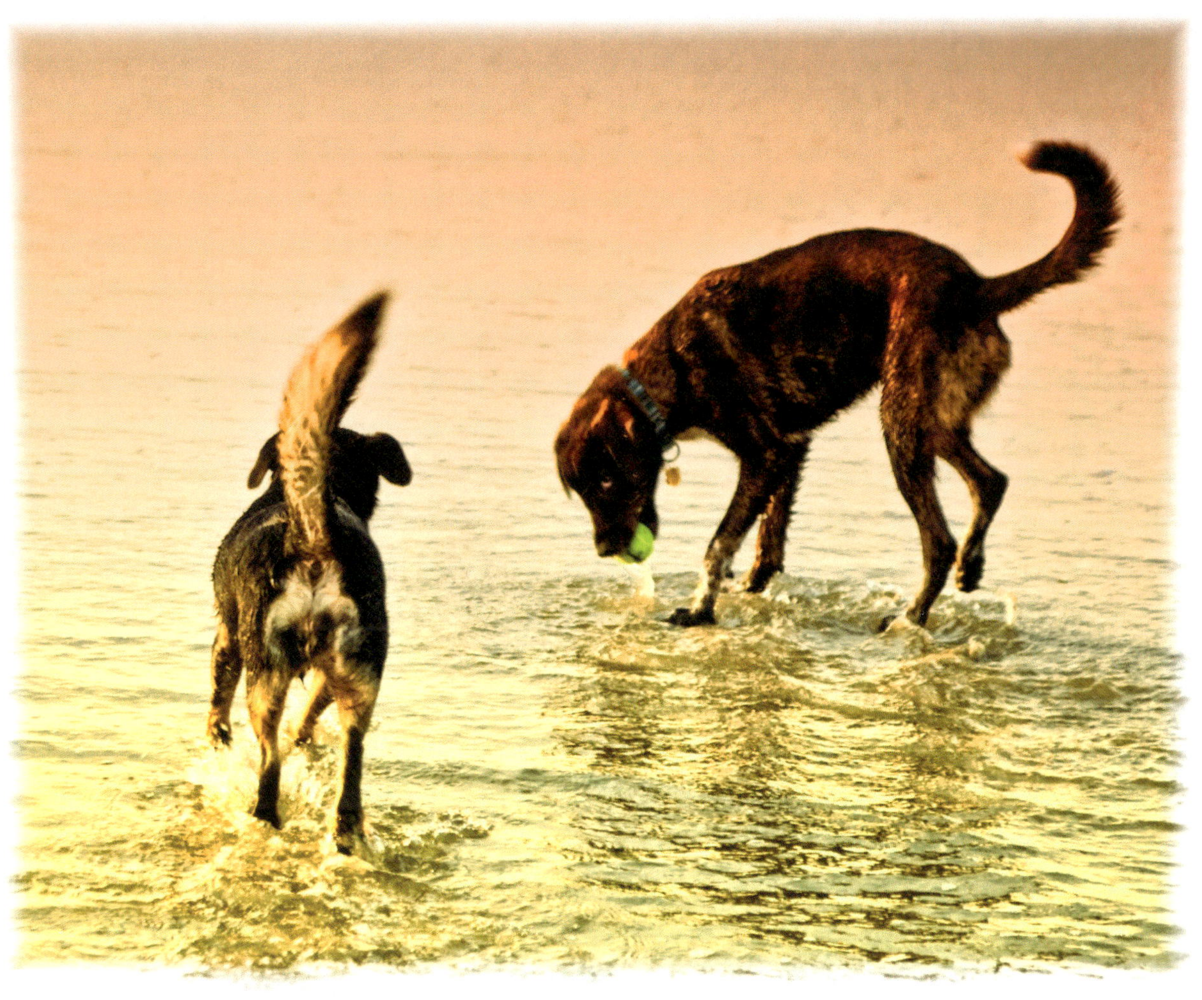

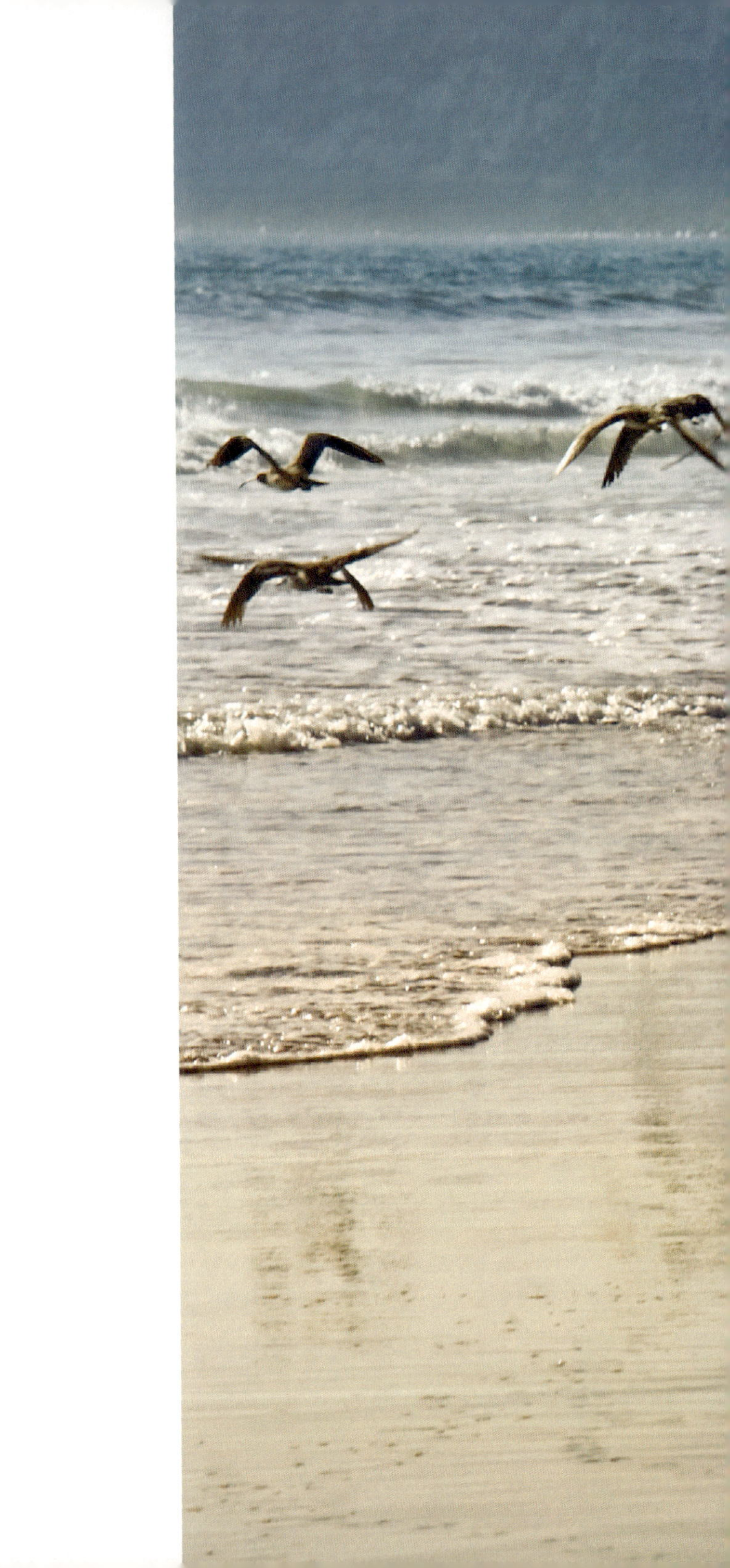

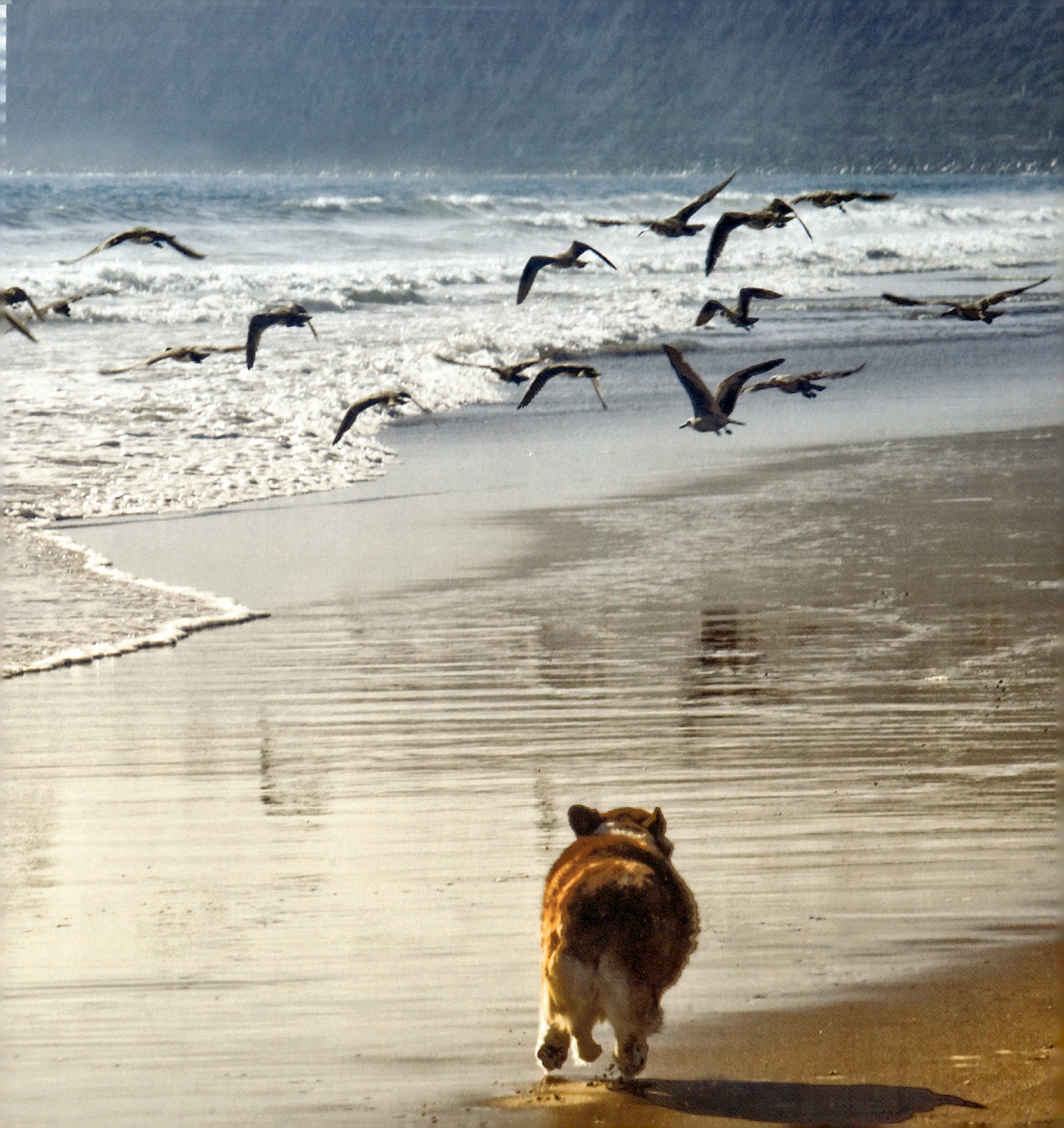

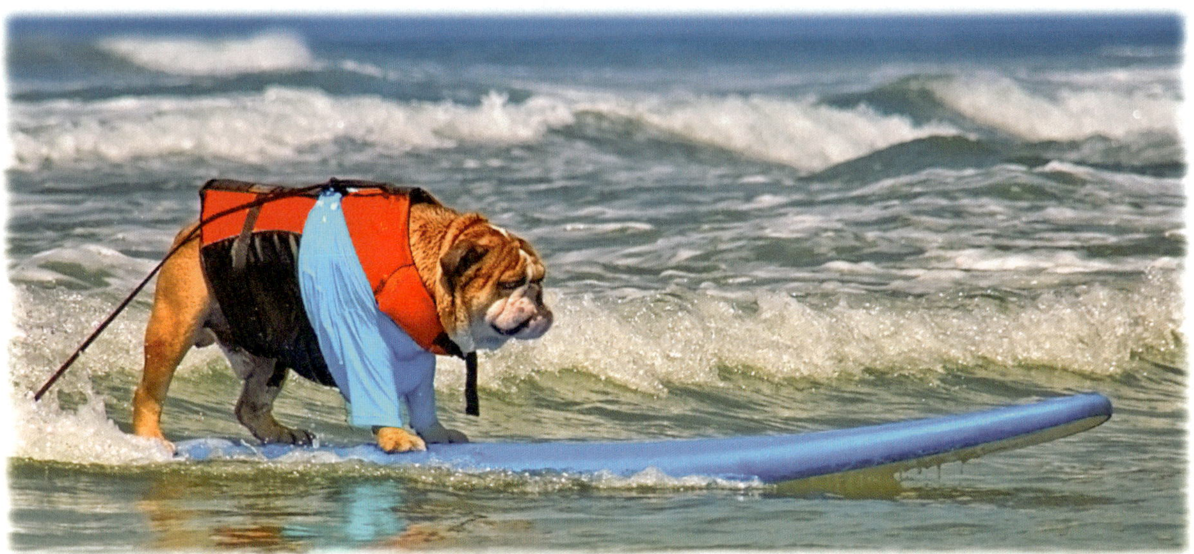

# The Helen Woodward Animal Center Surf-a-thon

Every year, sometime after Labor Day, when the dogs, once more, are allowed to roam Dog beach unleashed, the Helen Woodward Animal Center hosts a spectacular fund raiser—a dog surf-a-thon. It's a splendid event. The beach is crowded with spectators of every age and description and the ocean teeming with owners and dogs of all breeds and sizes.

Dog enthusiasts make a point of returning year after year and have a great time cheering for their favorite canine competitor.

I could go on and on about just how much fun attending the event is, but I think the photographs on the next pages speak best for themselves.

Instead let me fill you in on a few facts about the event I was given by John Van Zante from the Helen Woodward Animal Center.

- The Helen Woodward Animal Center's surf-a-thon  is now the largest and most popular event of its kind in the world.
- Inspired by the earliest surf-a-thons, similar events are now popping up all over the world, spreading like rings in the water.
- A world championship is under consideration for the future, but there are many logistics to be handled before it can actually happen.

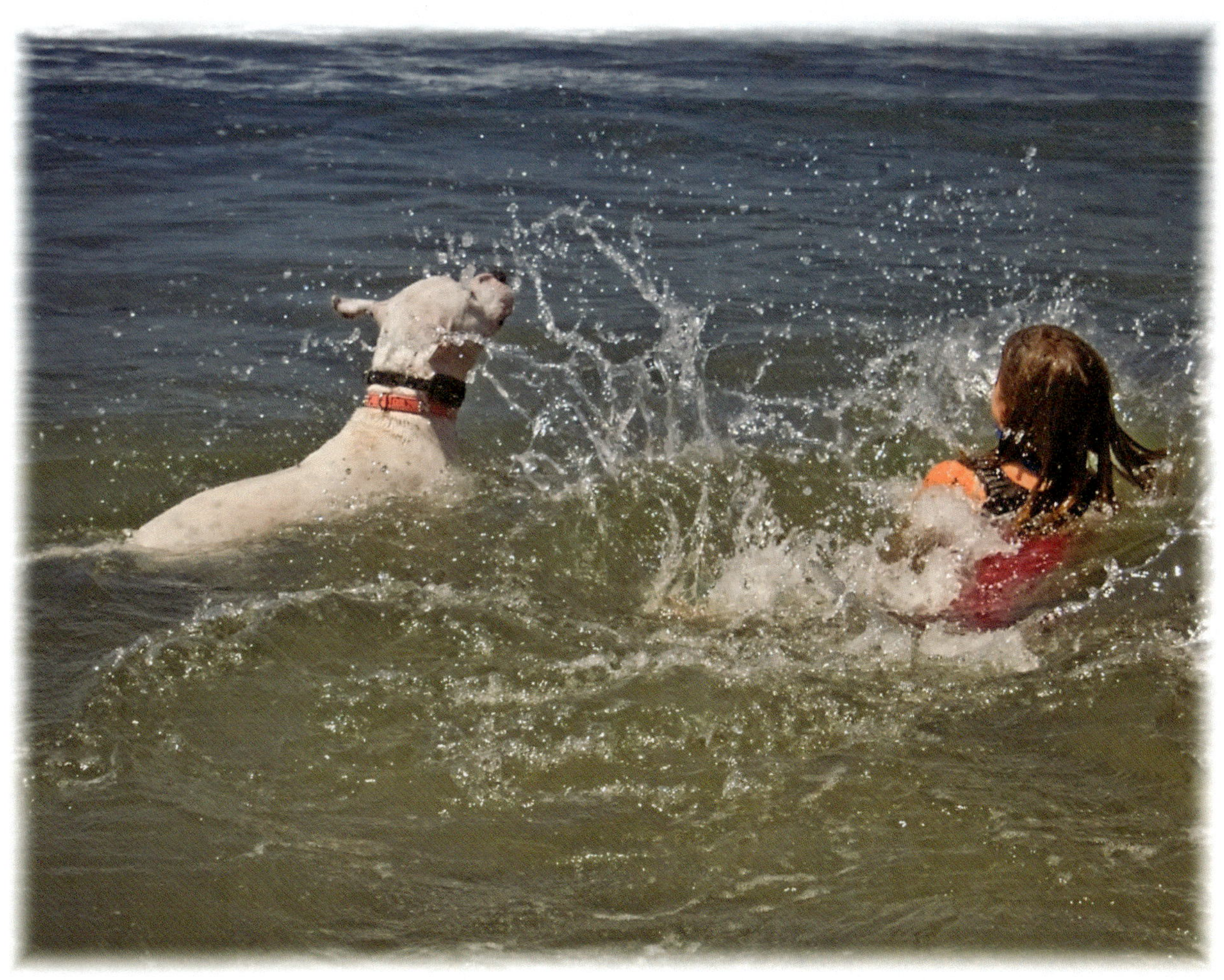

- The surf-a-thon that started out as merely a small, fun, informal event has garnered 165 million media impressions. That number is expected to rise to more than 200 million.
- The 2009 surf-a-thon drew television crews from Spain, Korea, France, and the United States.
- World famous "human surfers" brought their dogs to participate in the event.
- Special surfboards are now being constructed especially for dogs in order to improve their balance as they ride the waves.
- Although it's a competition, the surf-a-thon is more about showing off the dogs and enjoying the fun and companionship than about actually winning.
- Dog surfing is all about trust. It's a  wonderful way of enhancing the bond between a dog and his family.
- Dog surfing is a fun way to exercise and enjoy the water.
- The Helen Woodward Animal Center offers surfing lessons—a great way to have fun and unite the family.
- When asked why he wanted to cover a seemingly trivial event so far away, a London journalist smiled. "Because it's so typically Californian," he said.

For more information about the surf-a-thon go to:
**http://www.animalcenter.org/events/surfdog/**

For more information about Helen Woodward Animal Center go to:
**http://www.animalcenter.org**

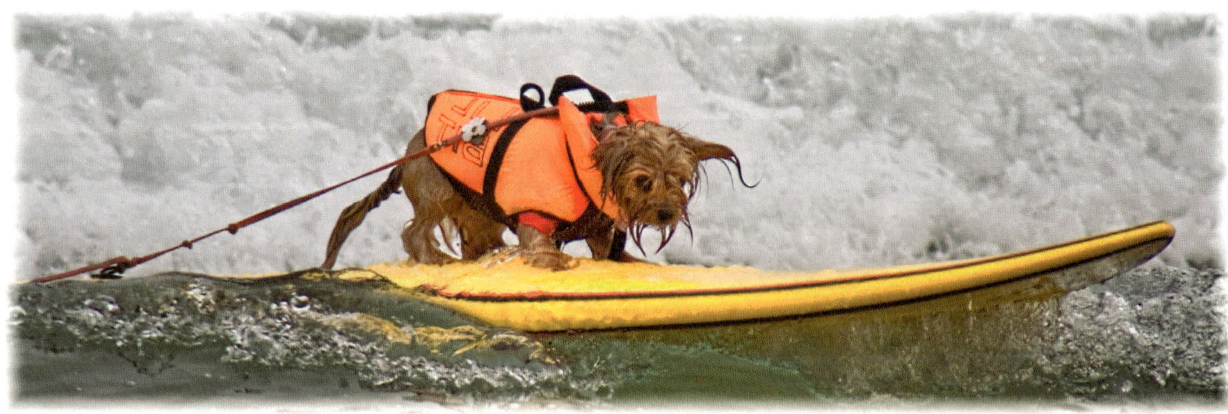

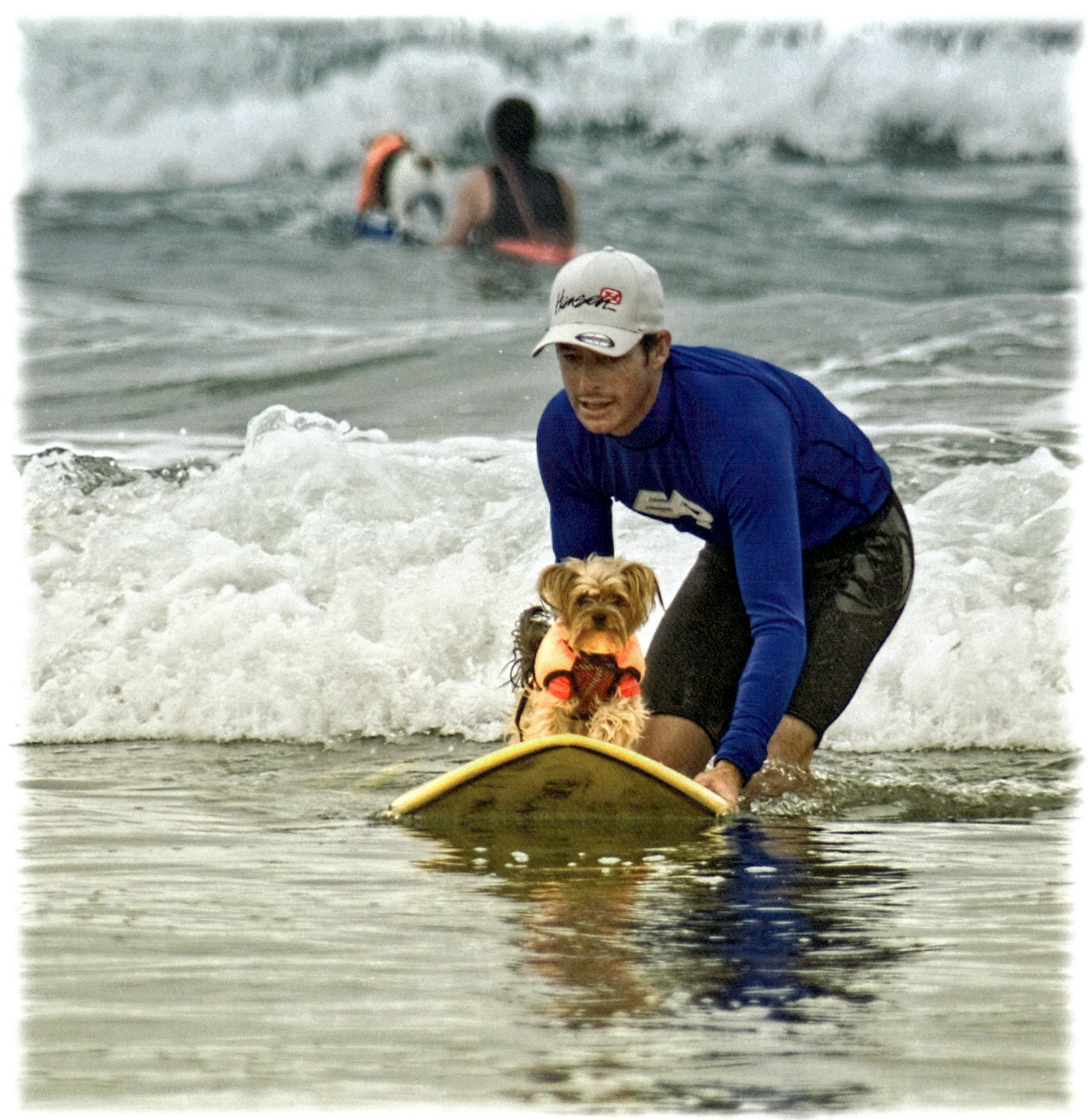

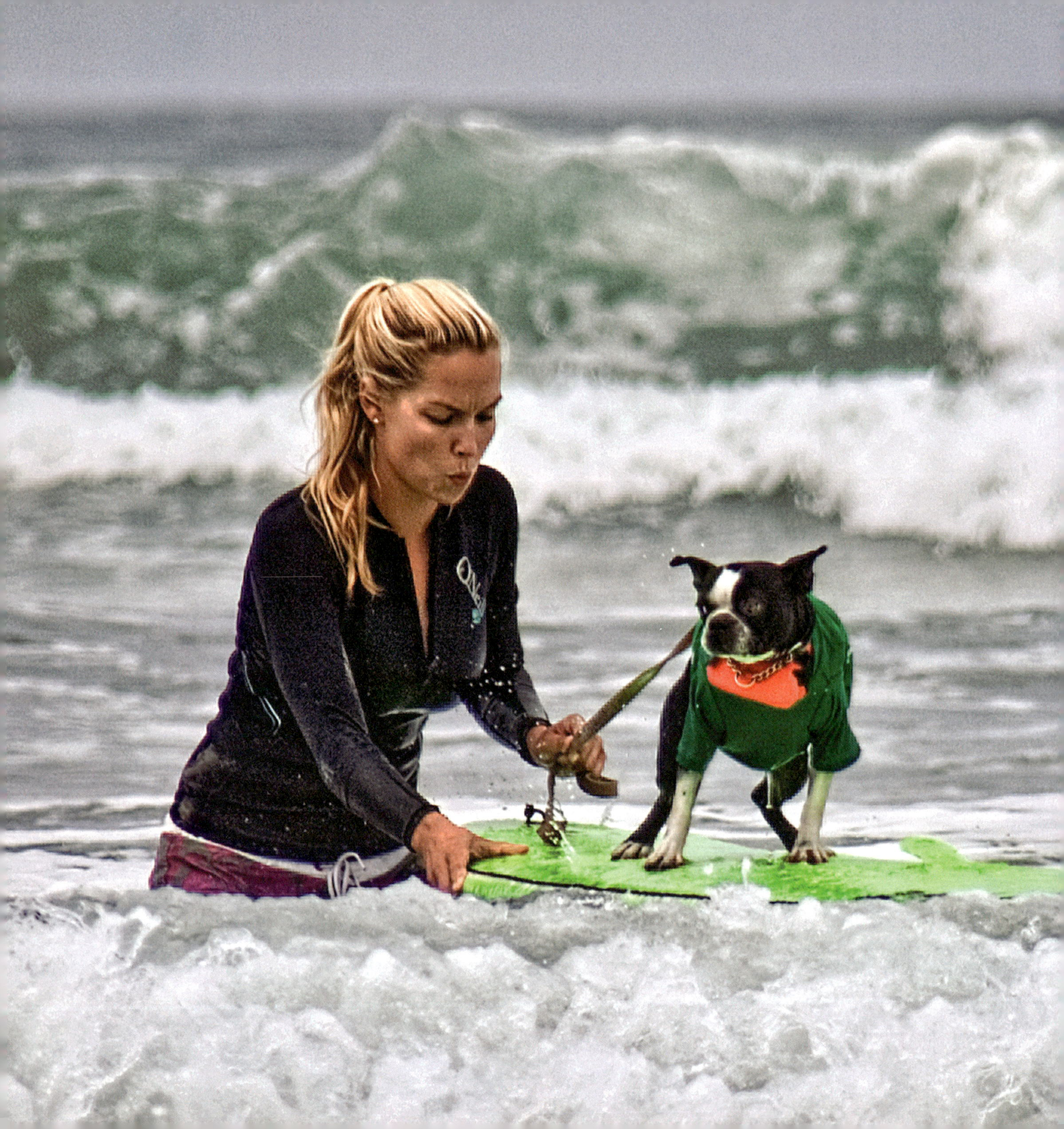

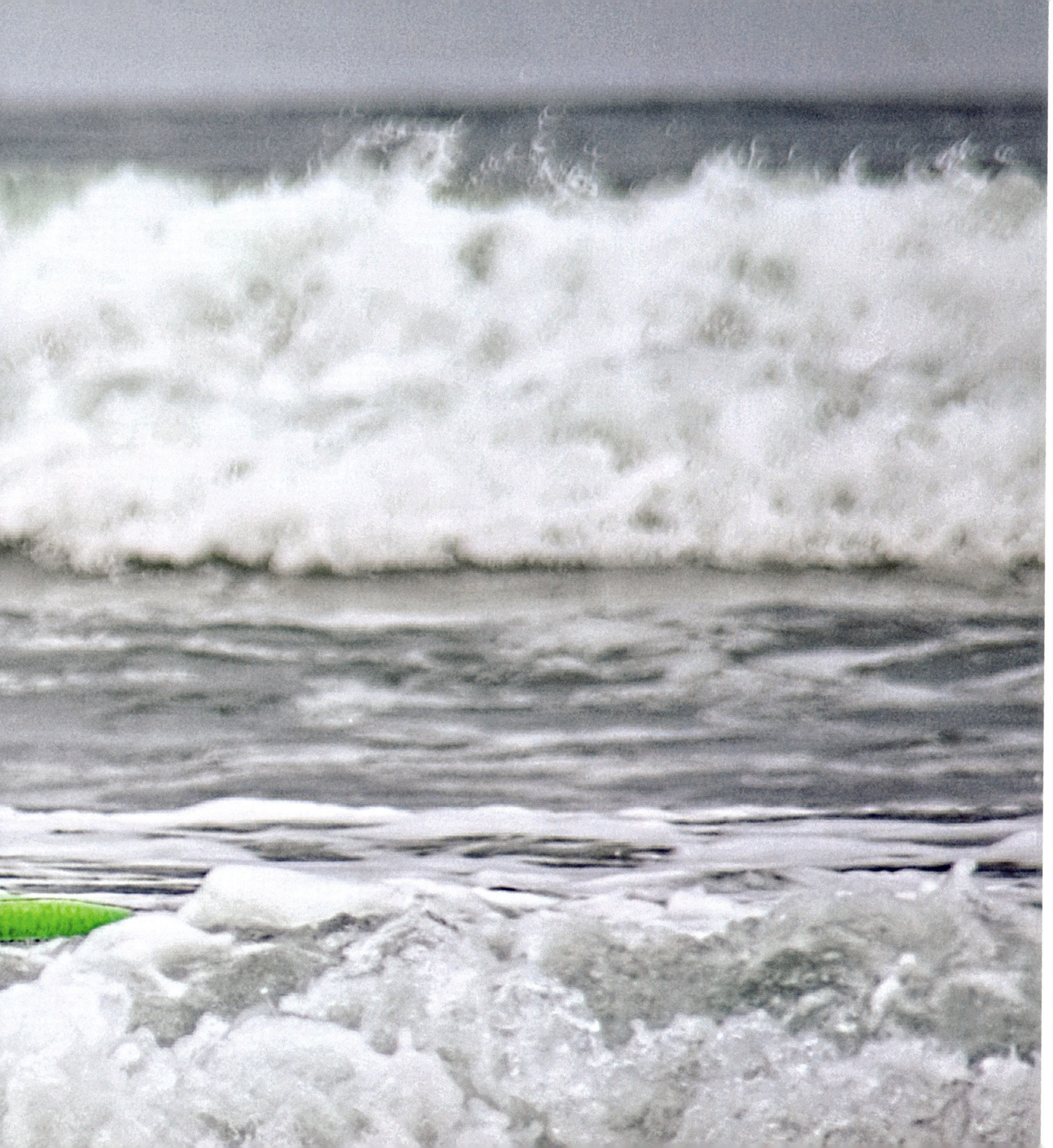

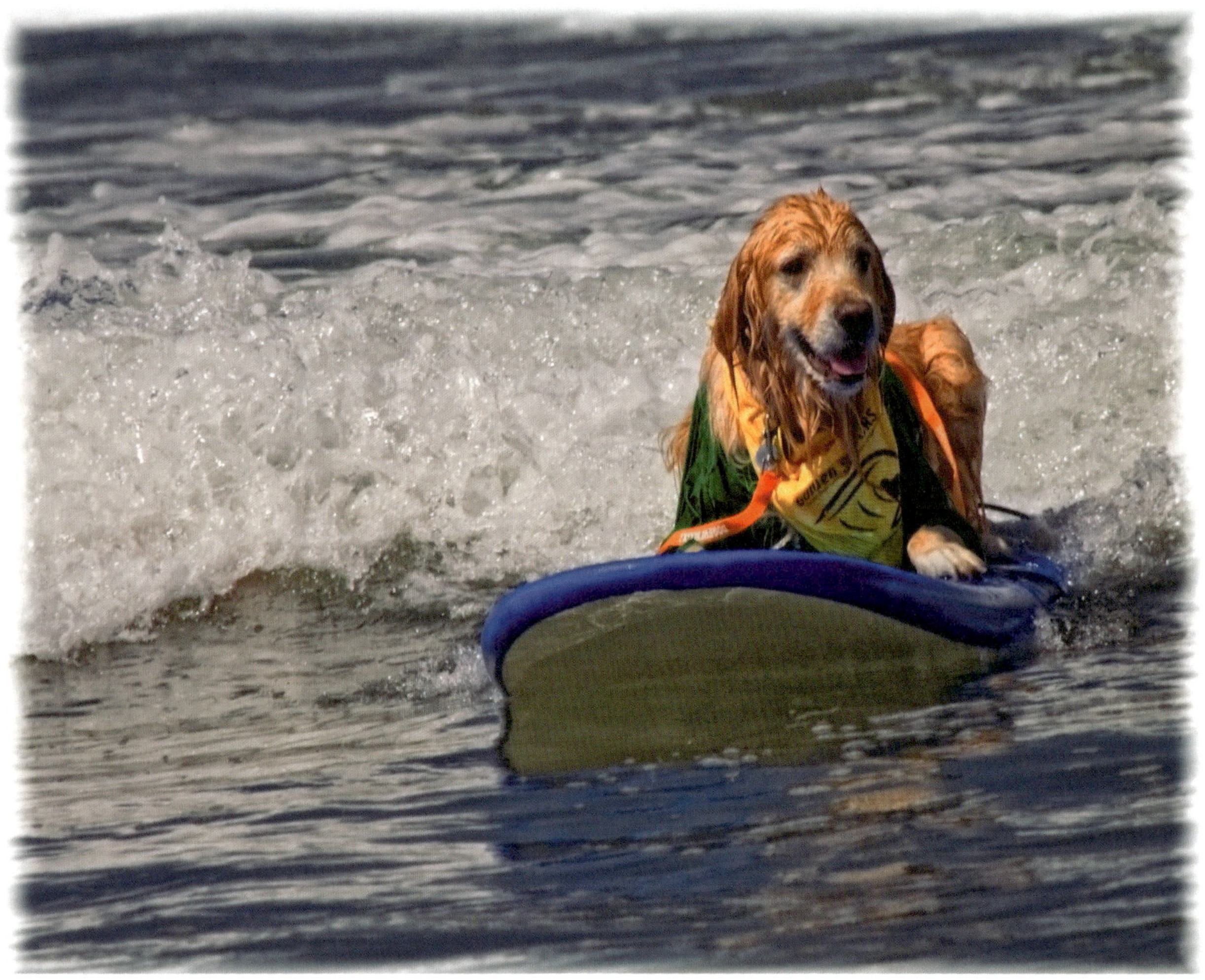

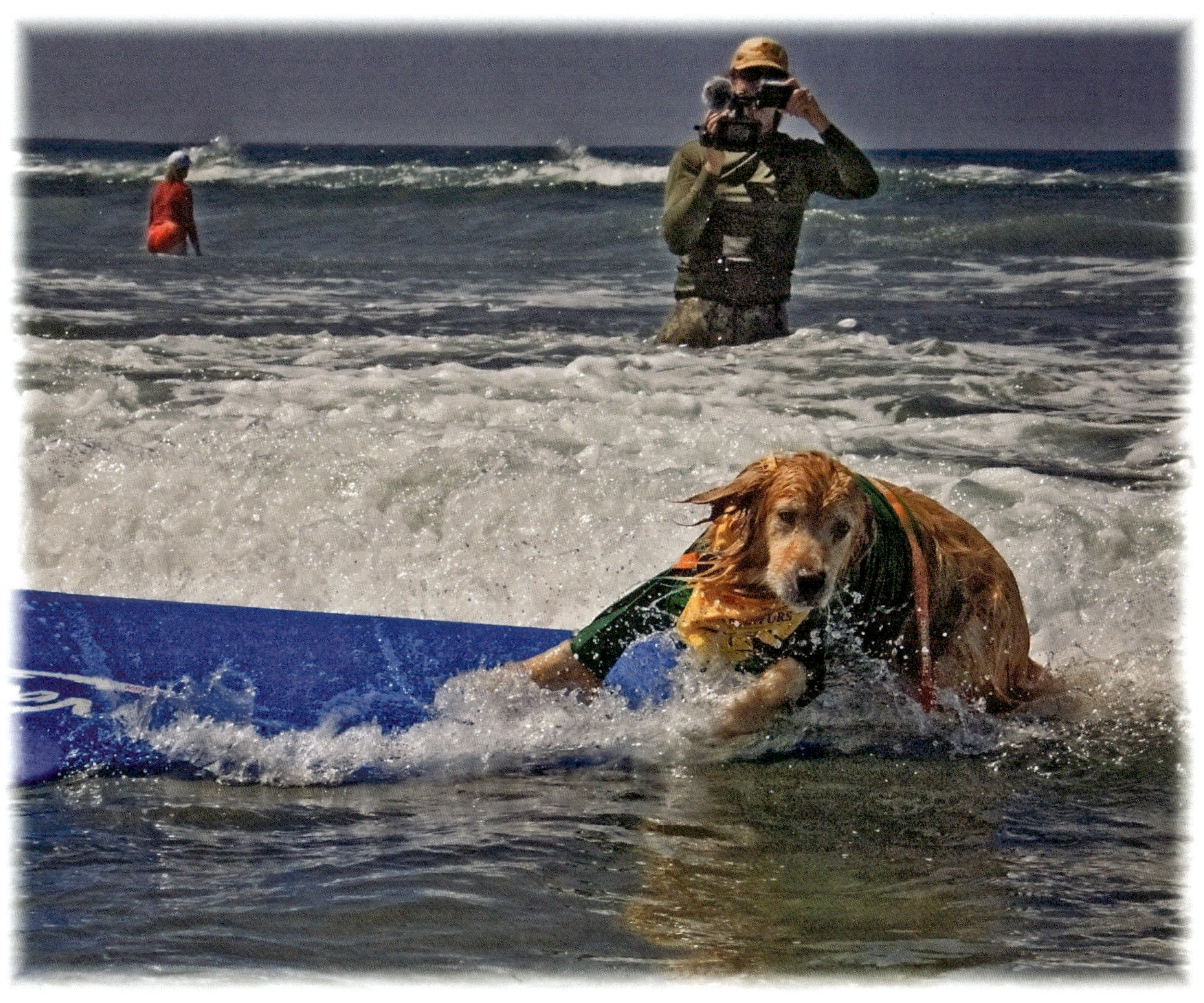

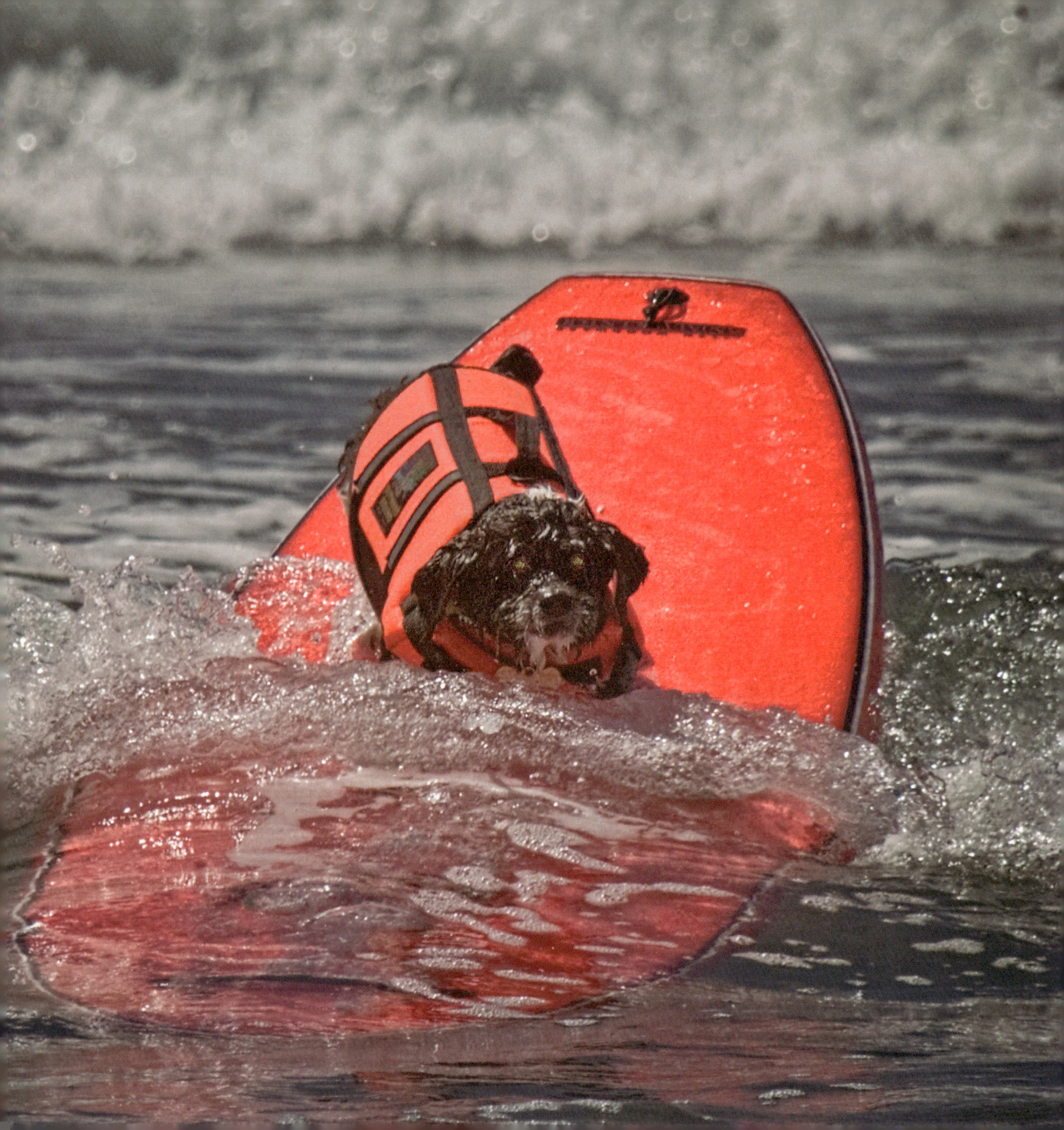

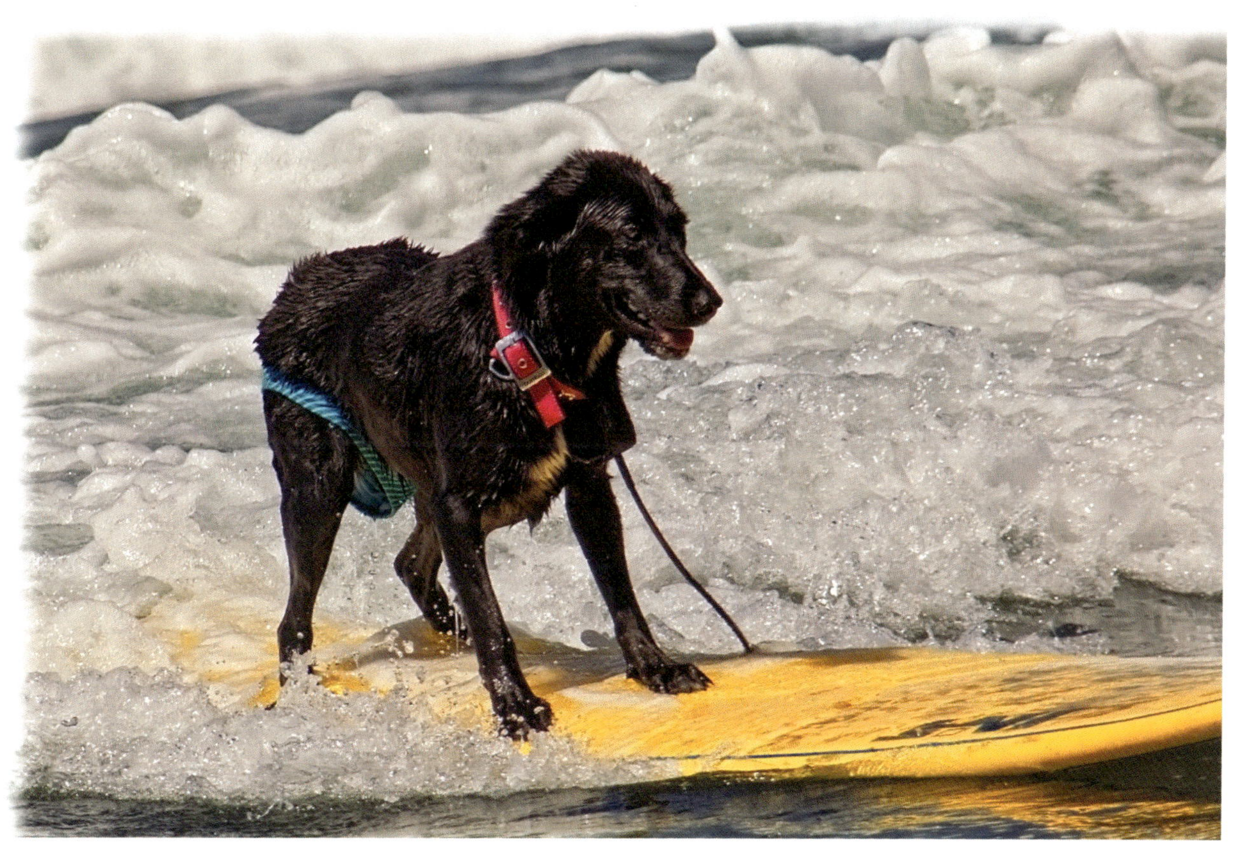

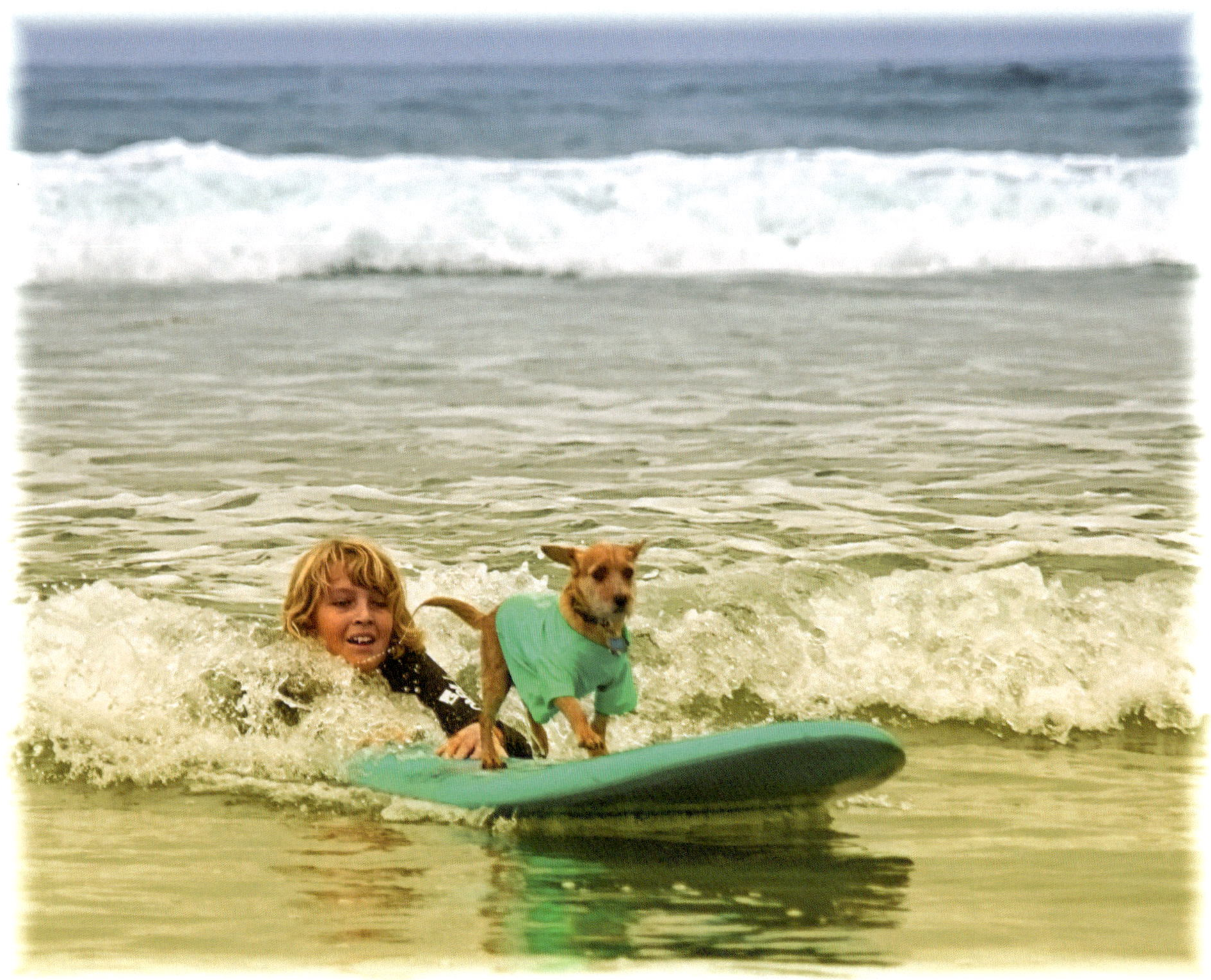

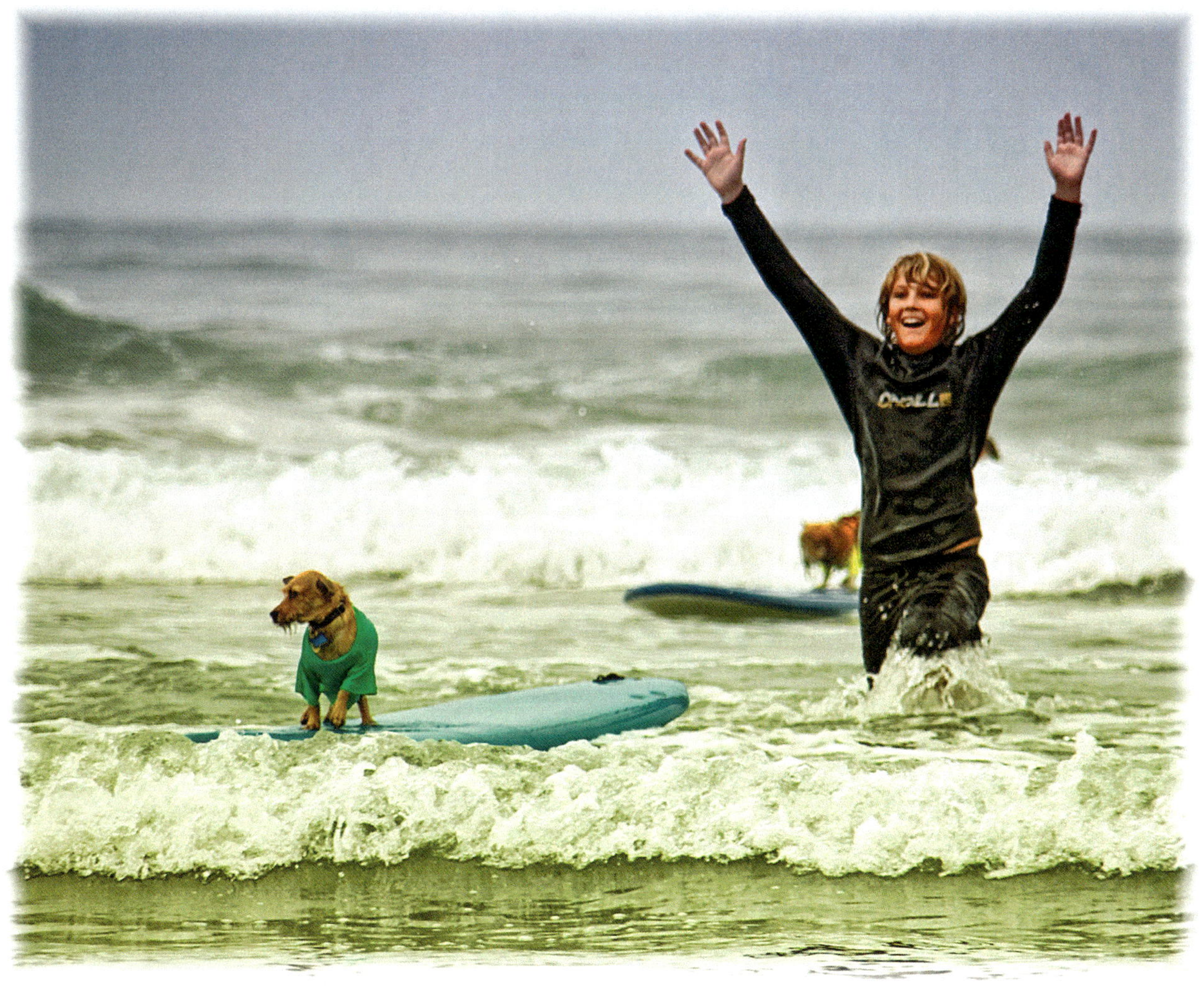

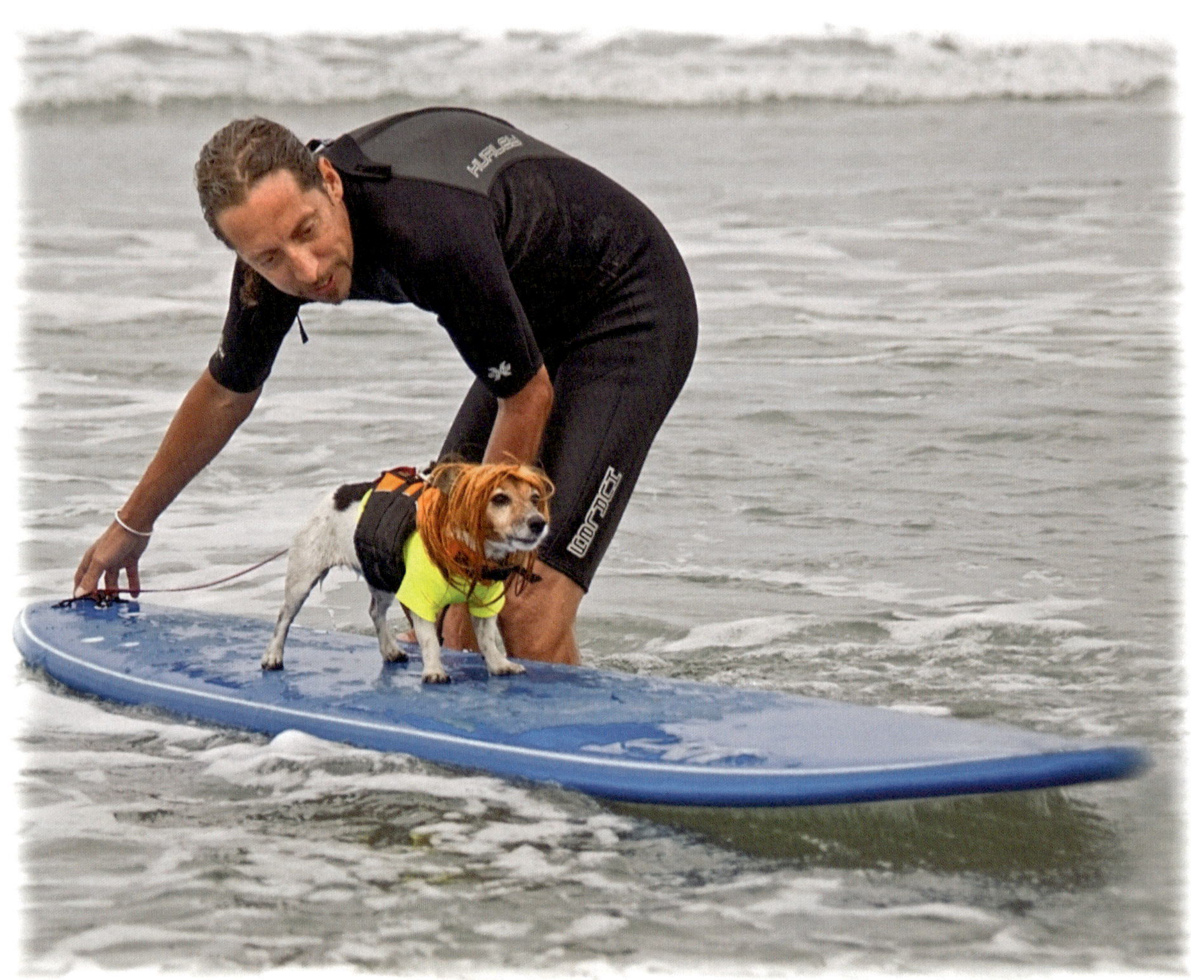

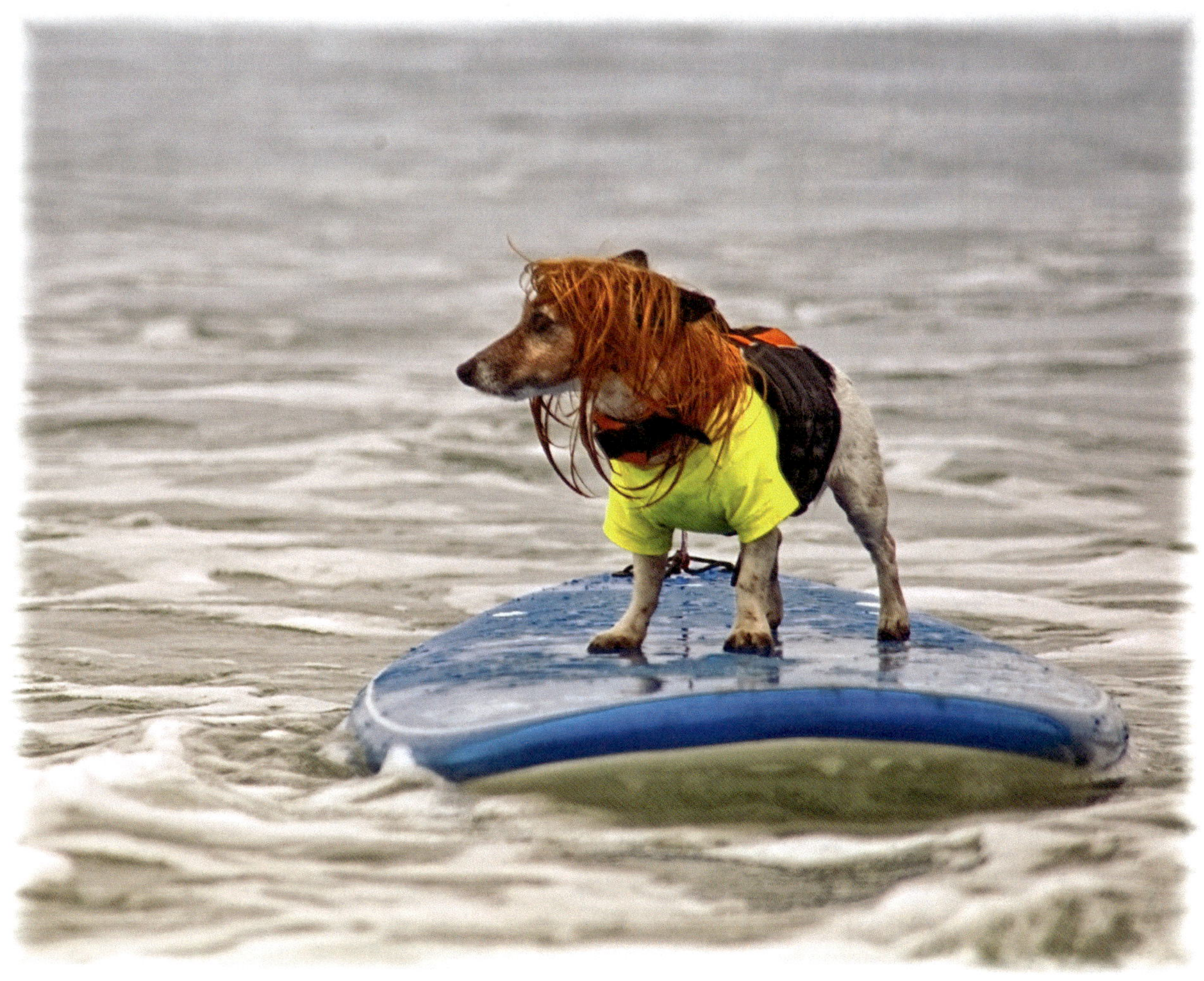

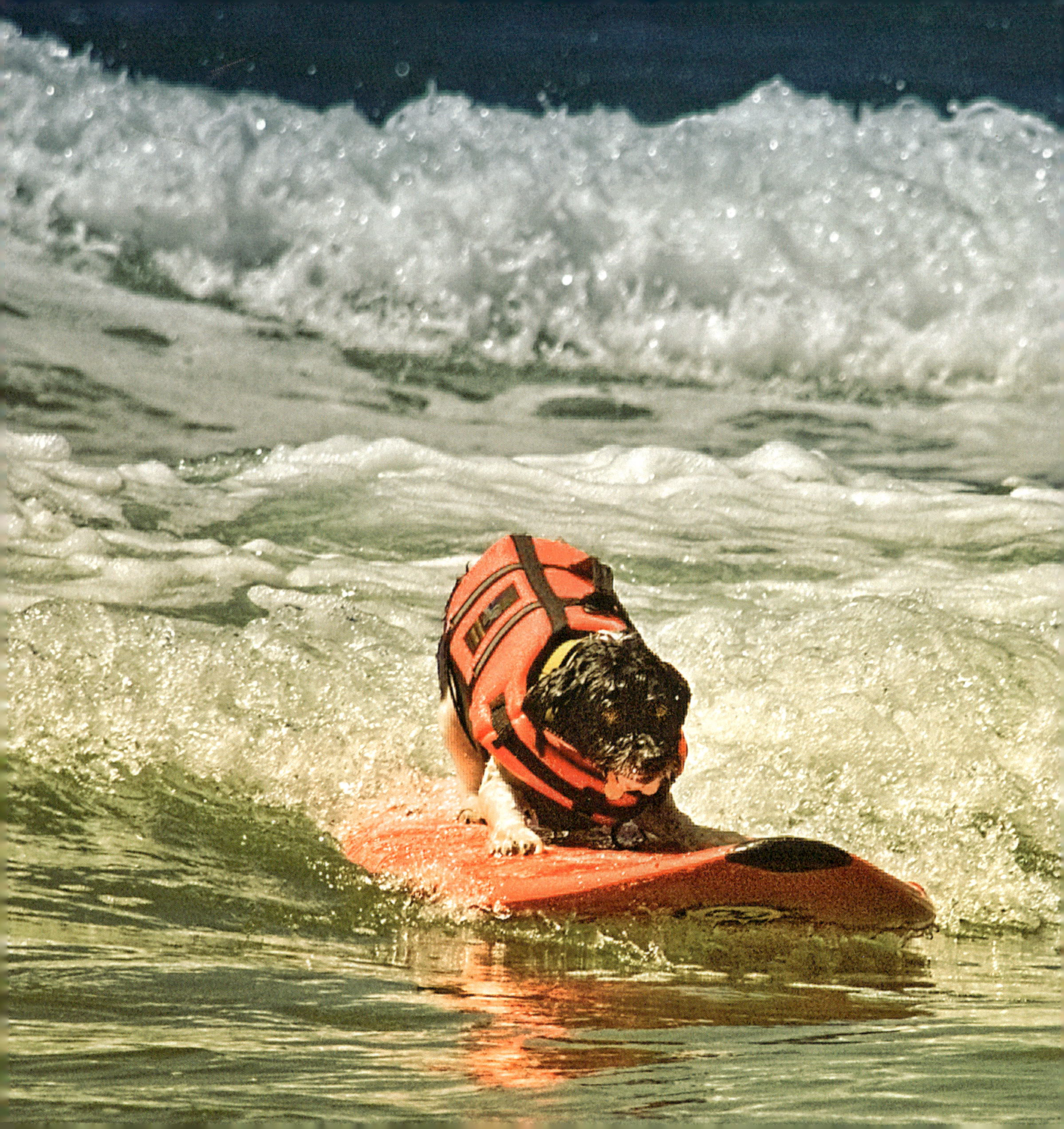

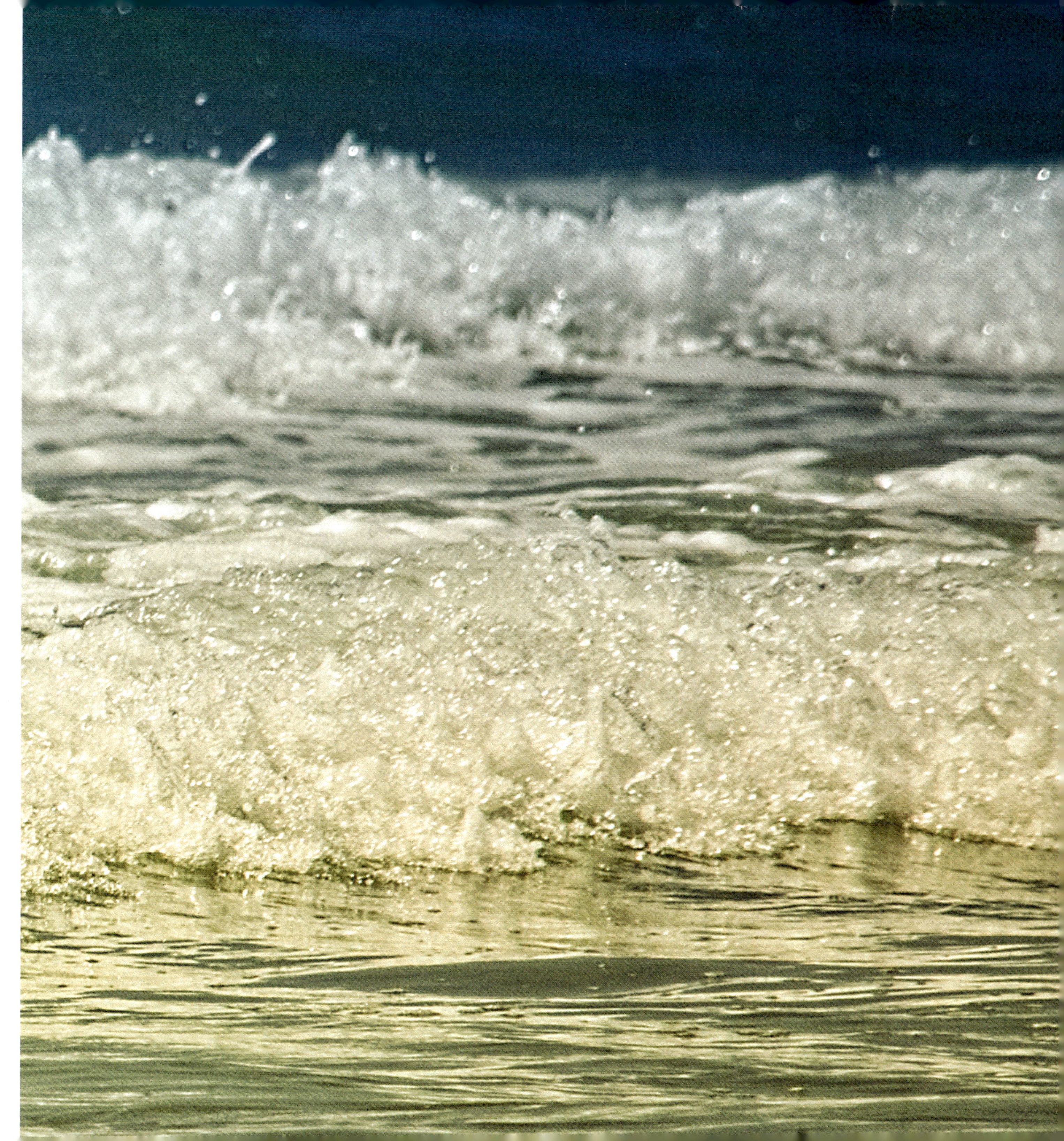

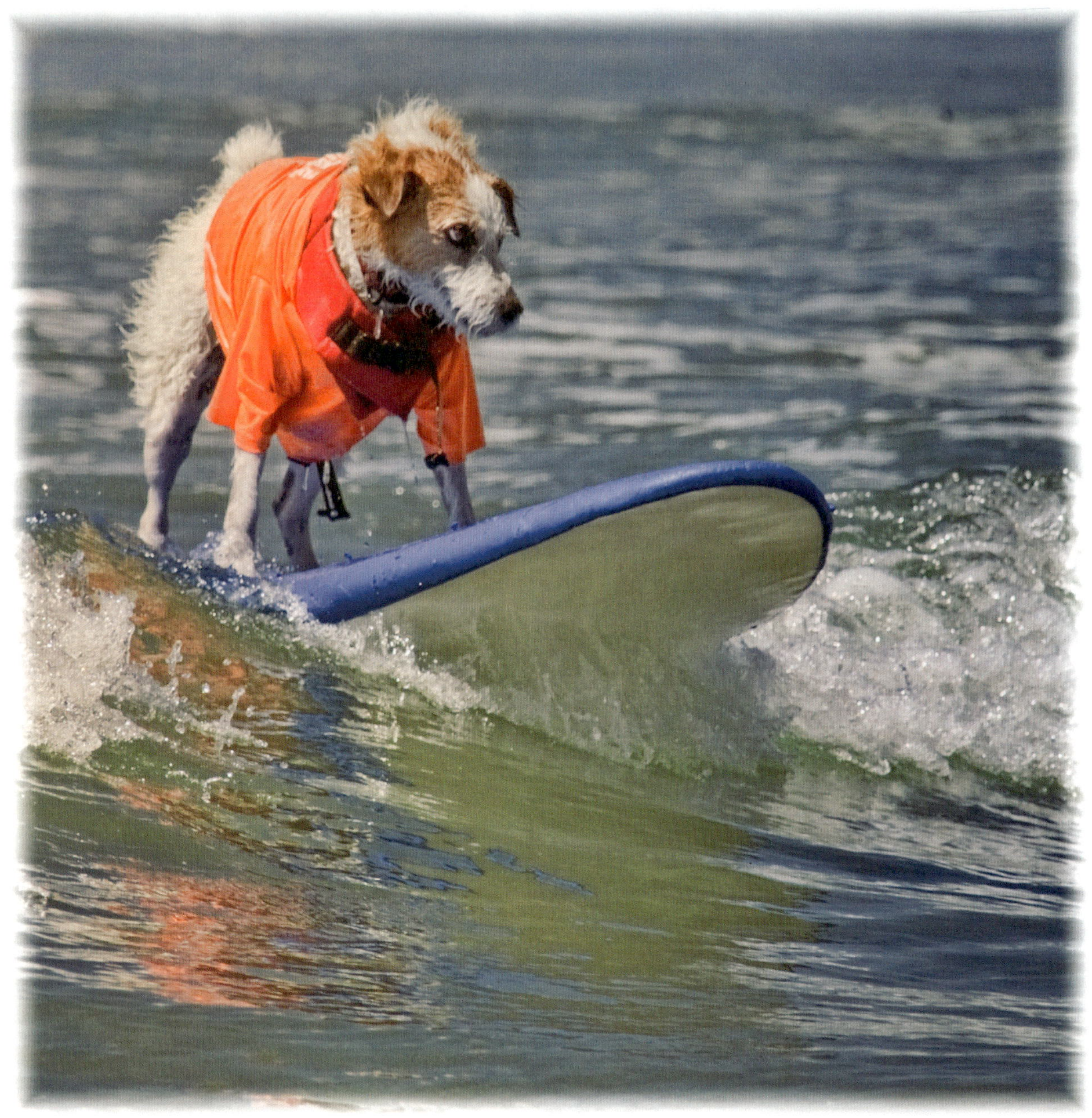

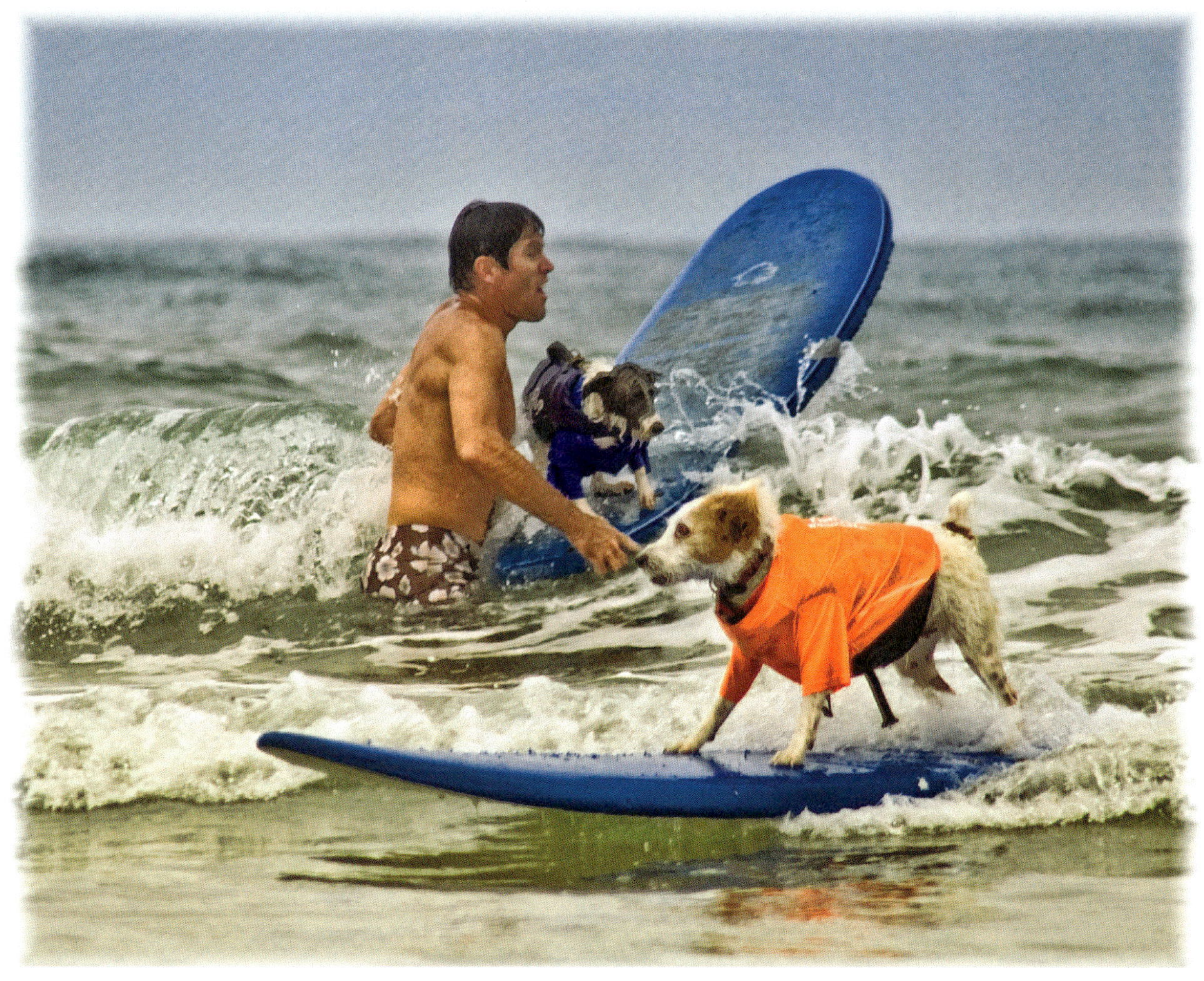

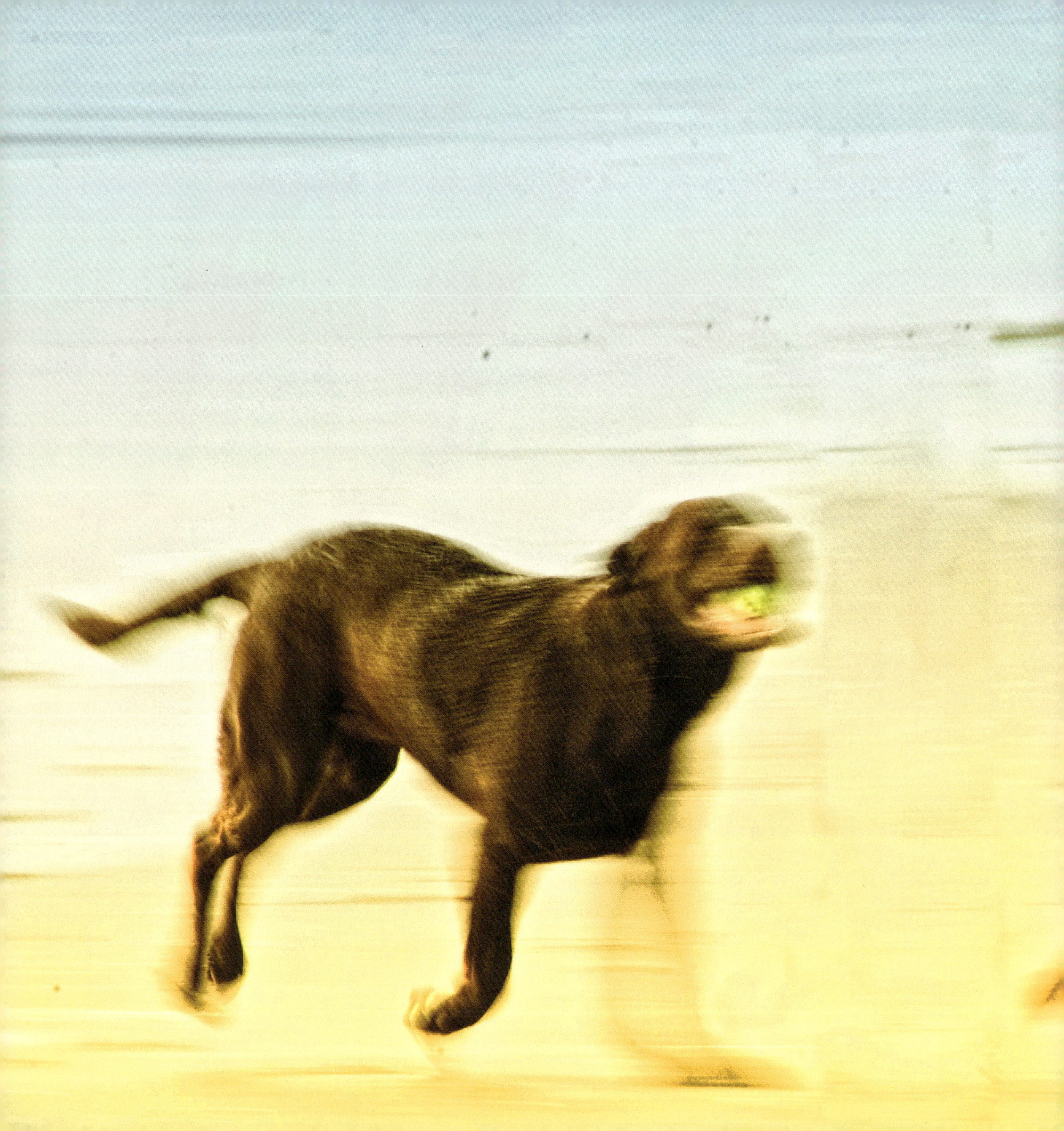

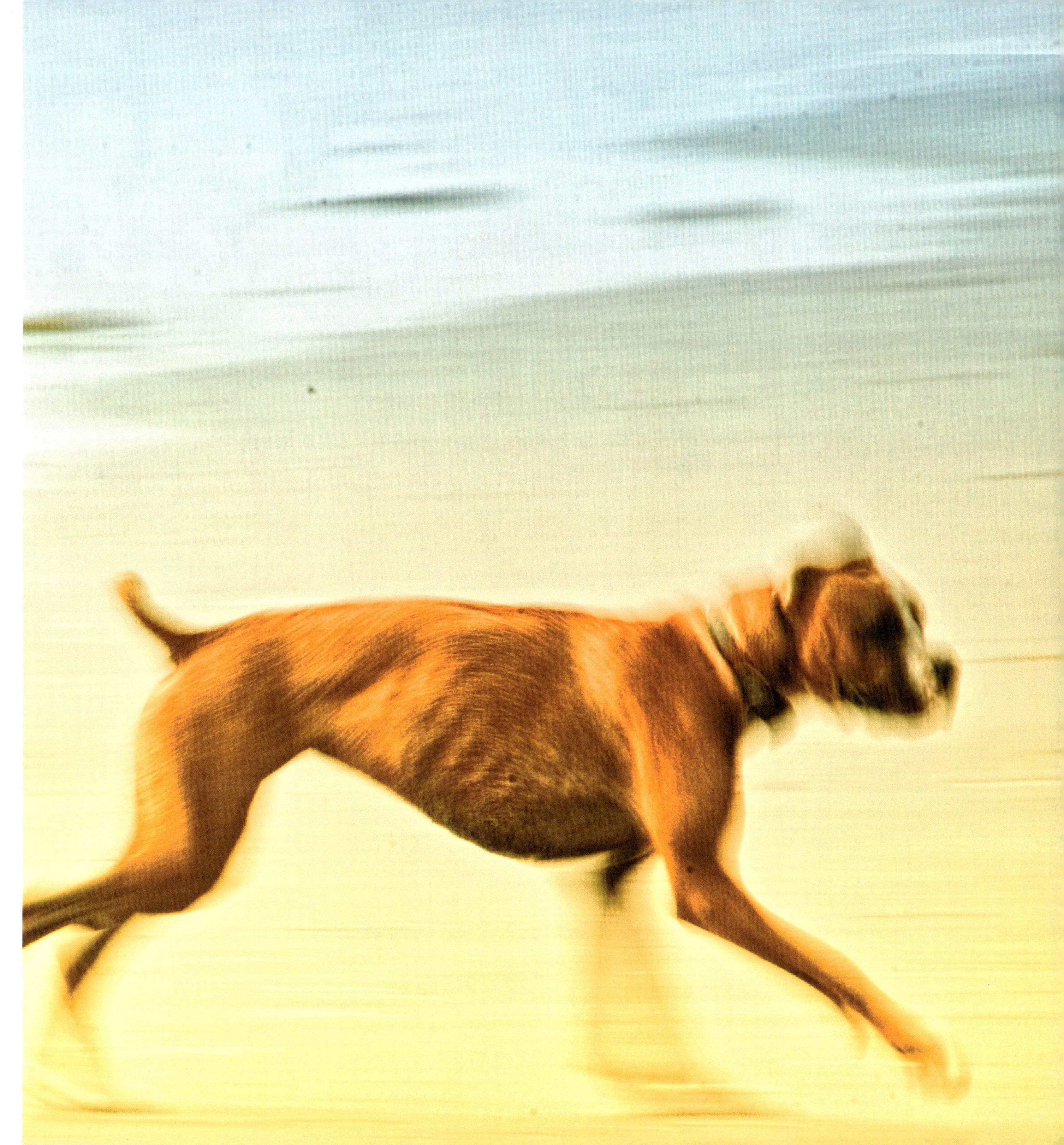

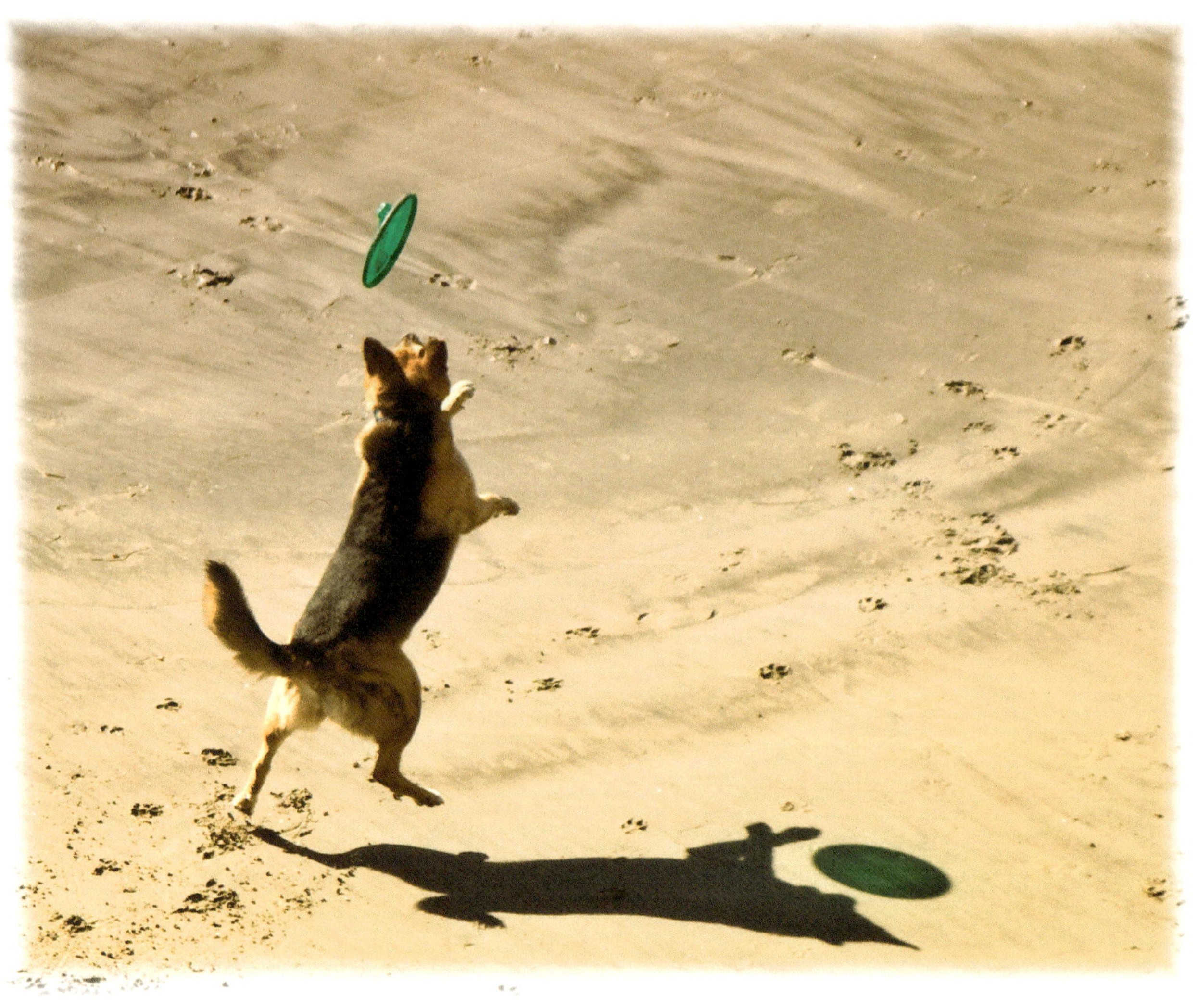

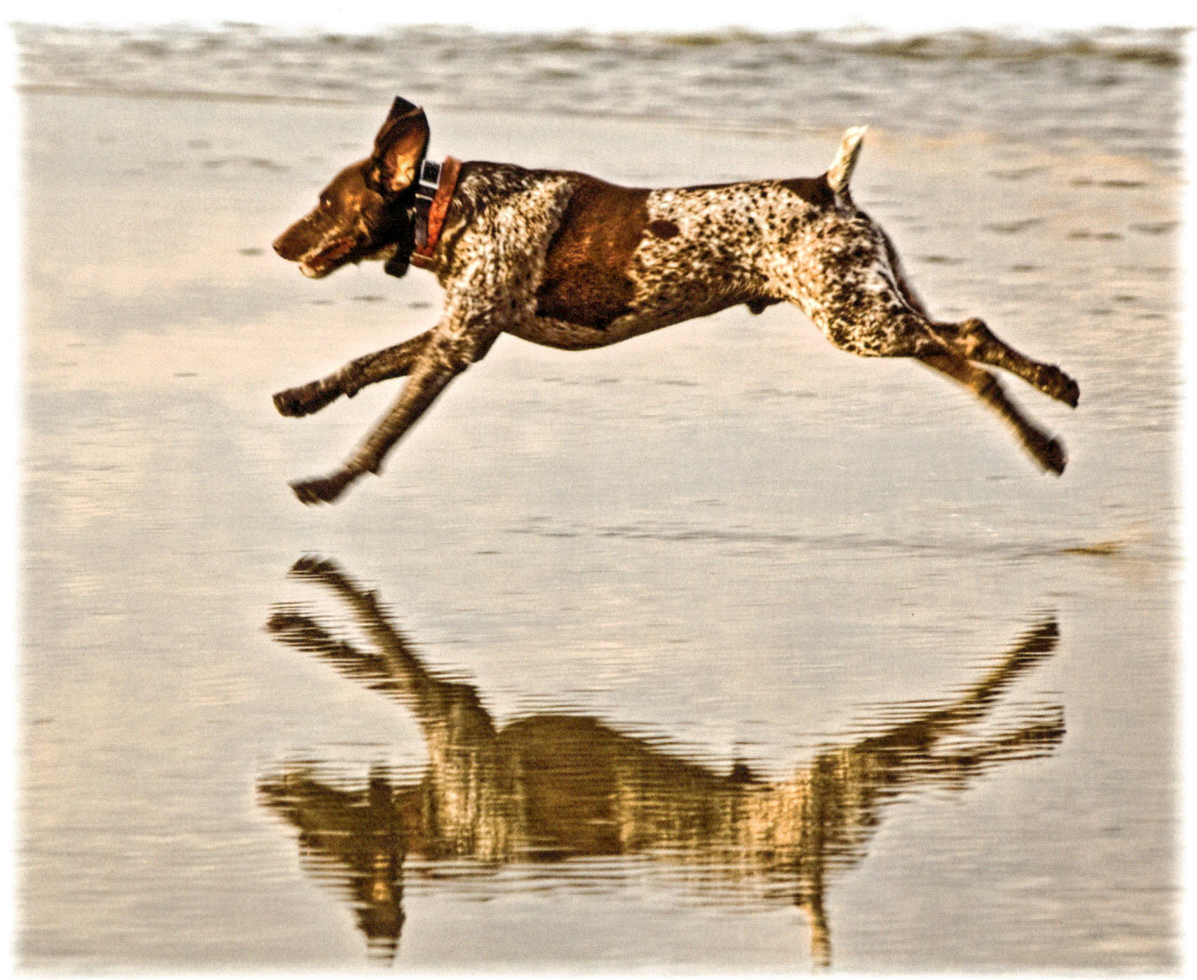

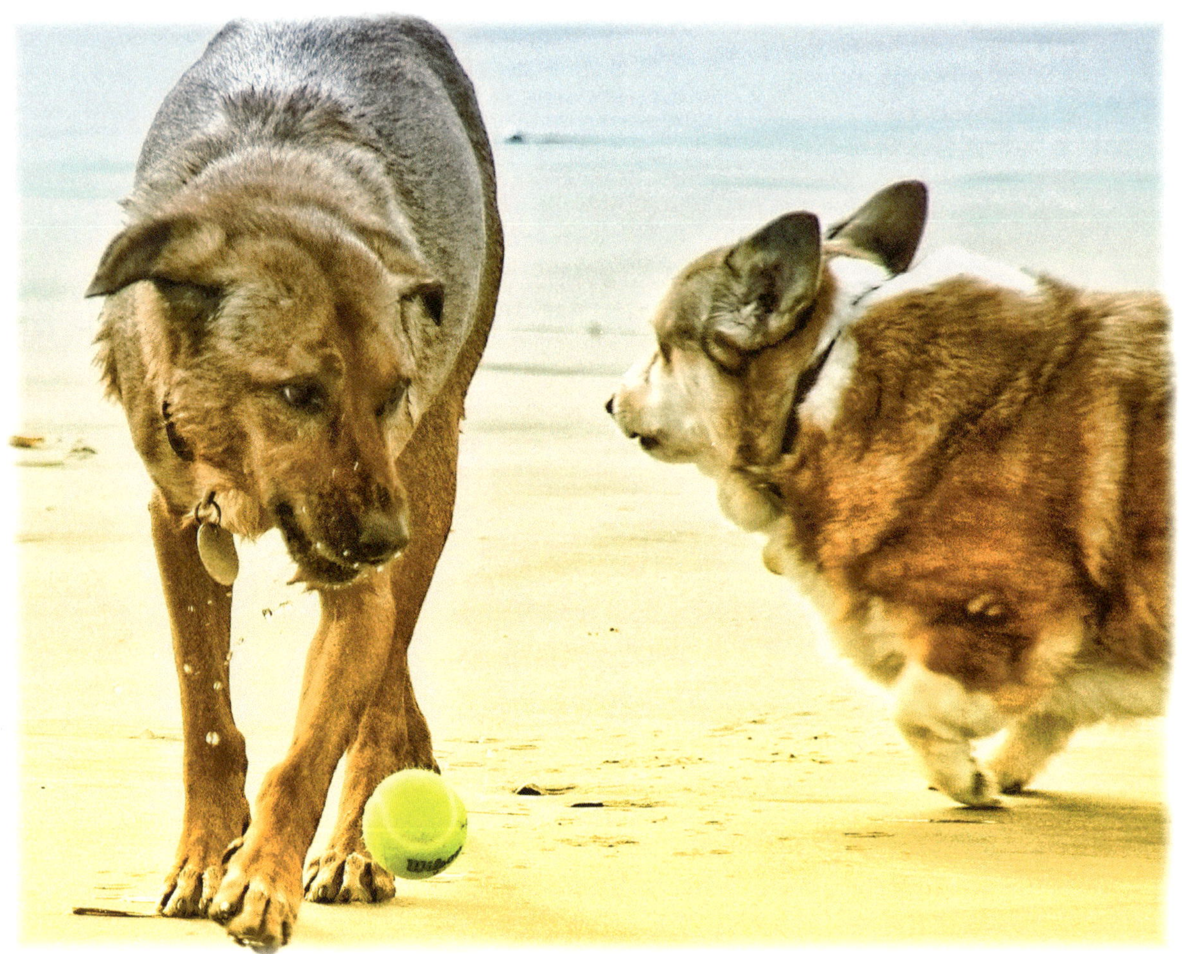

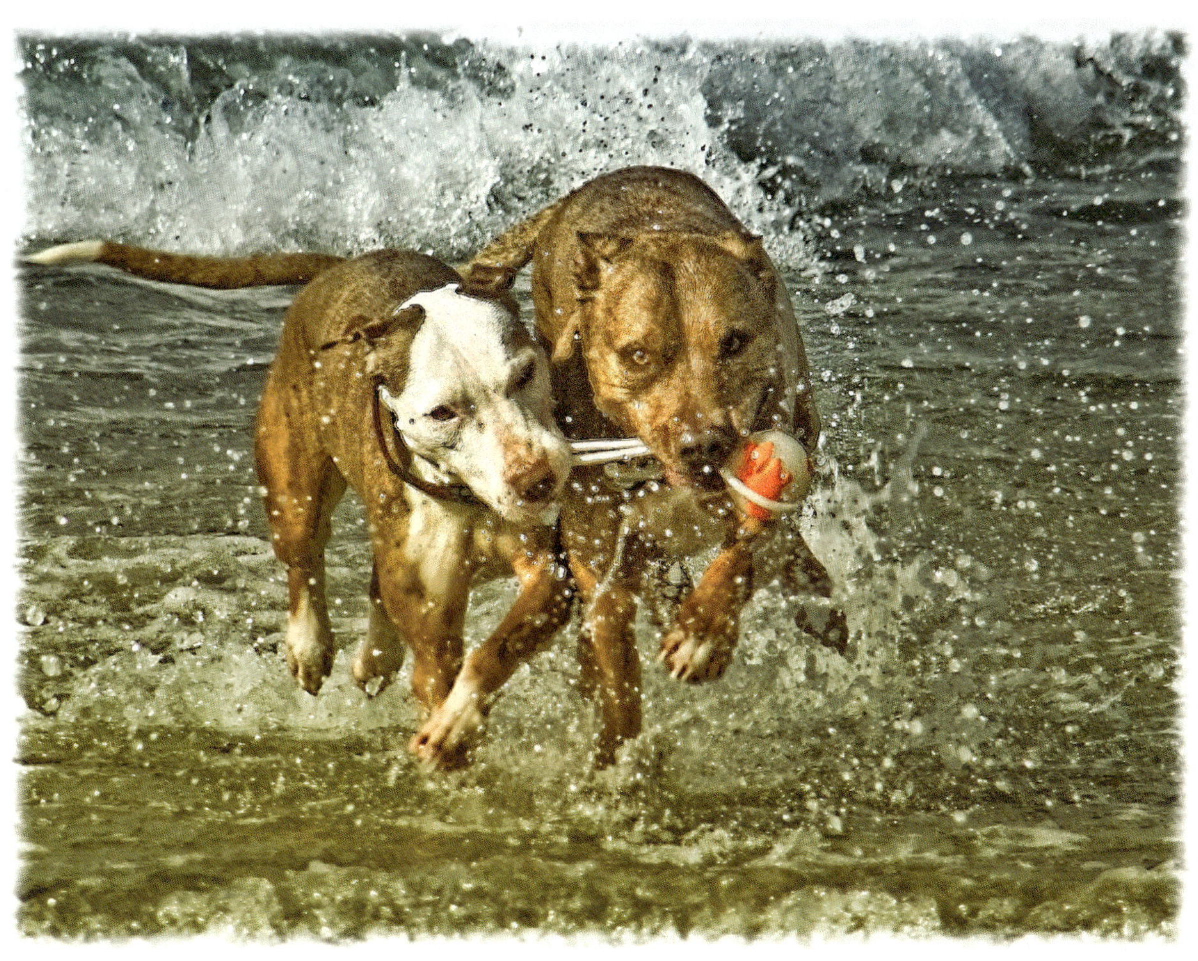

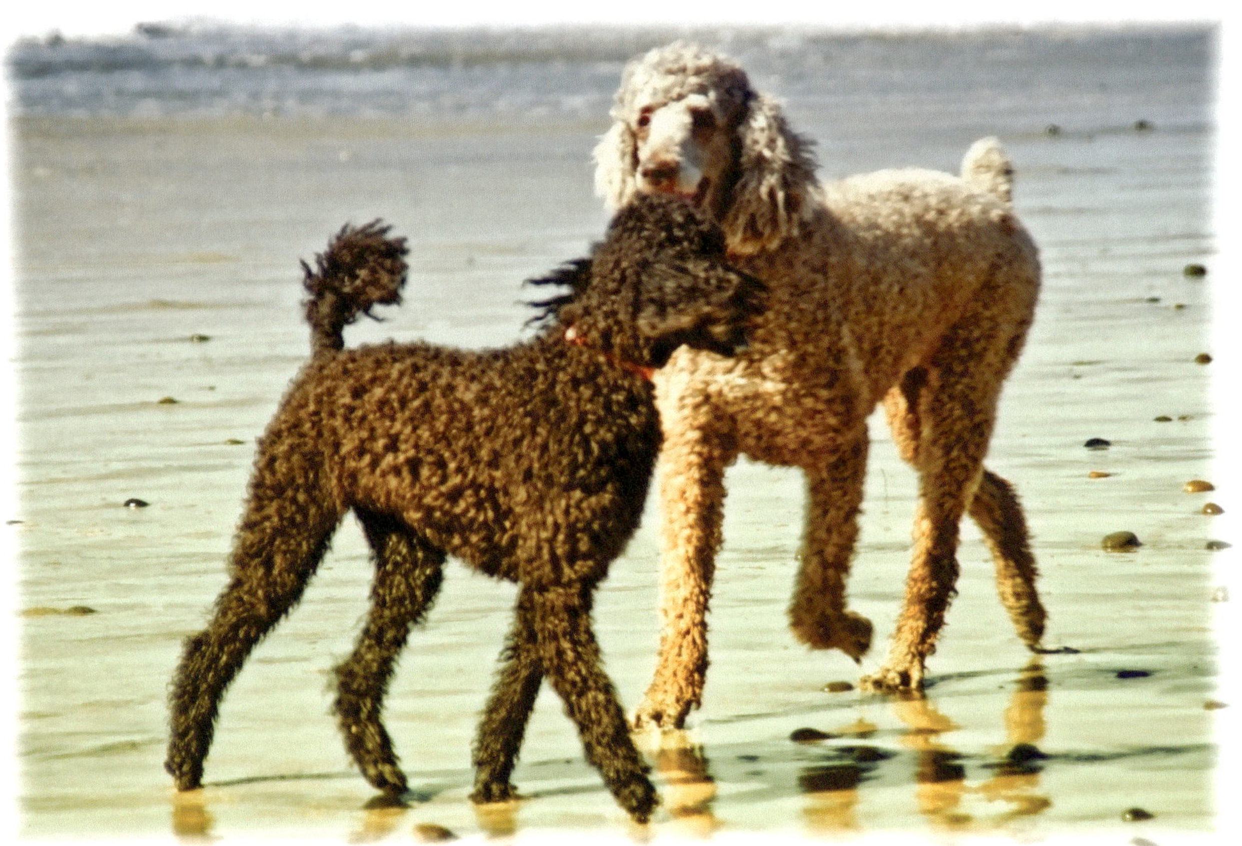

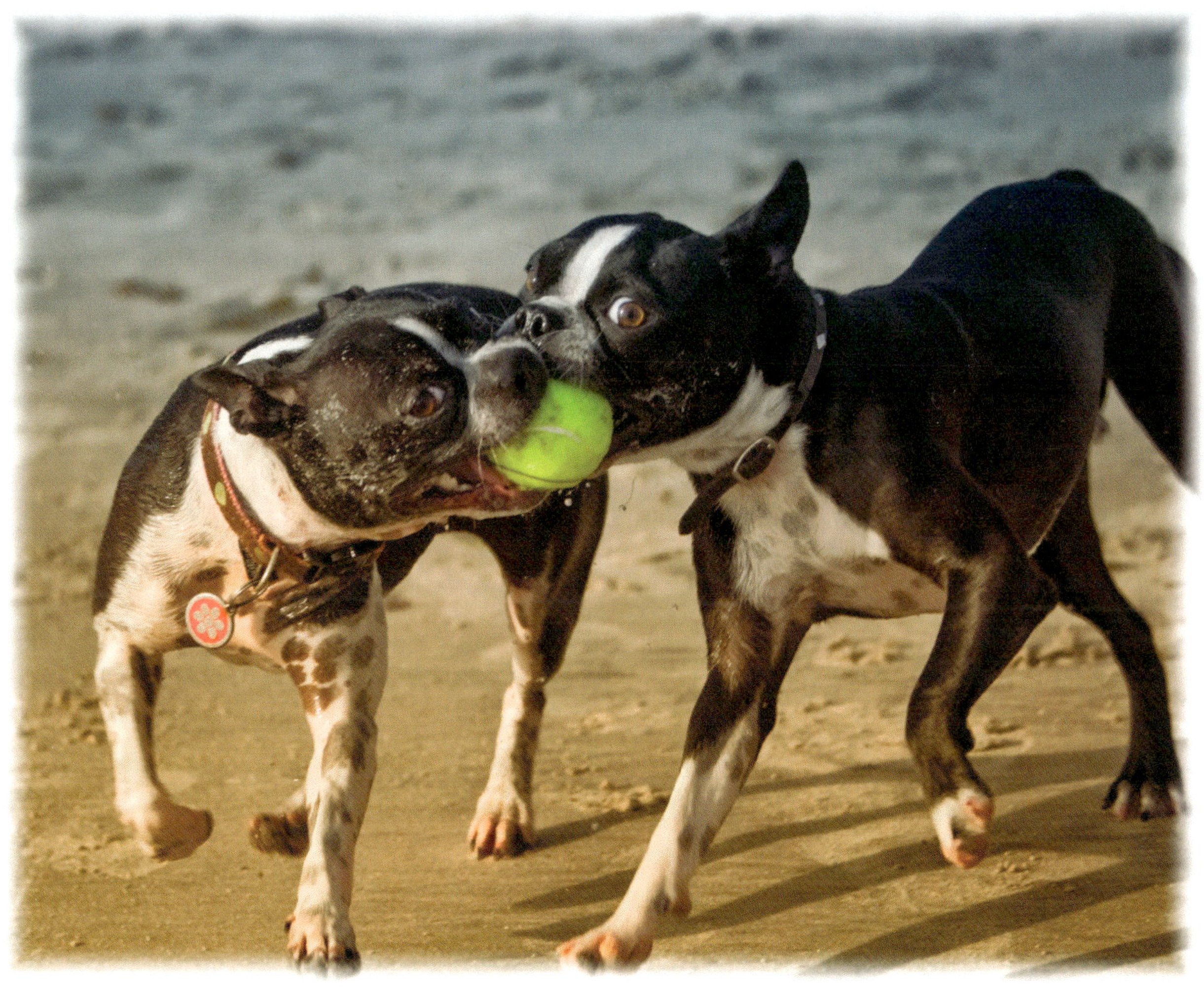

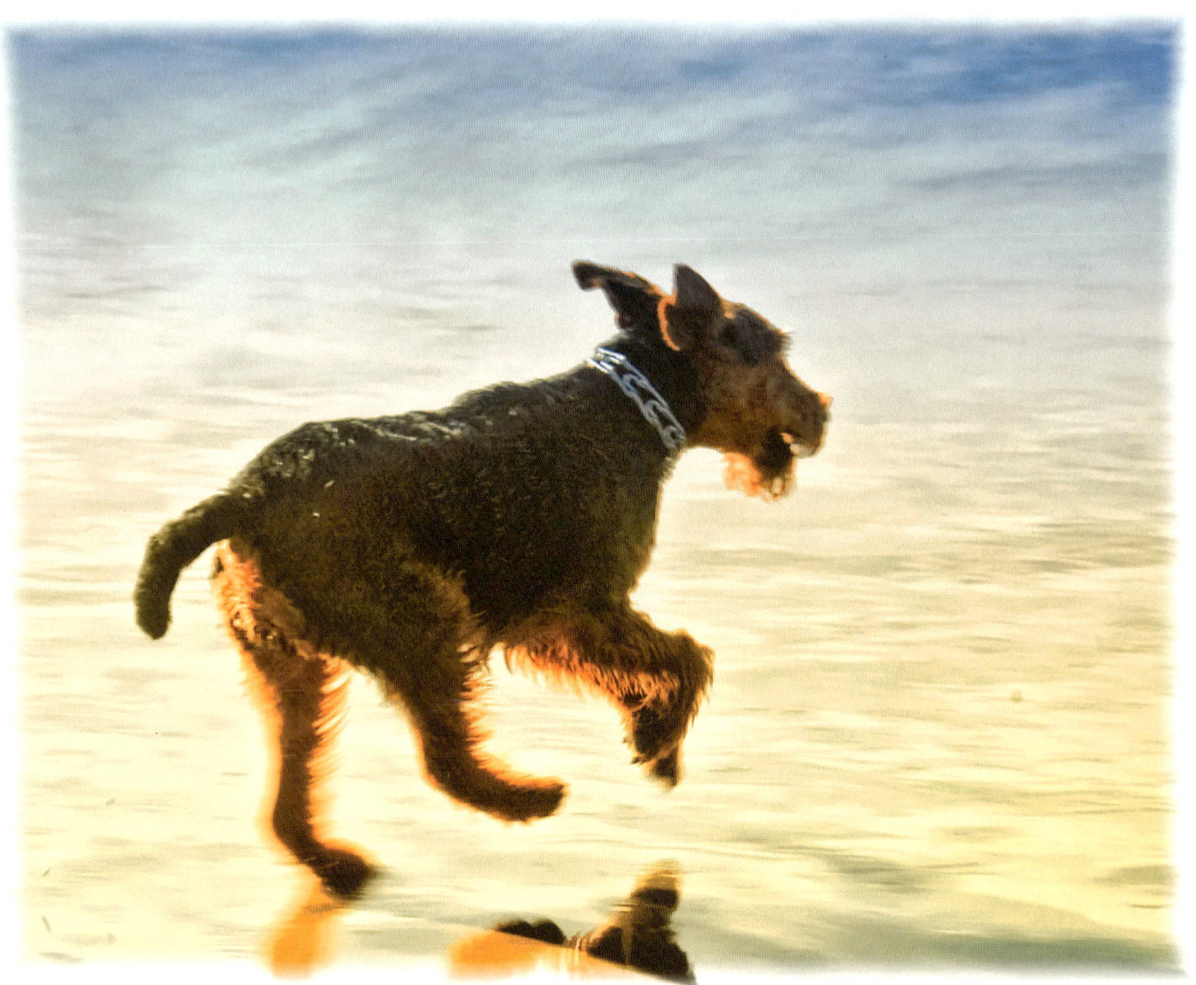

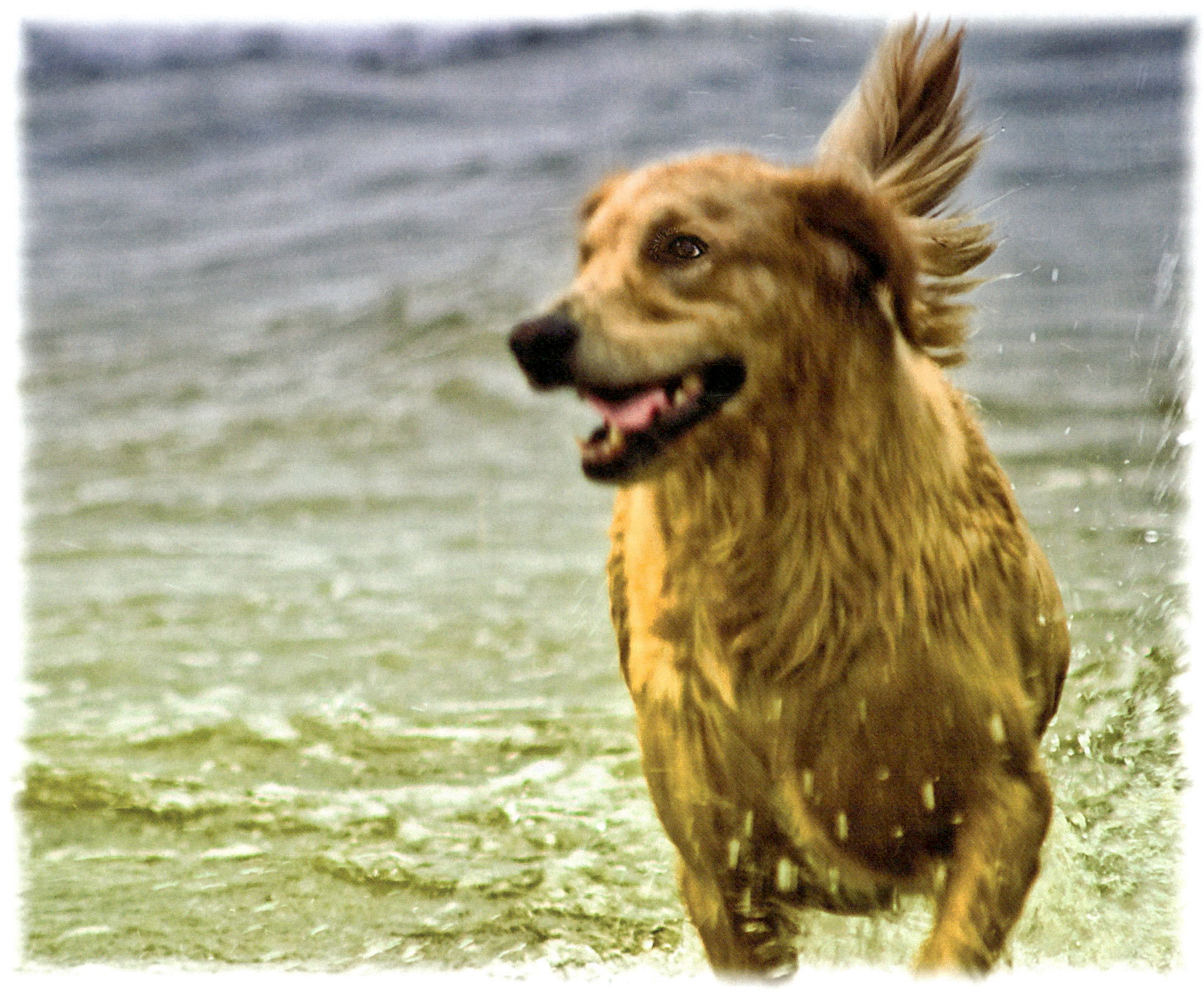

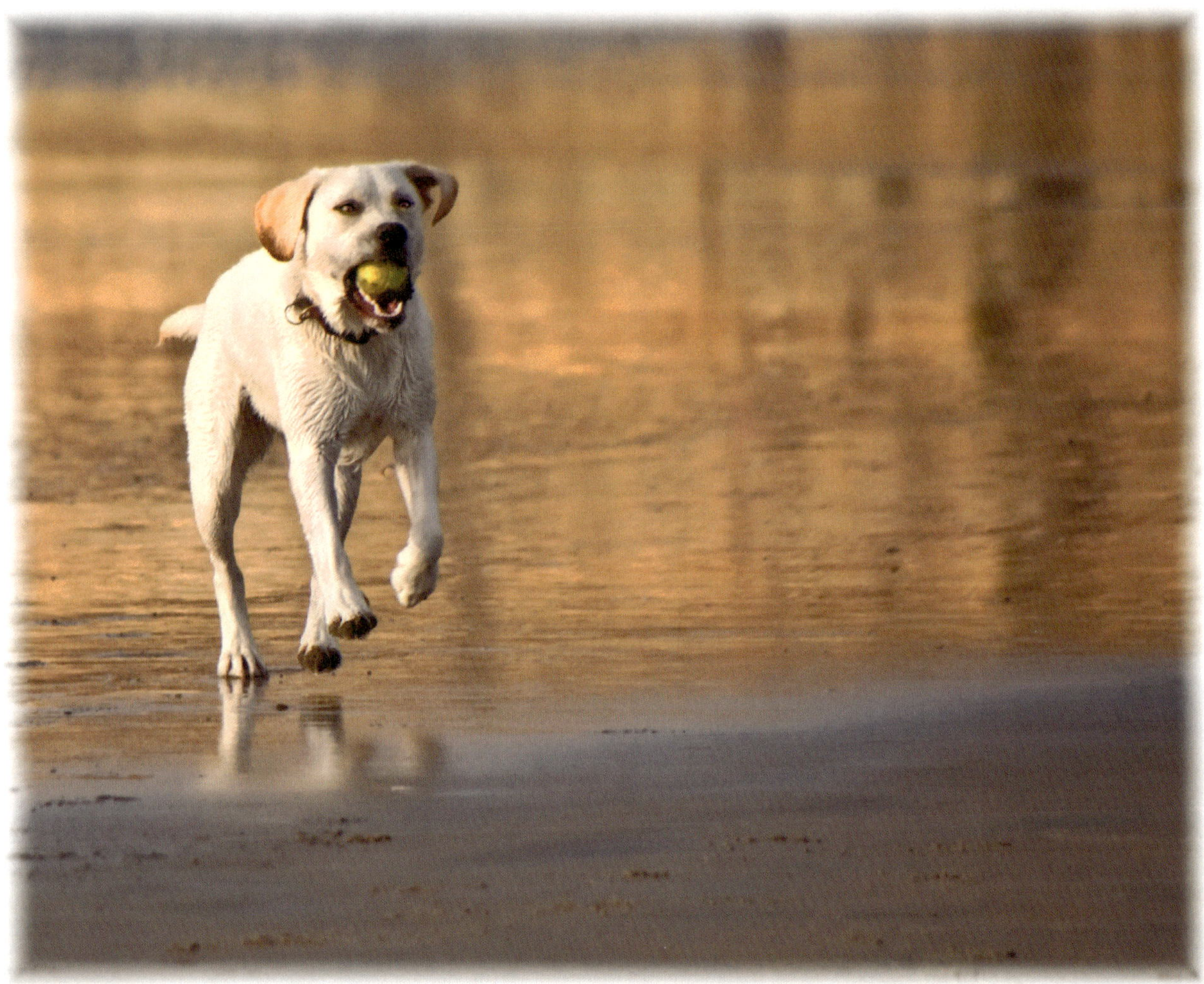

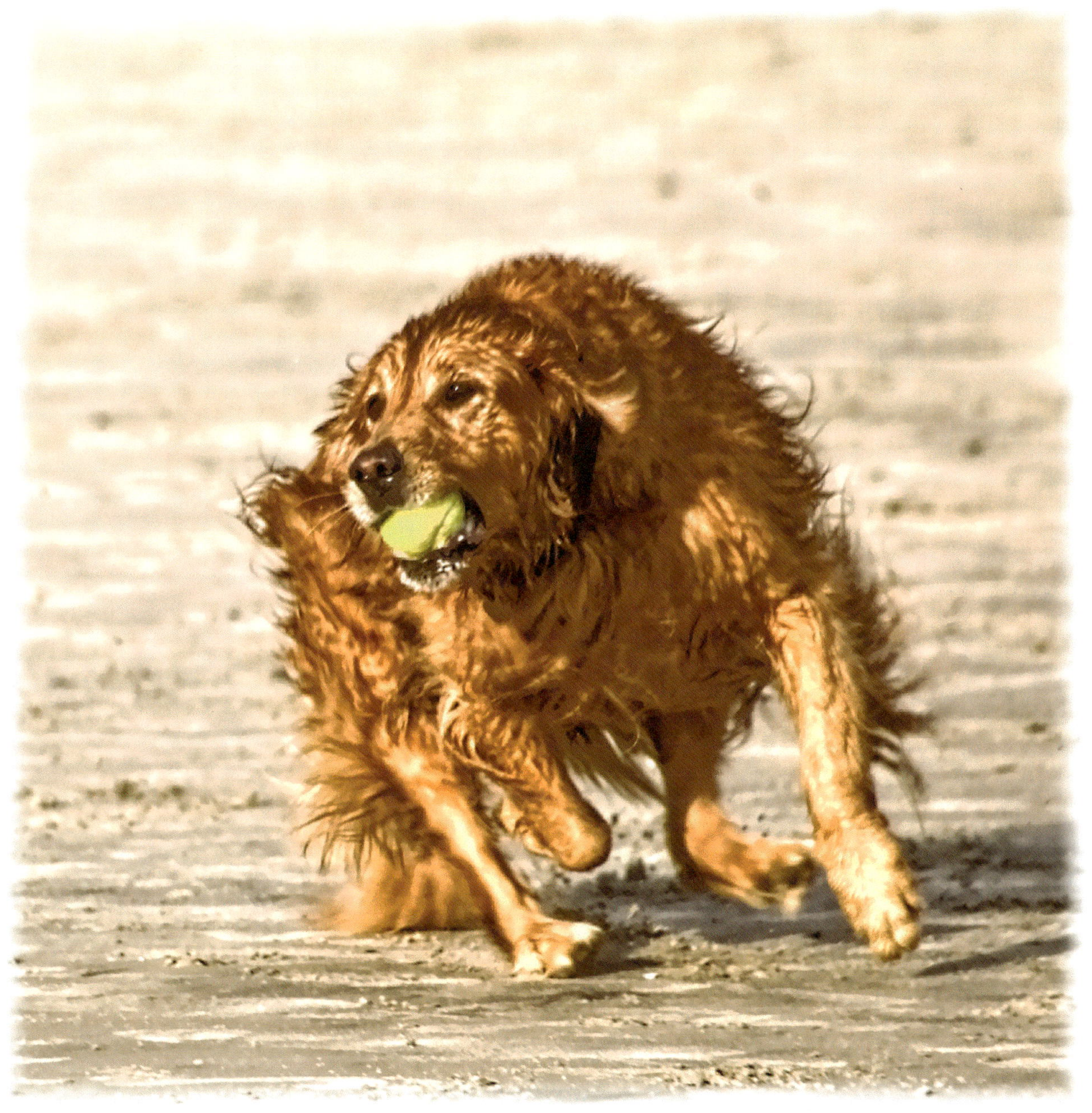

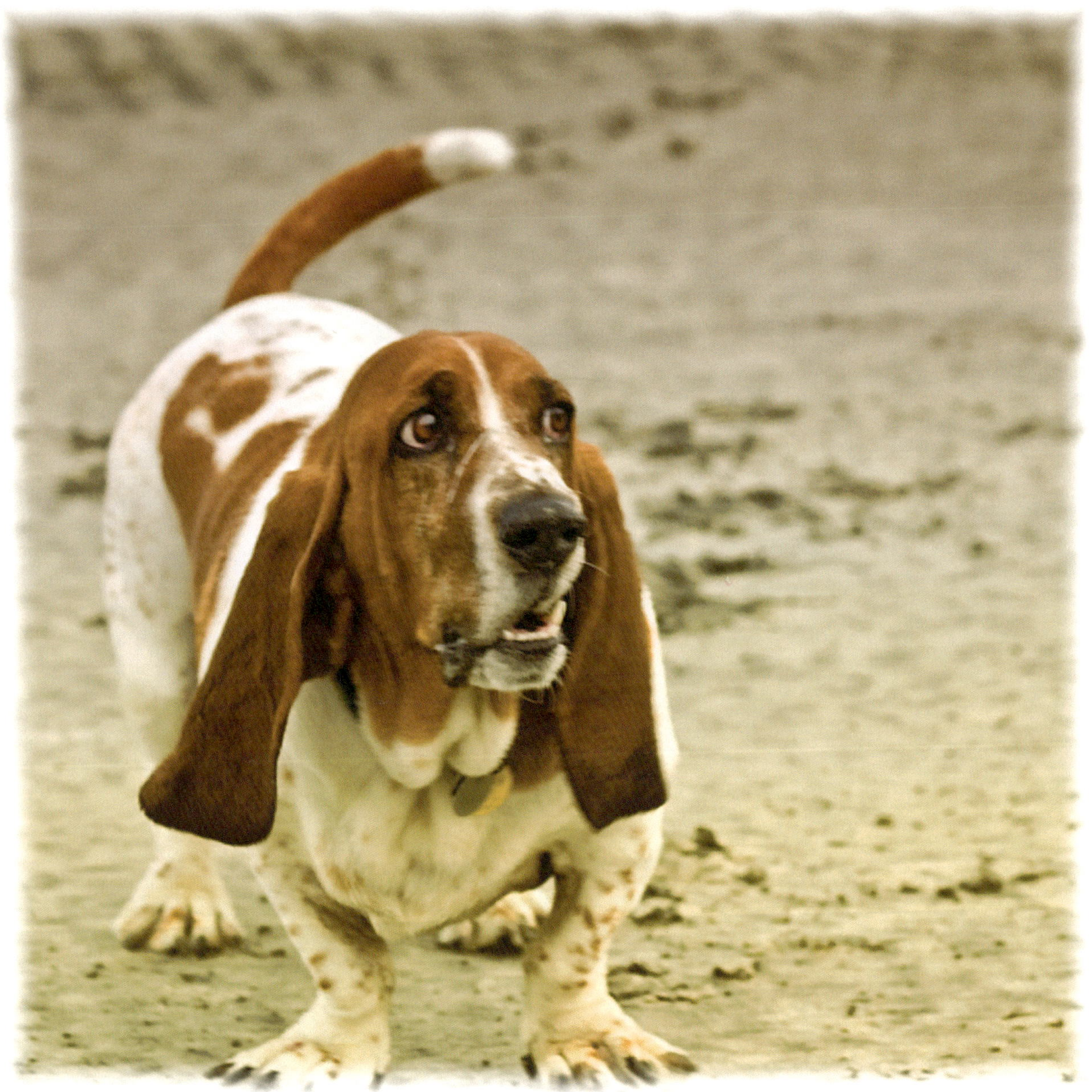

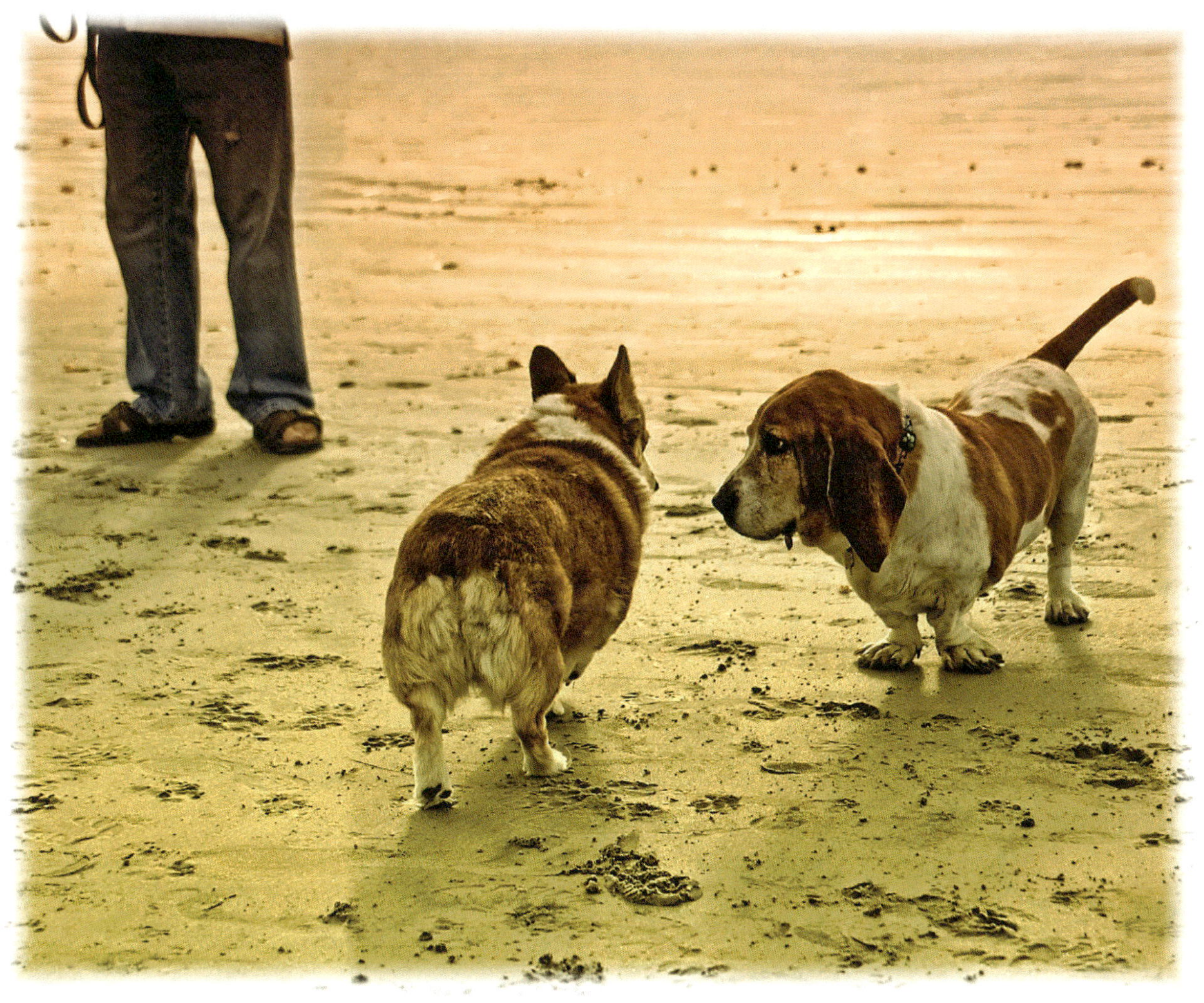

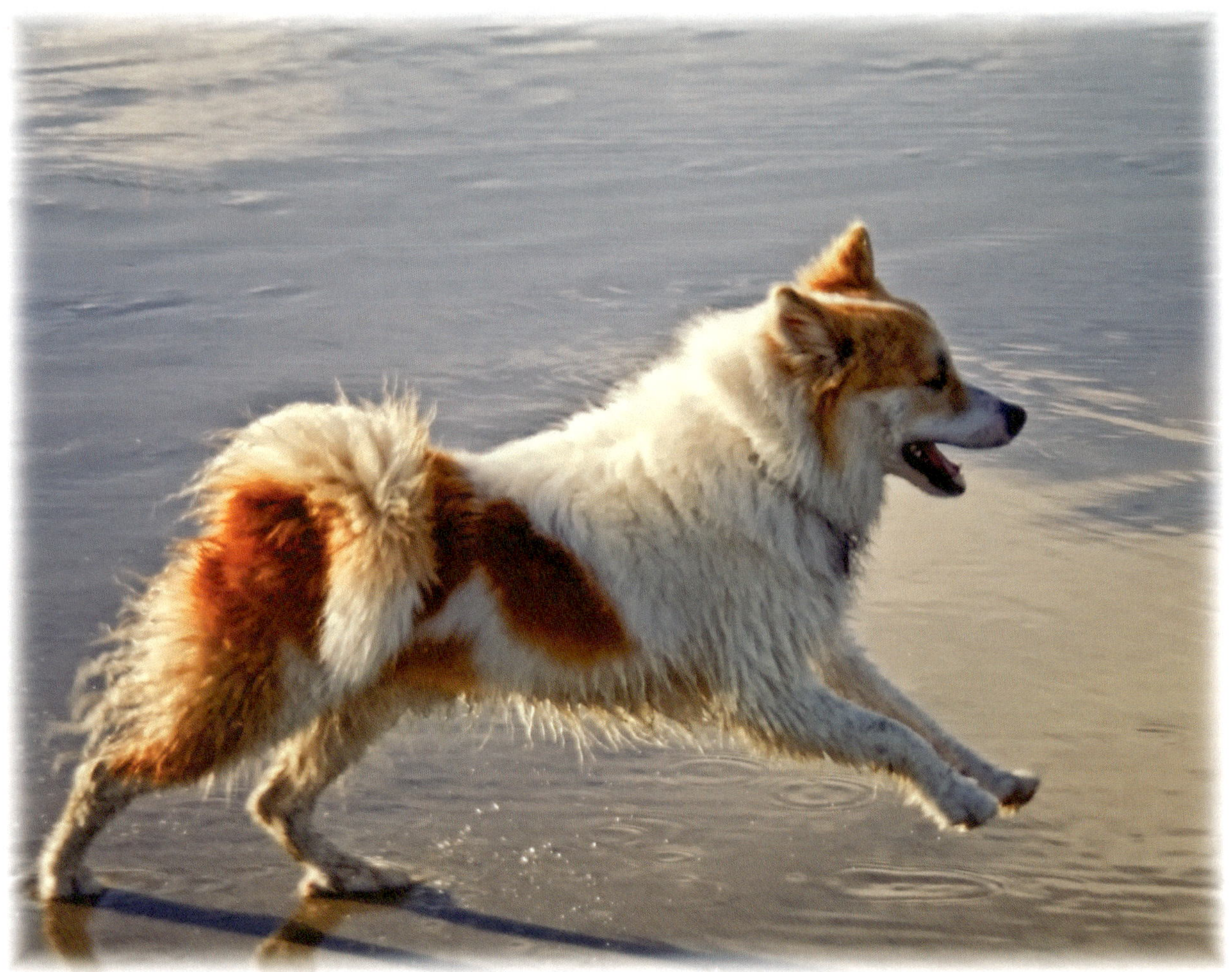

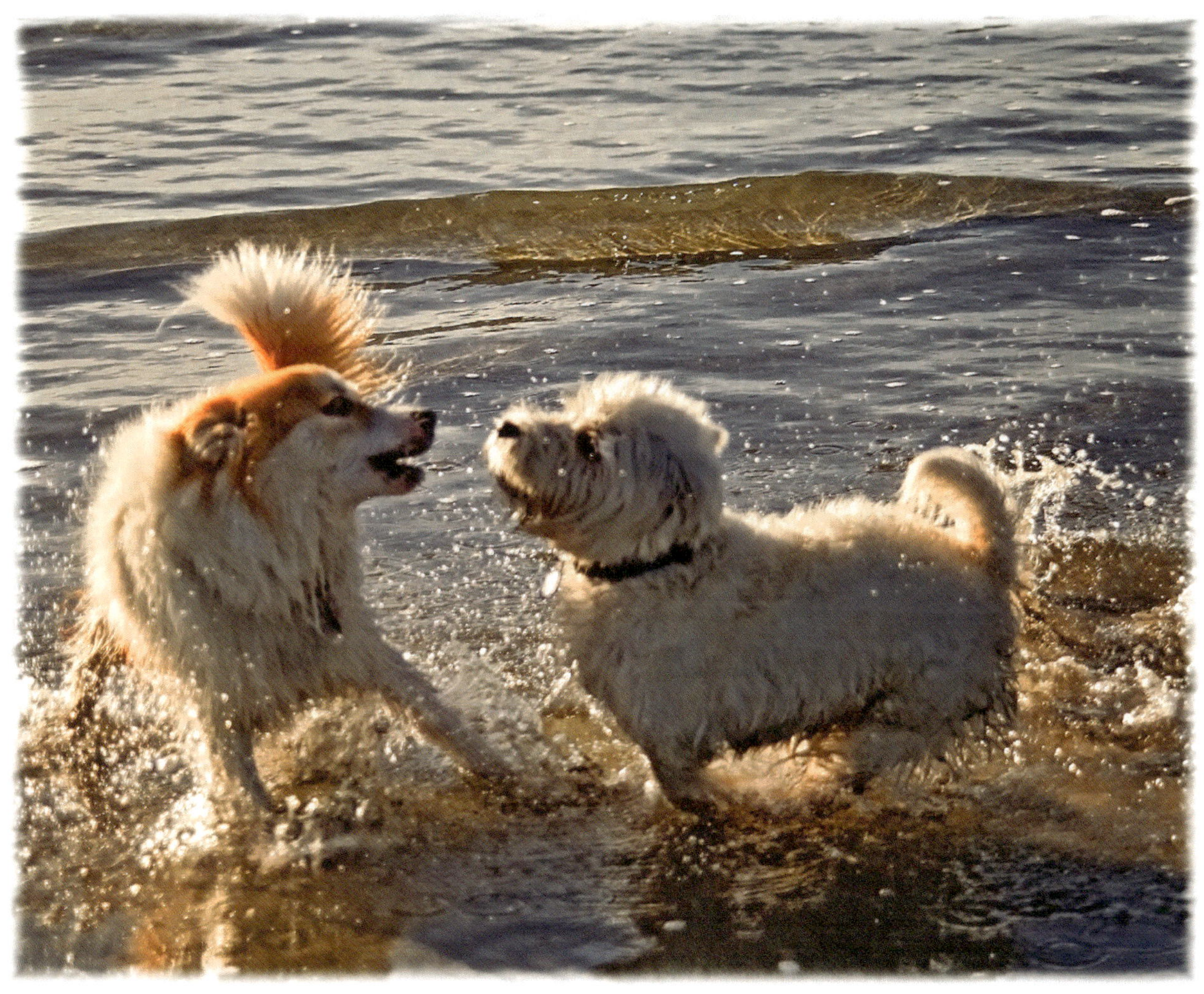

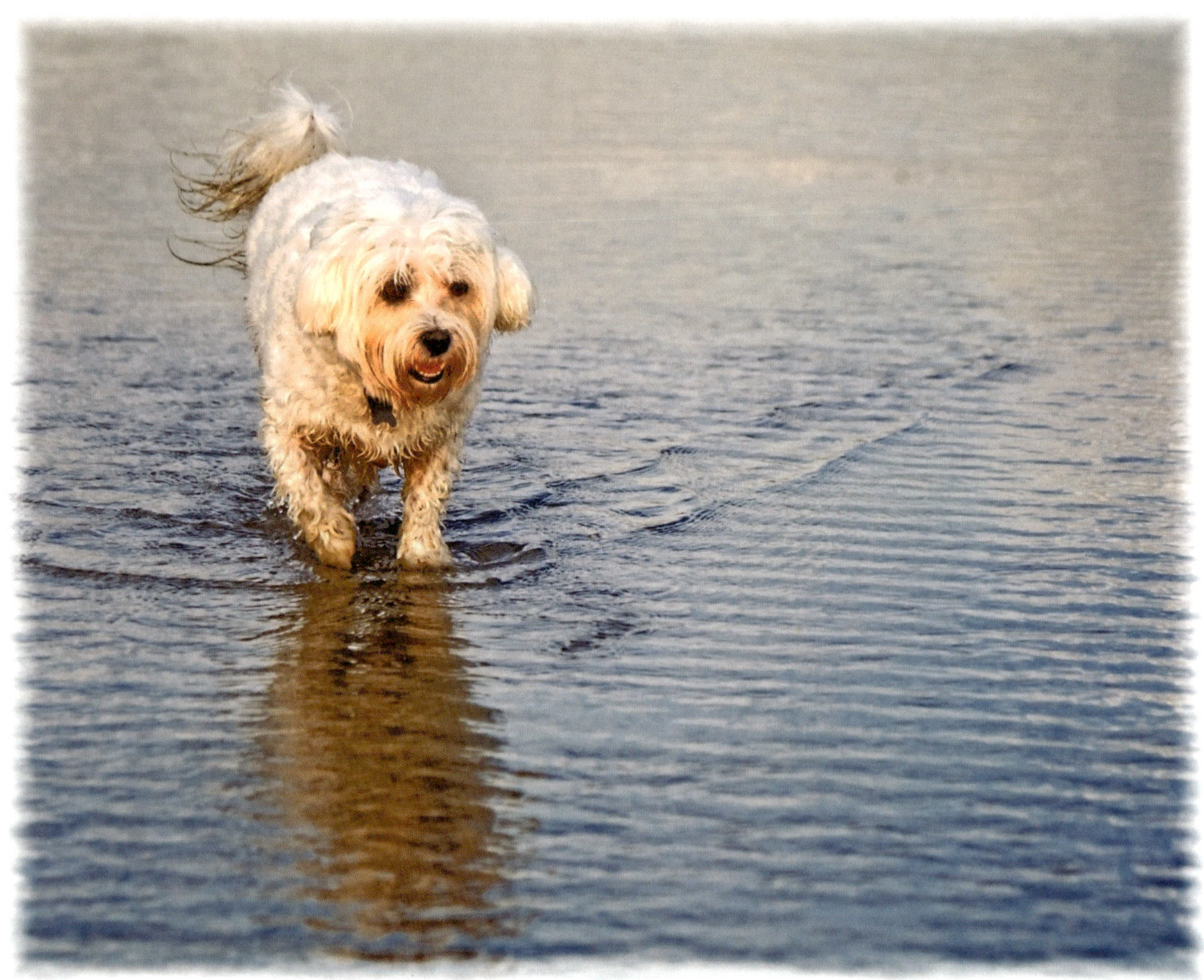

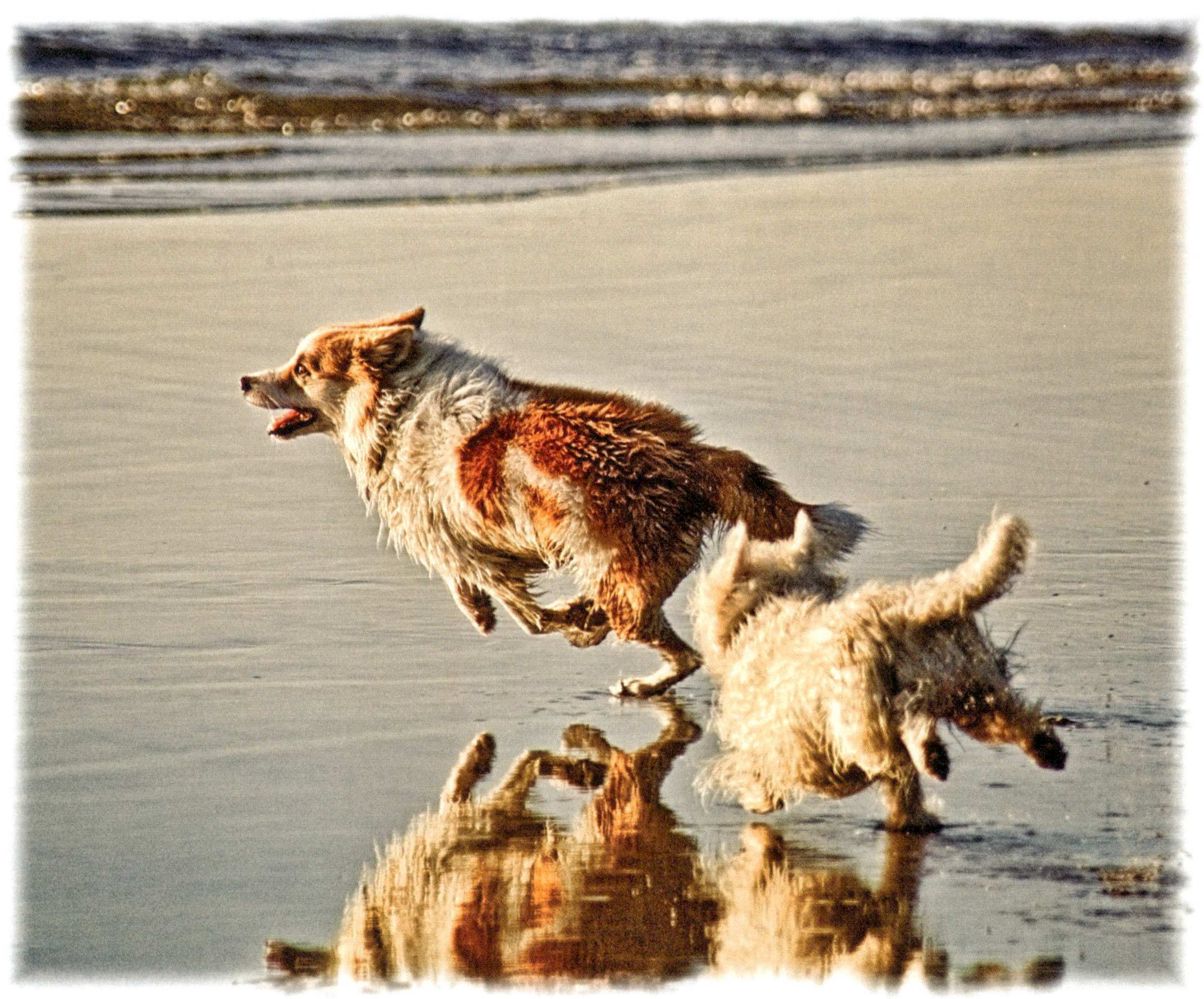

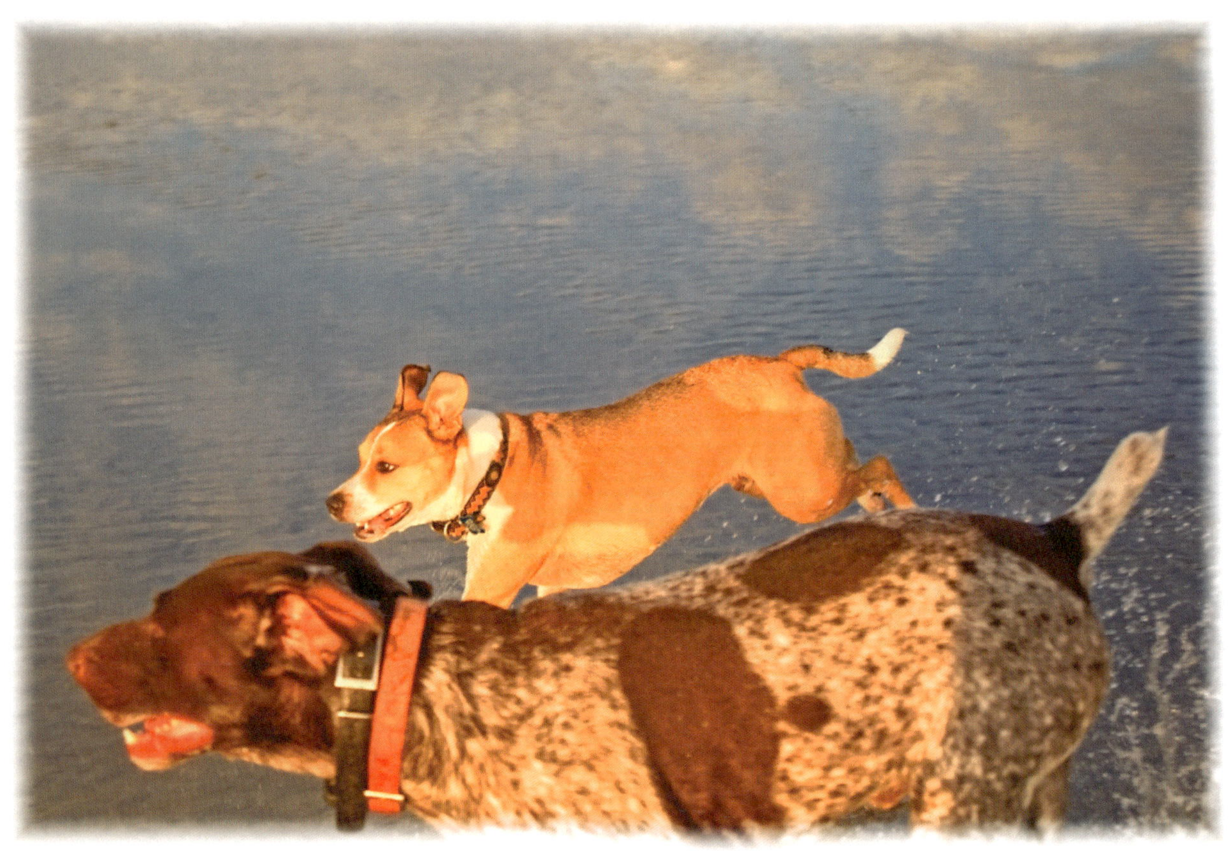

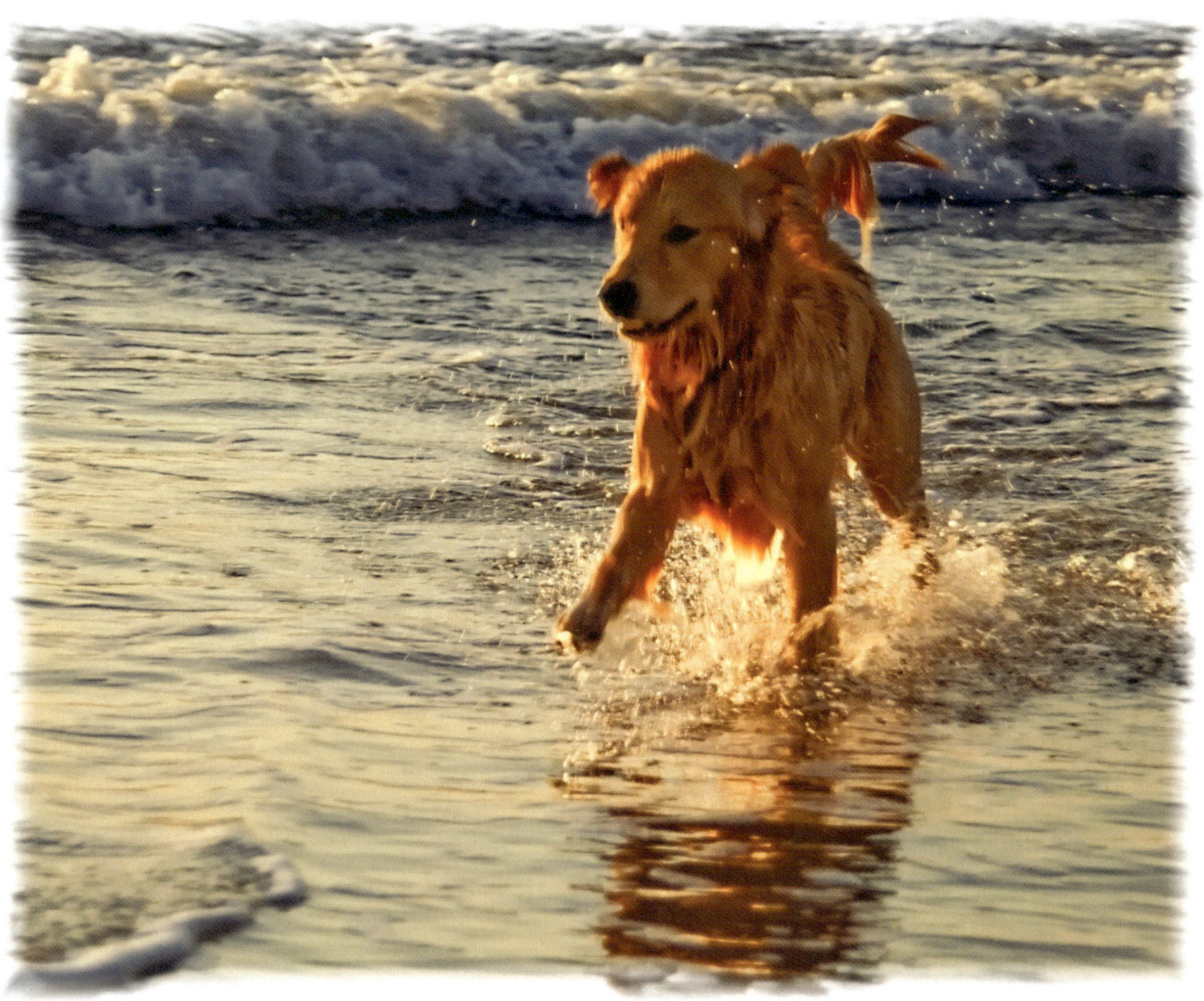

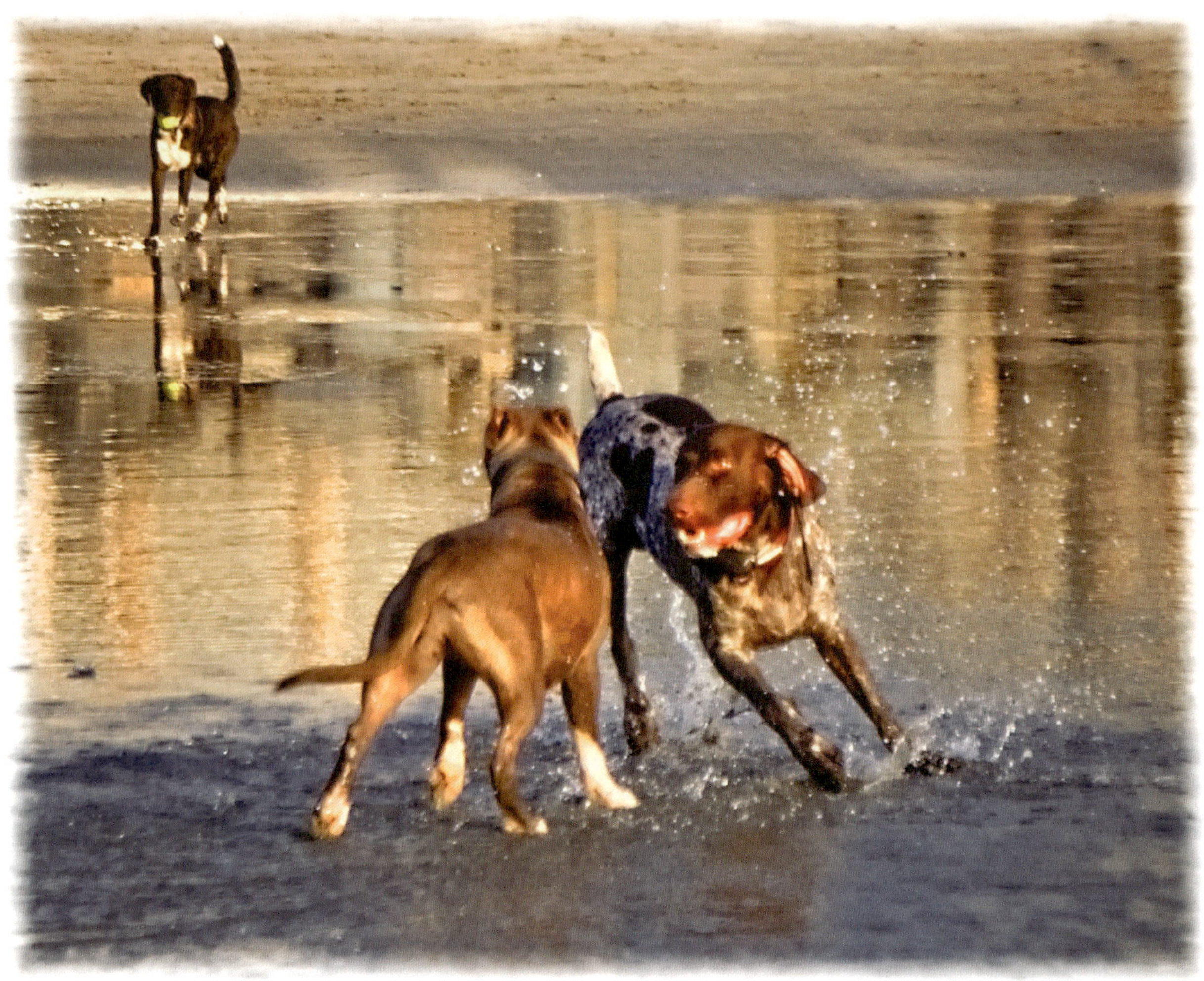

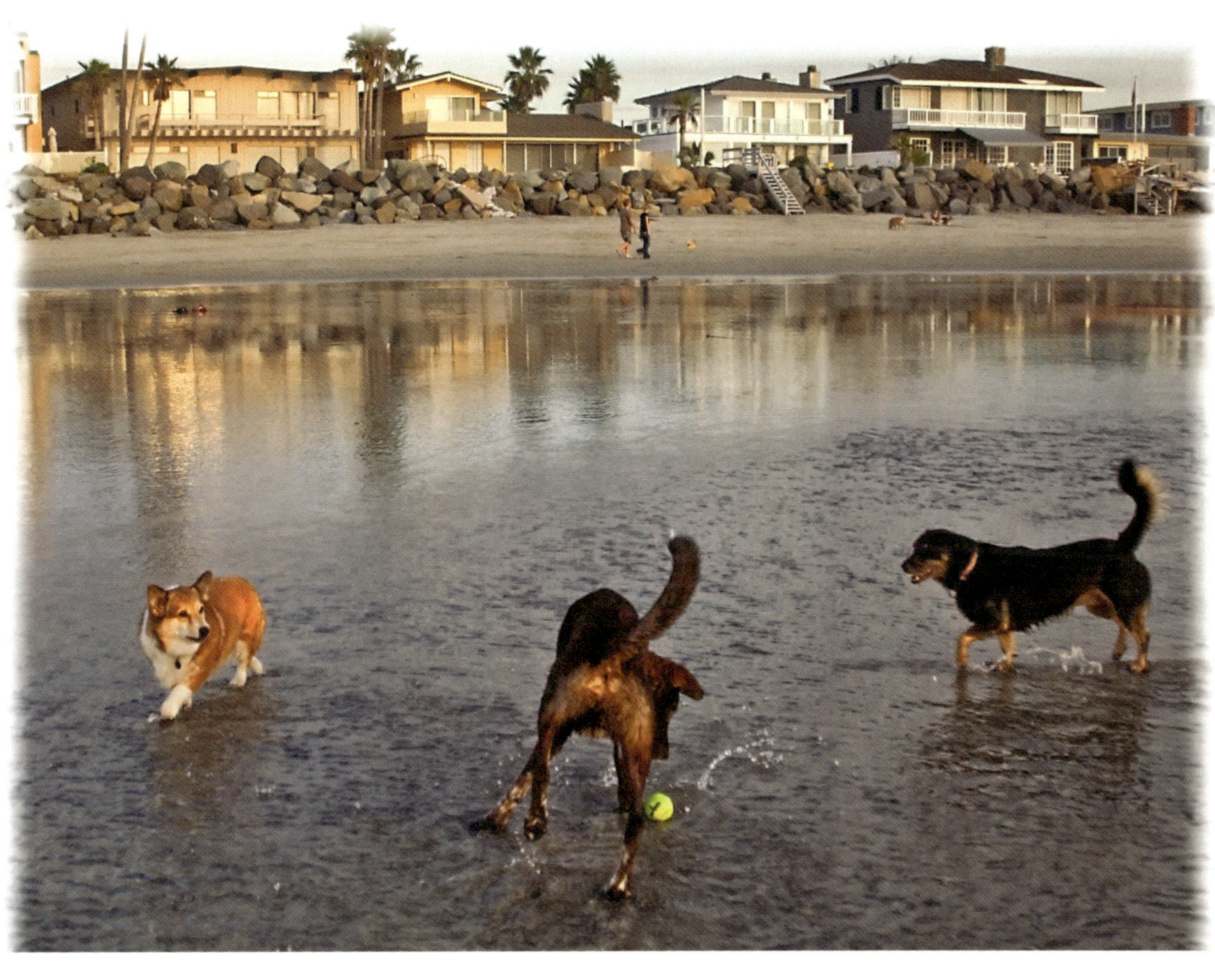

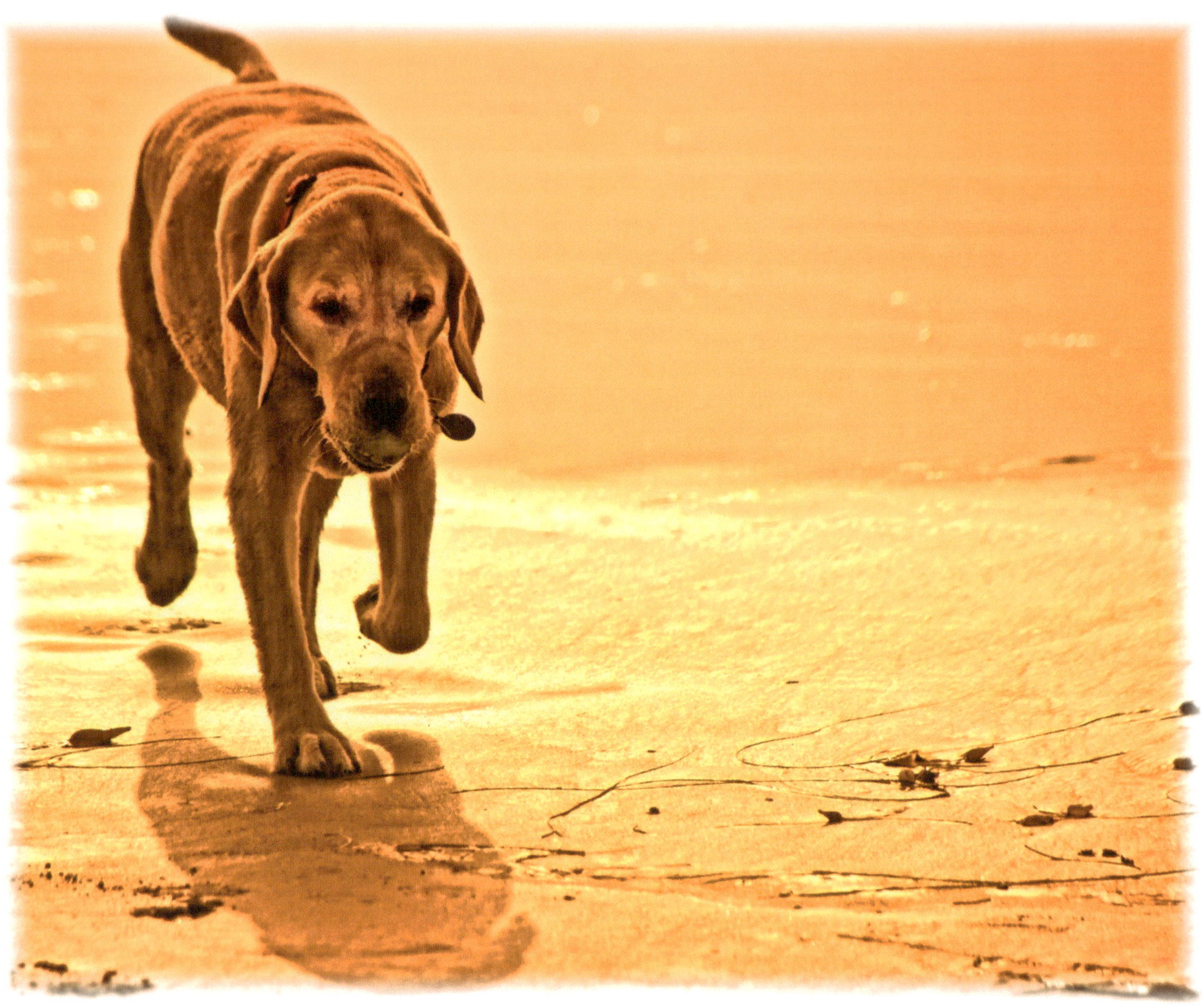

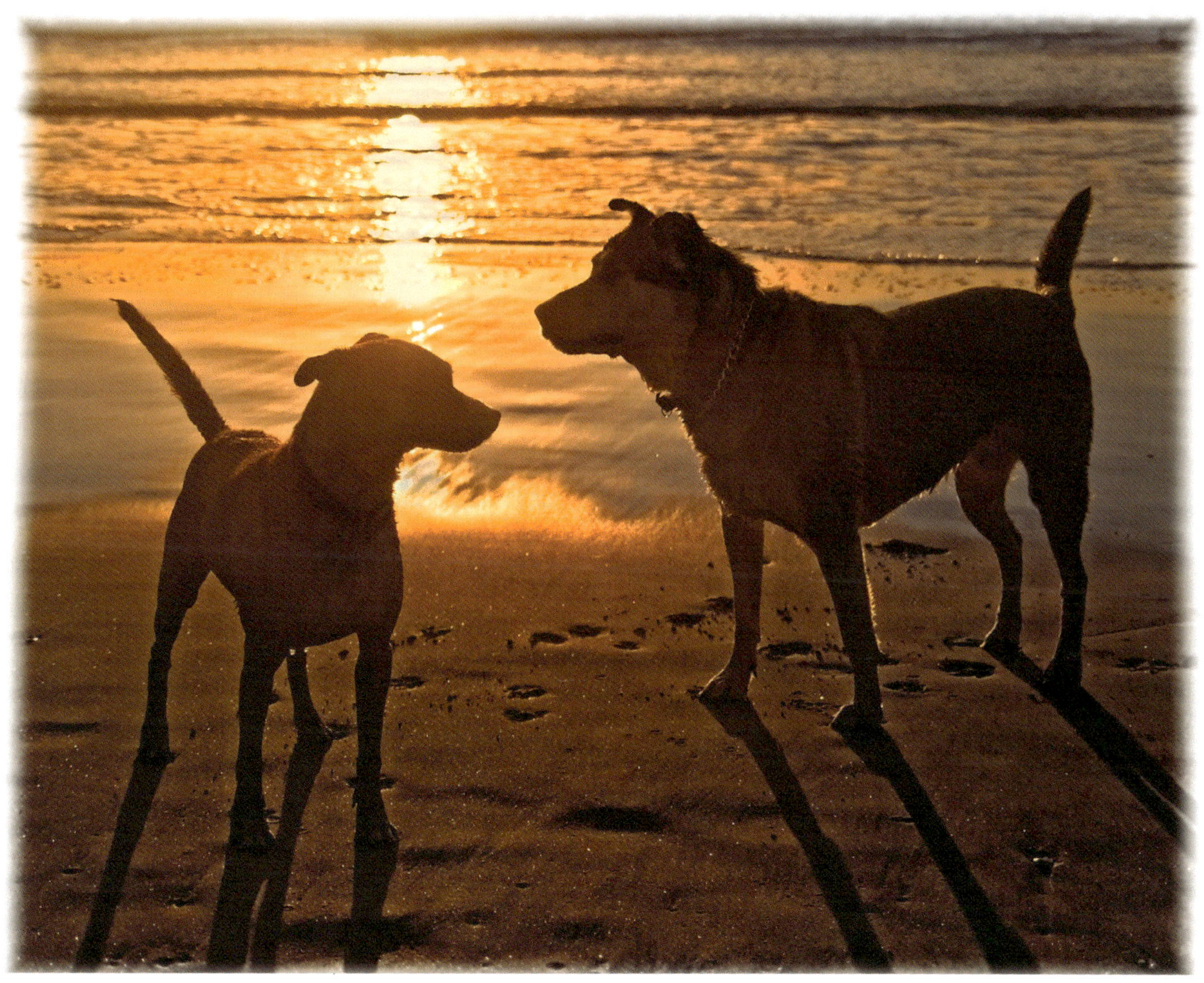

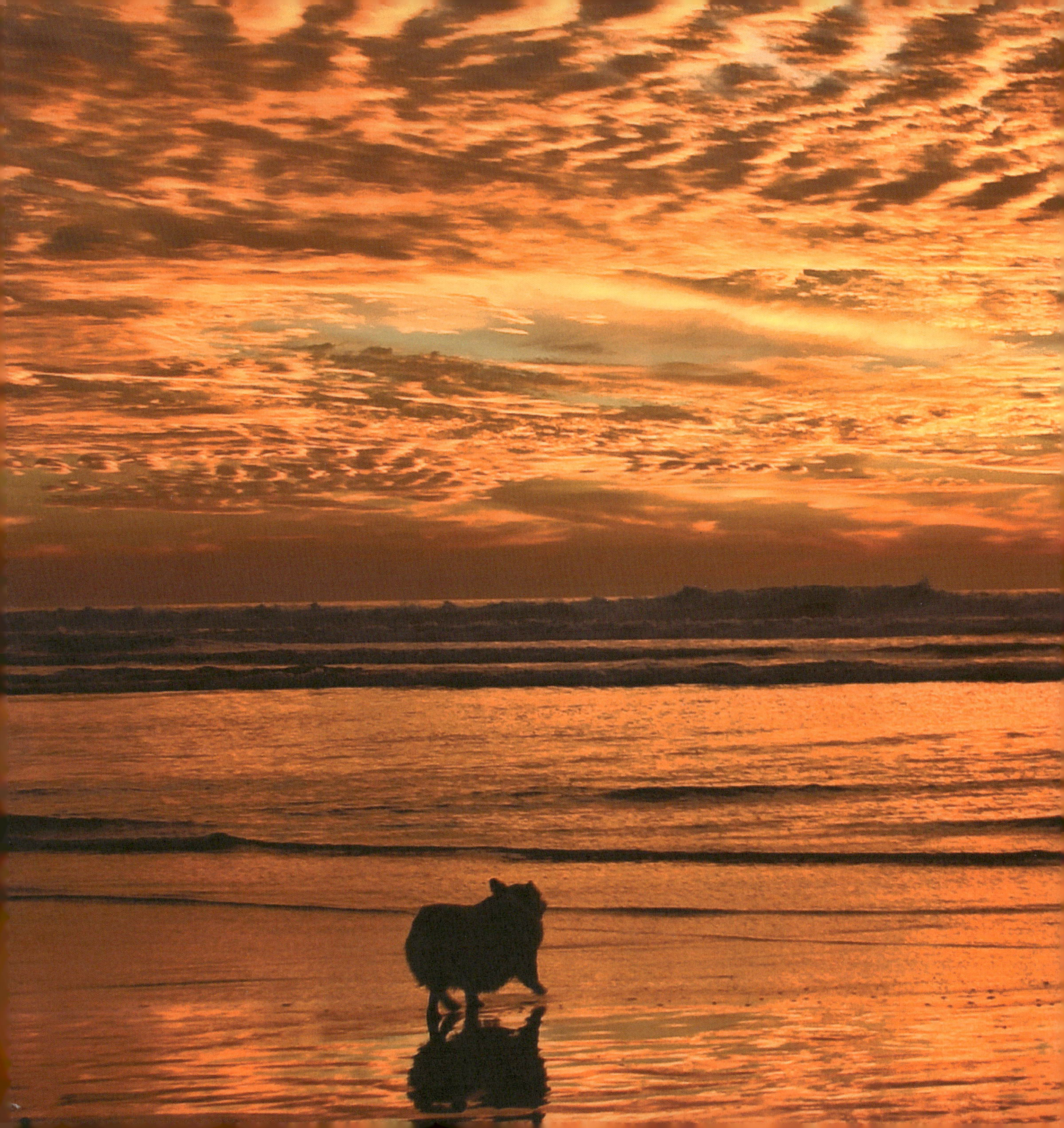

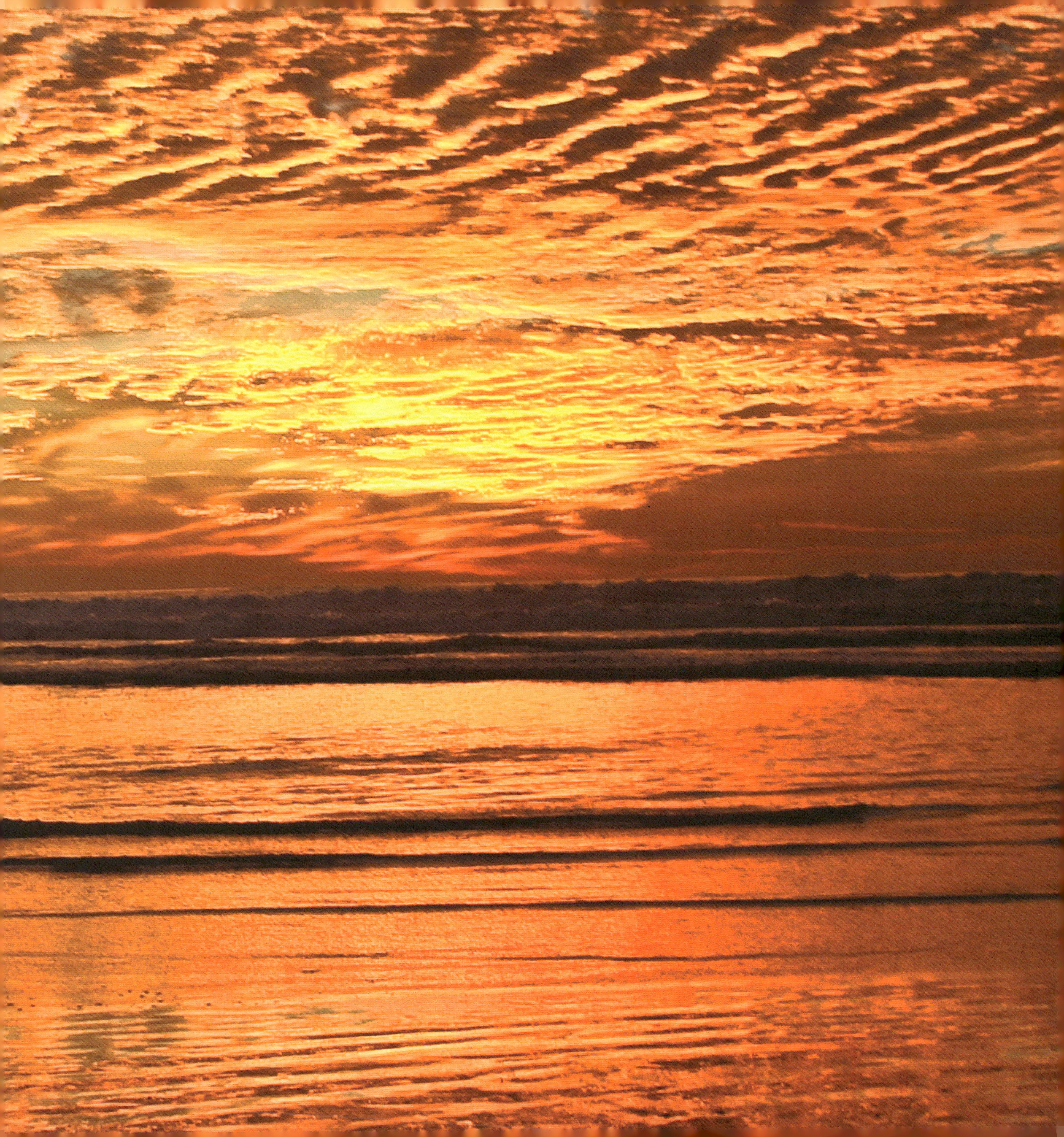

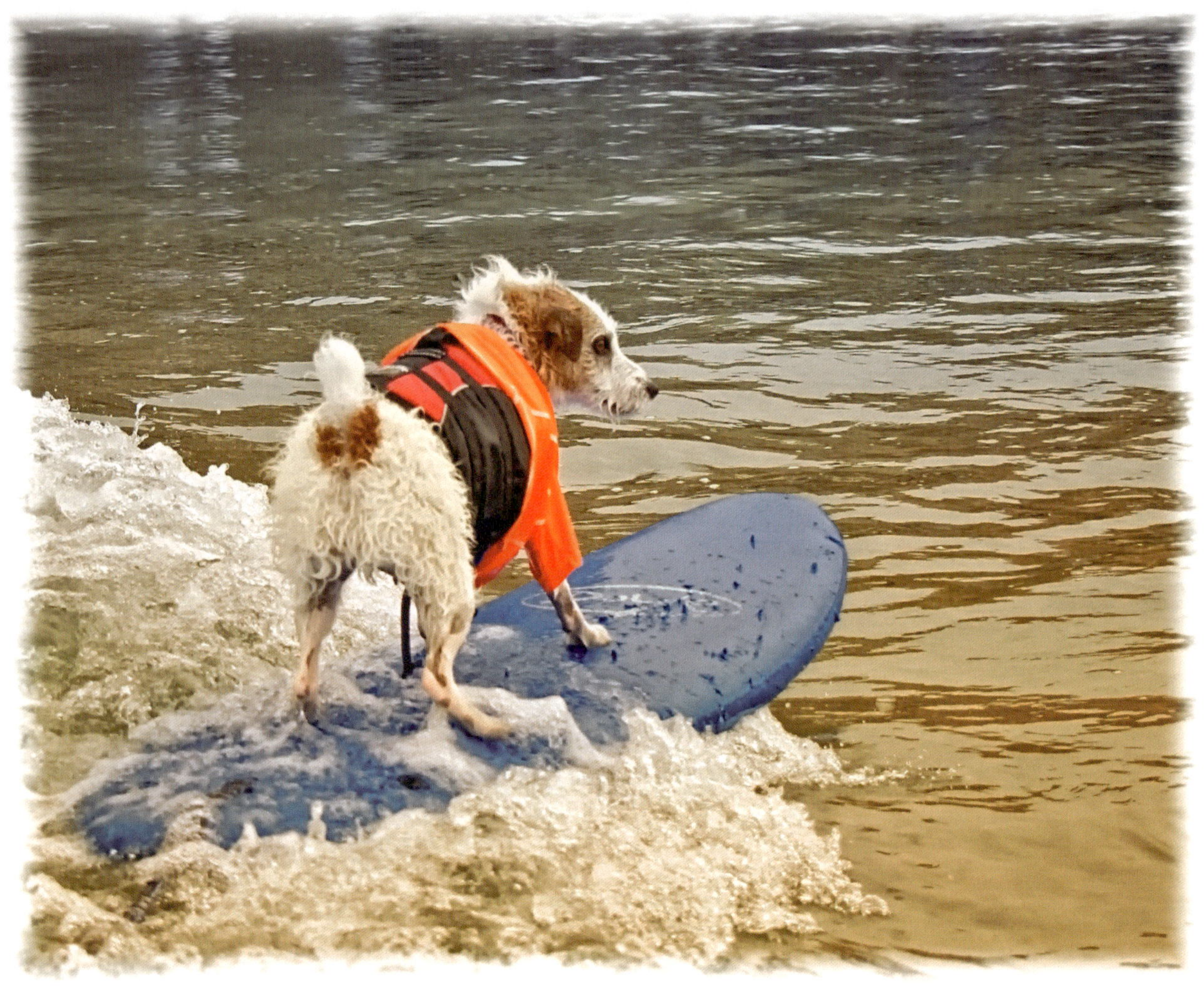

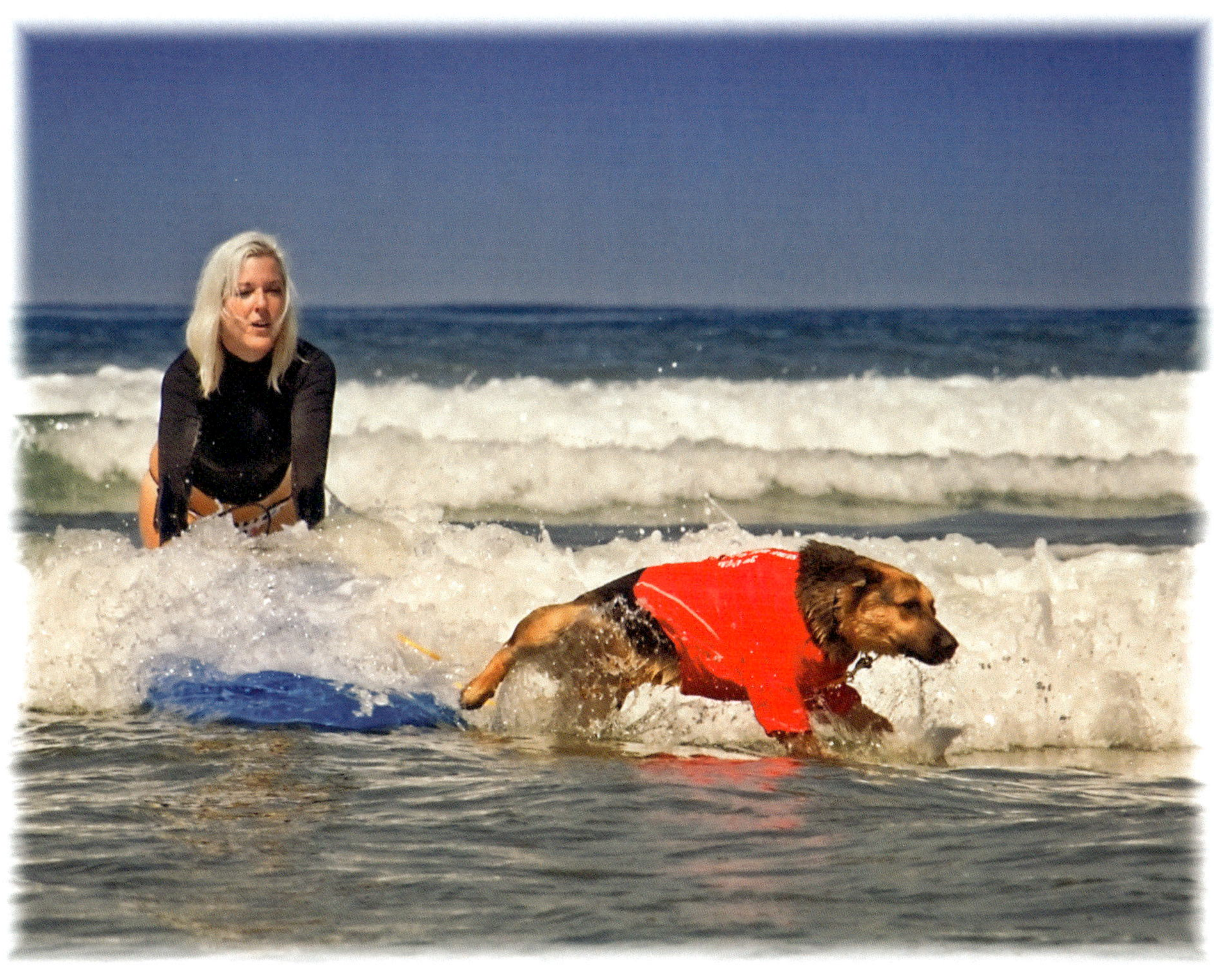

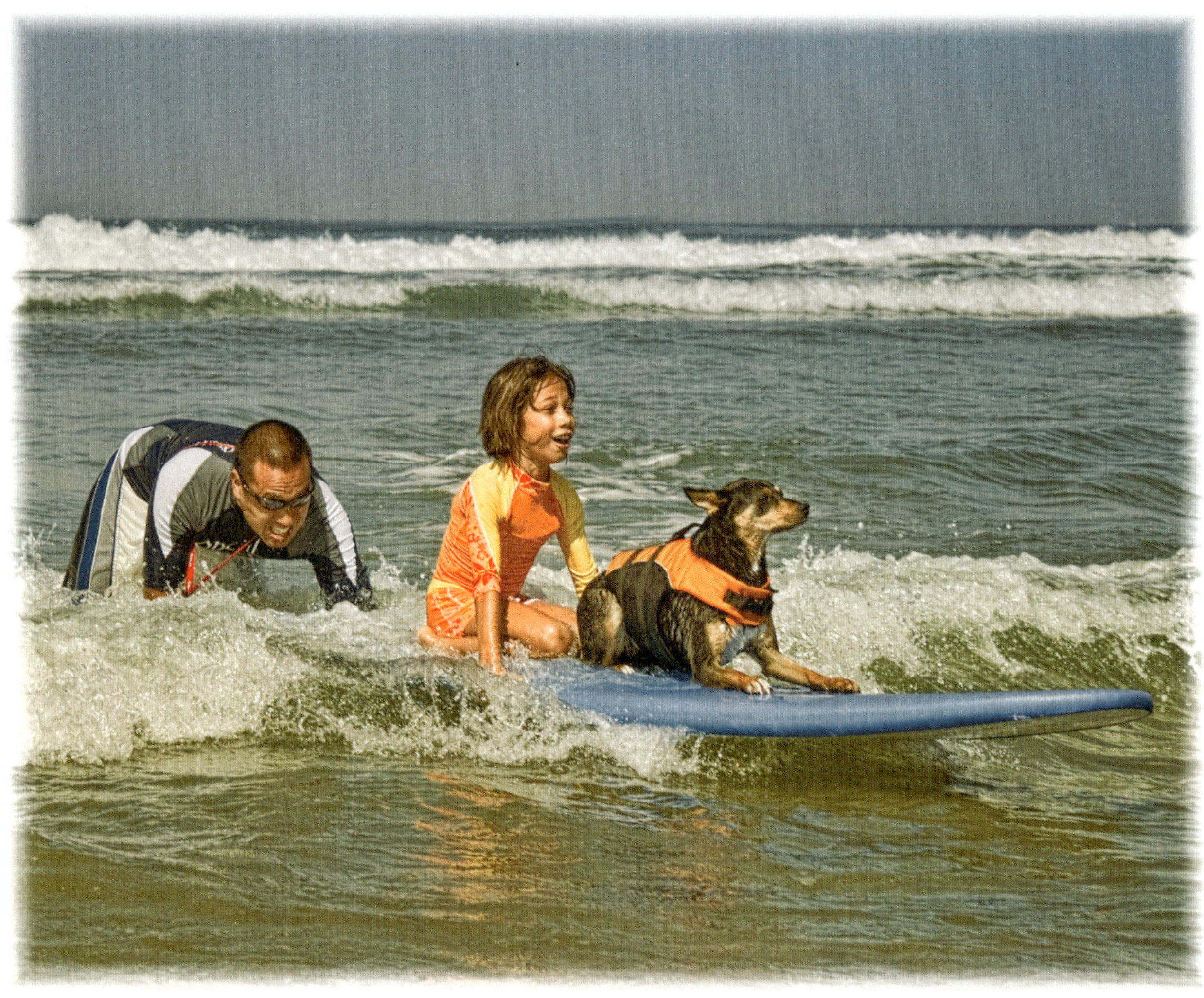

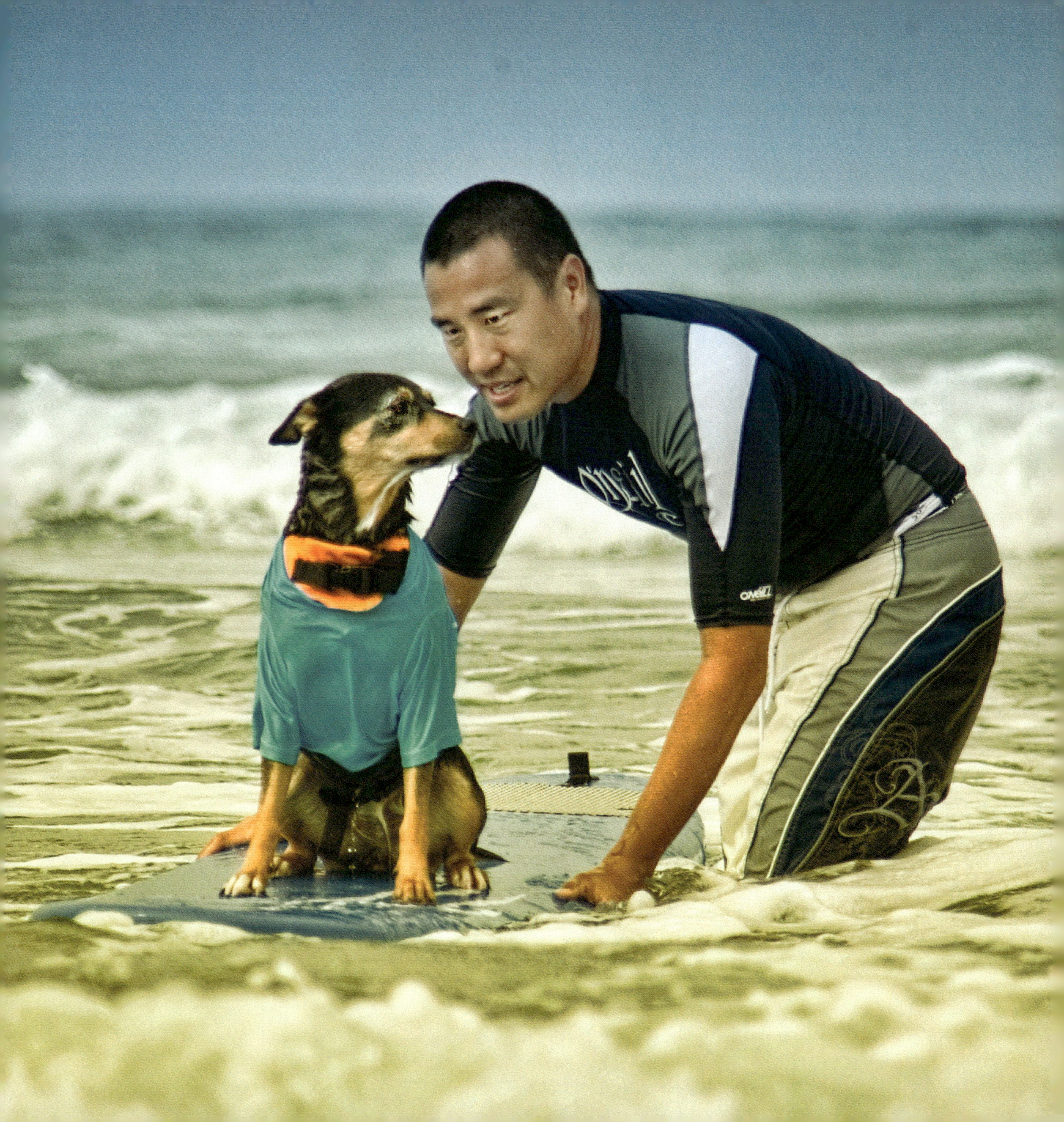

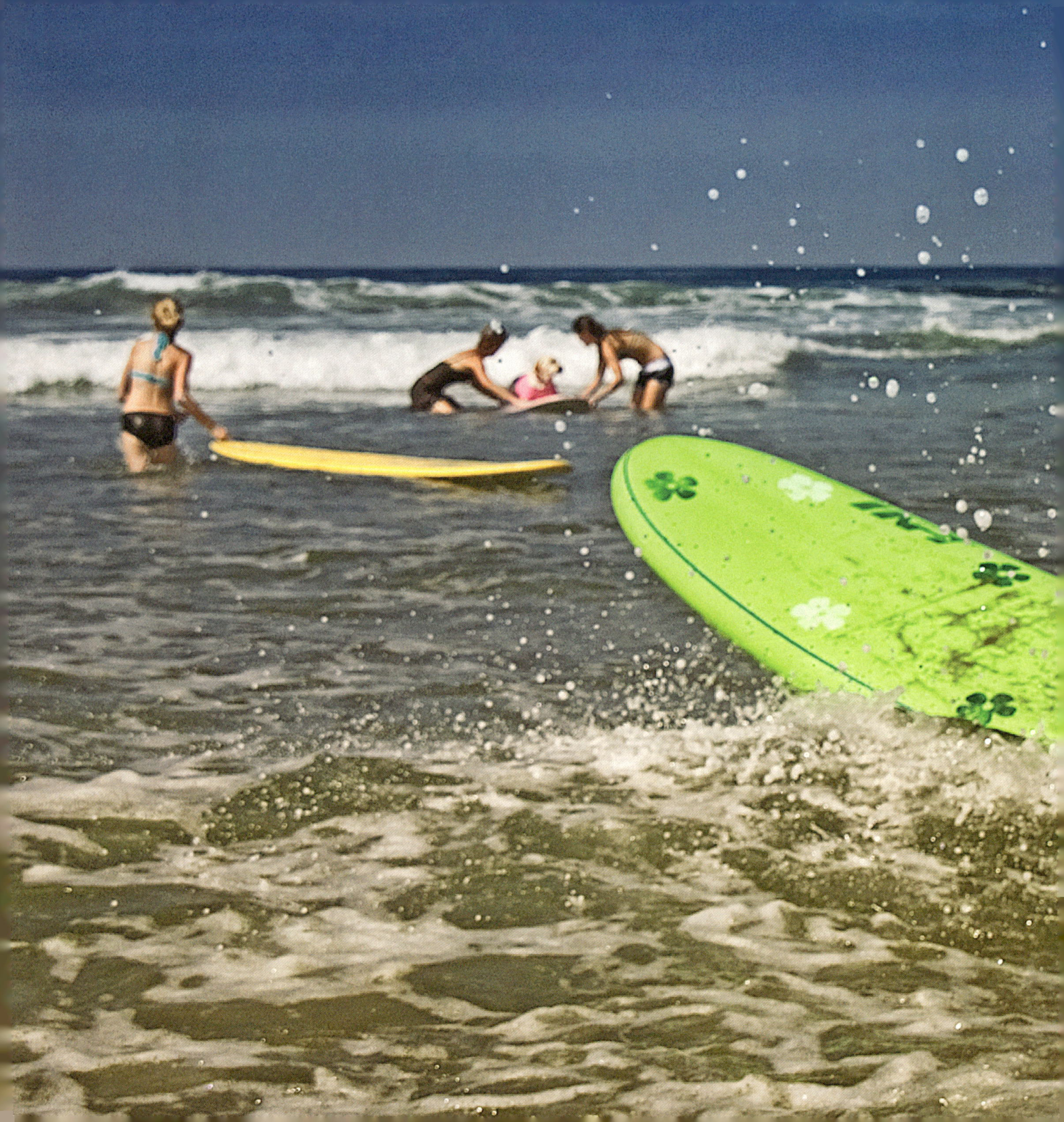

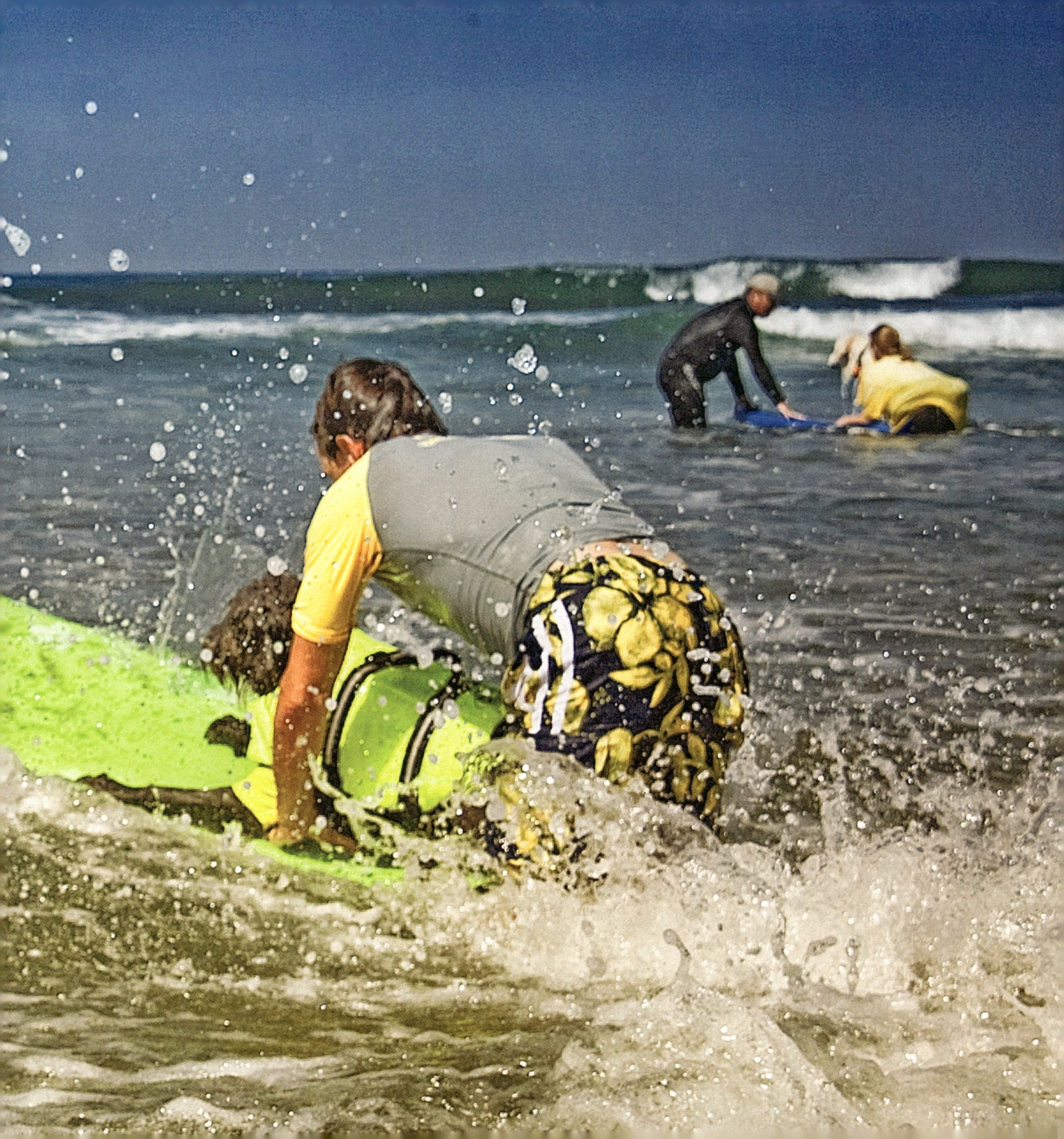

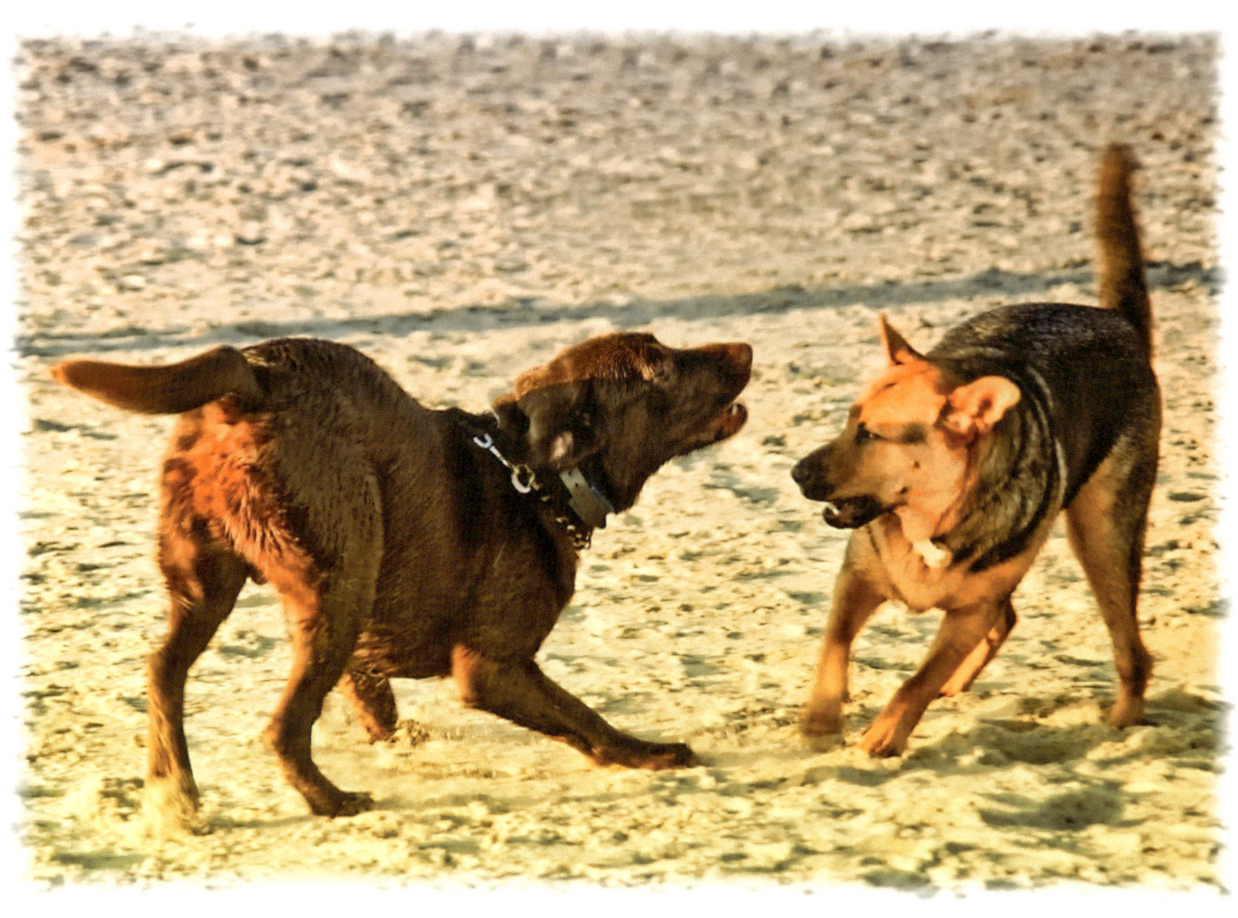

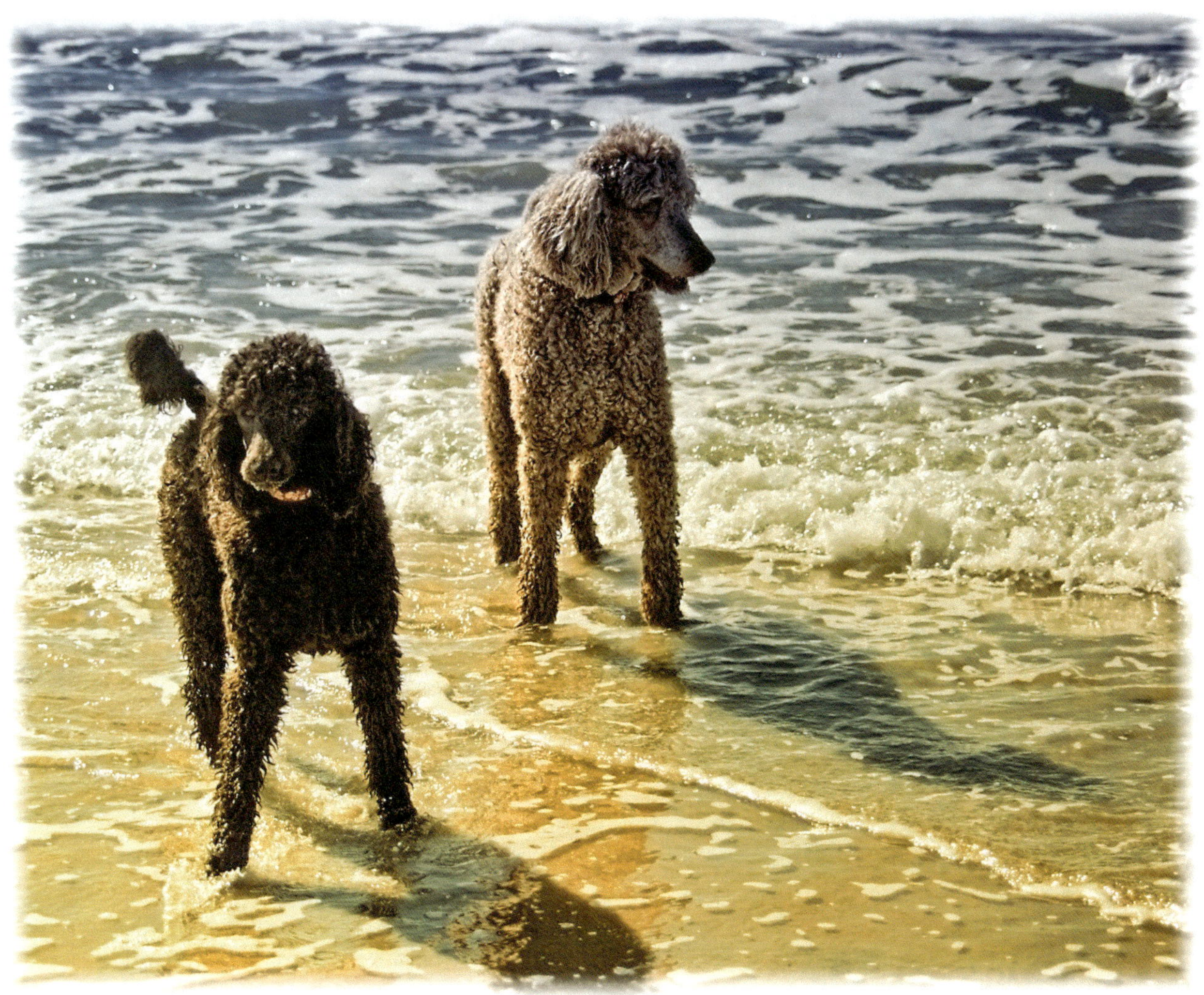

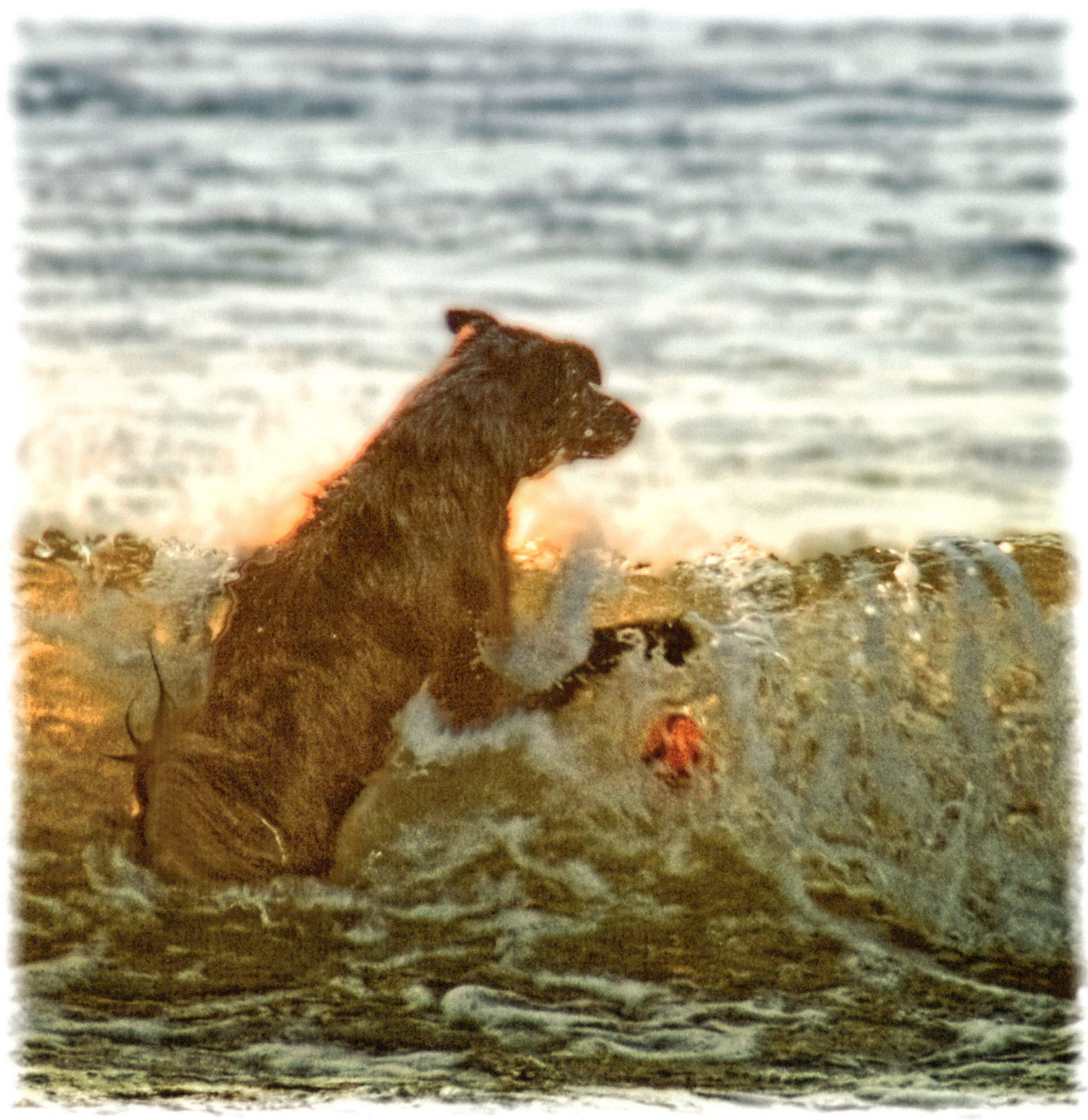

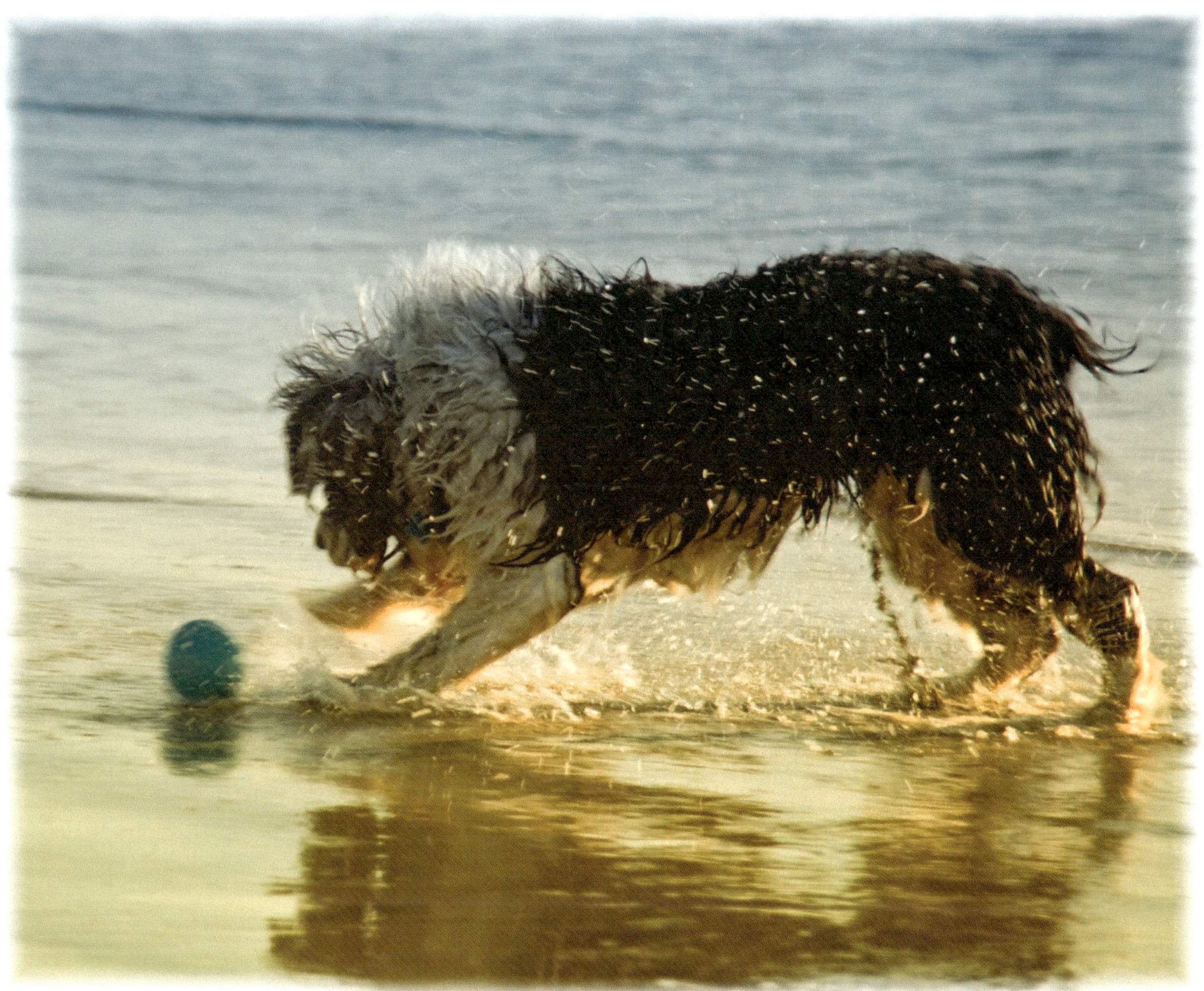

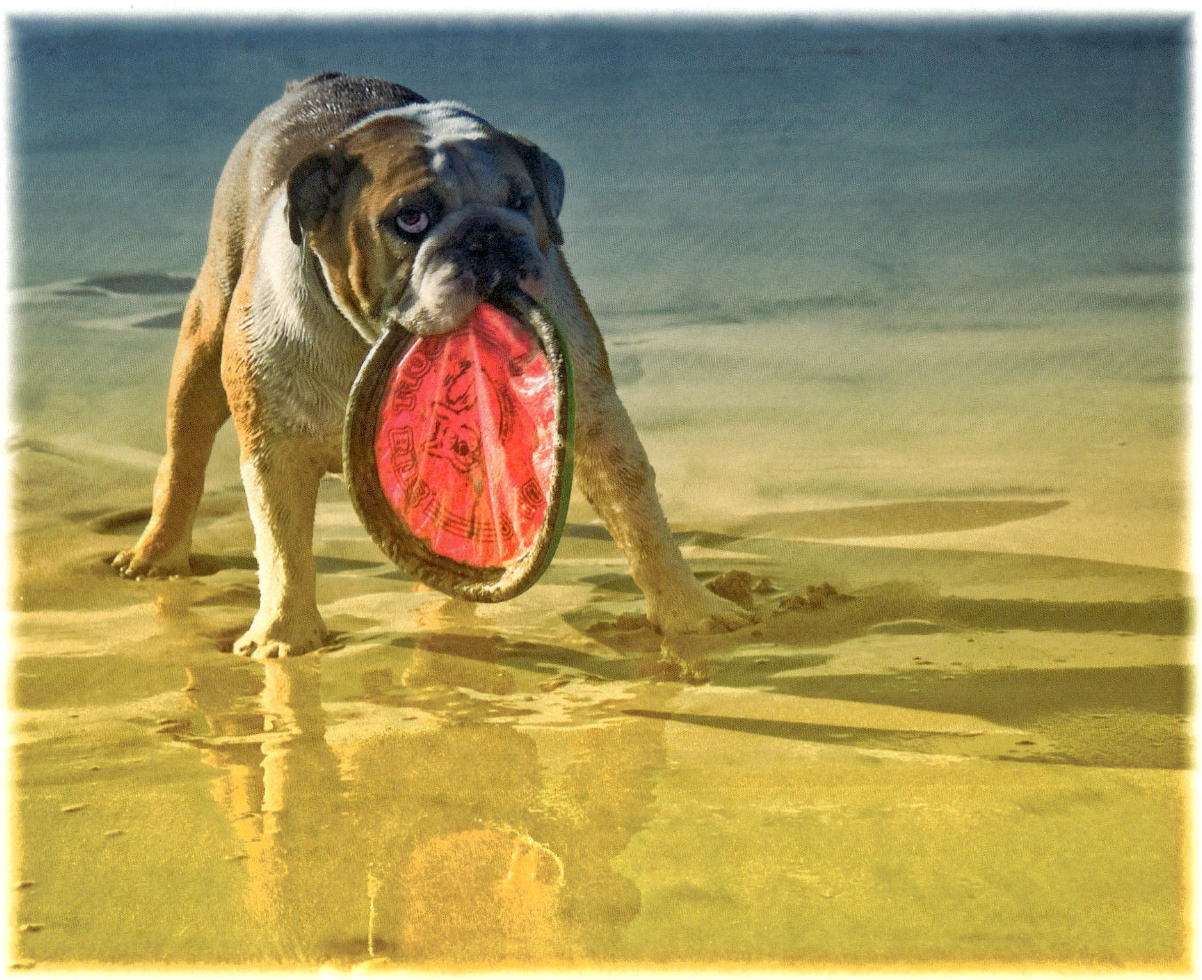

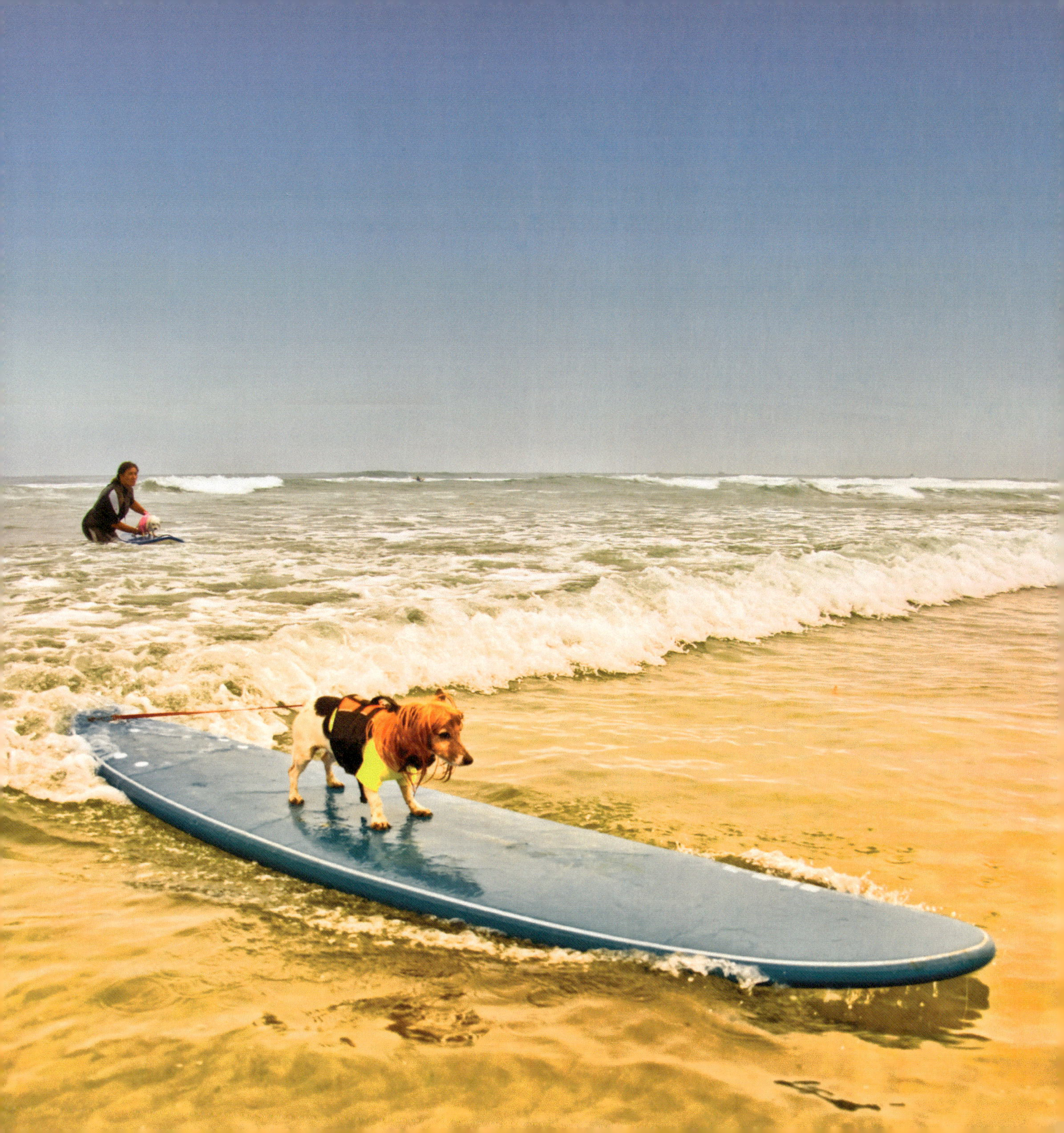

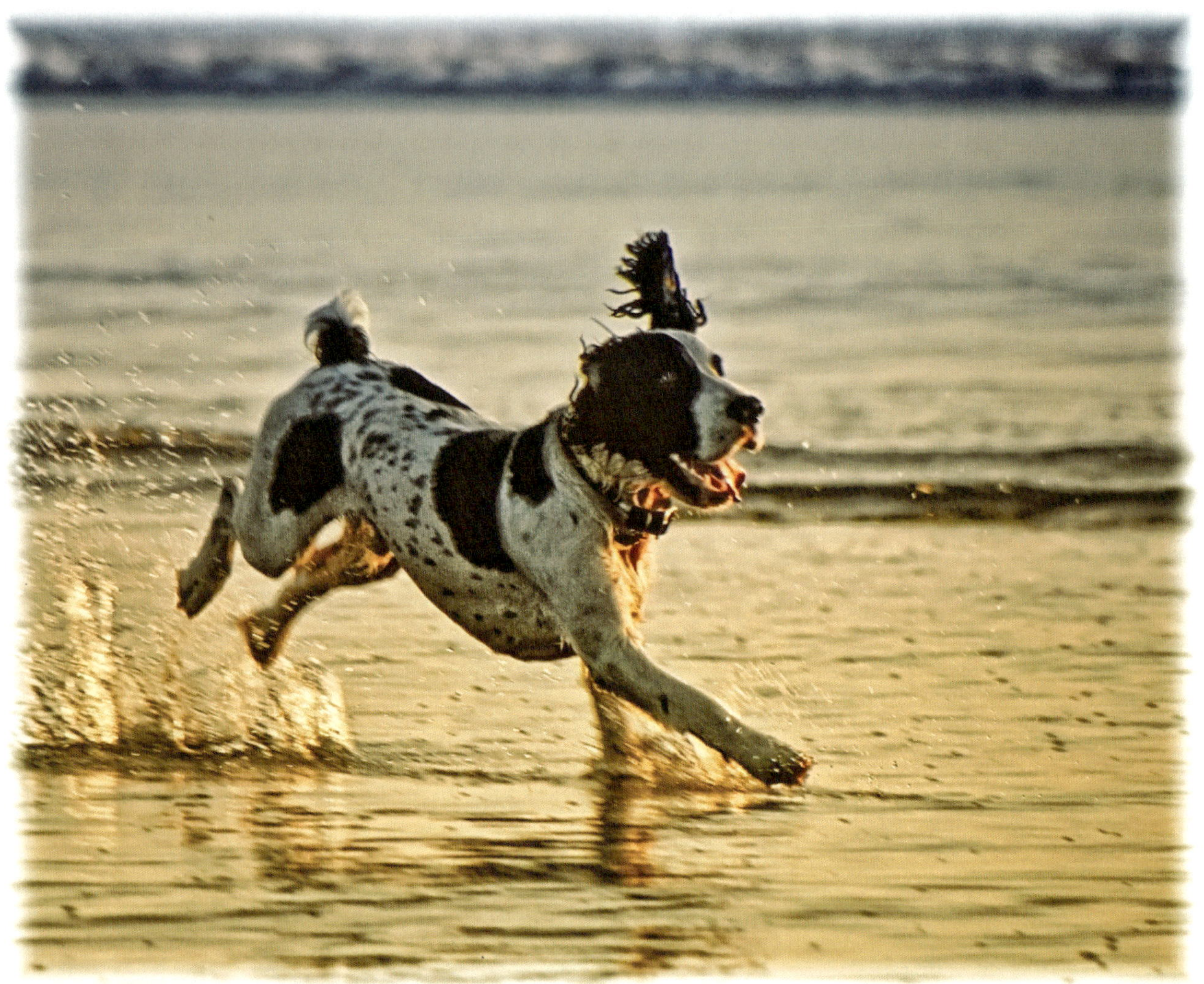

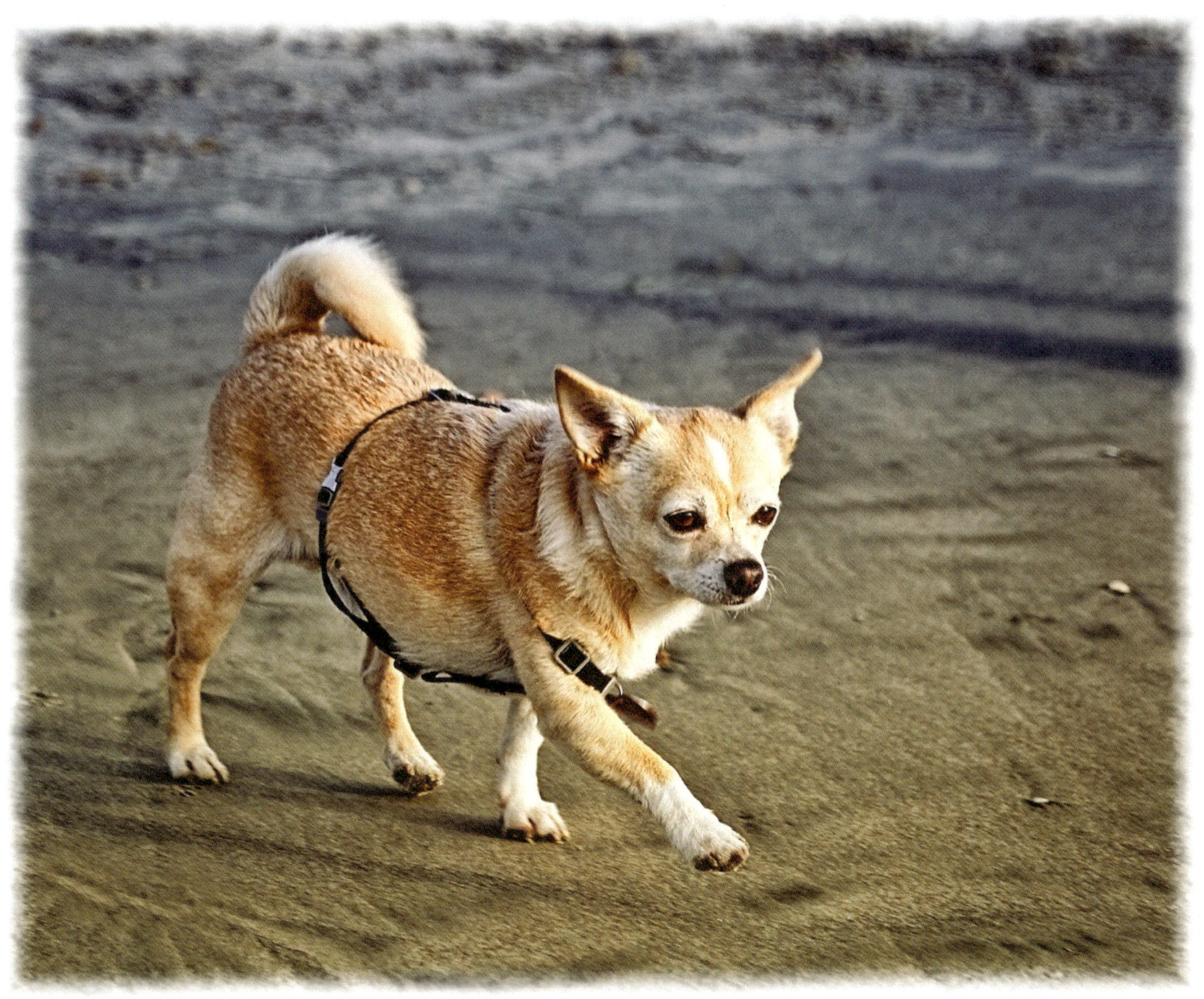

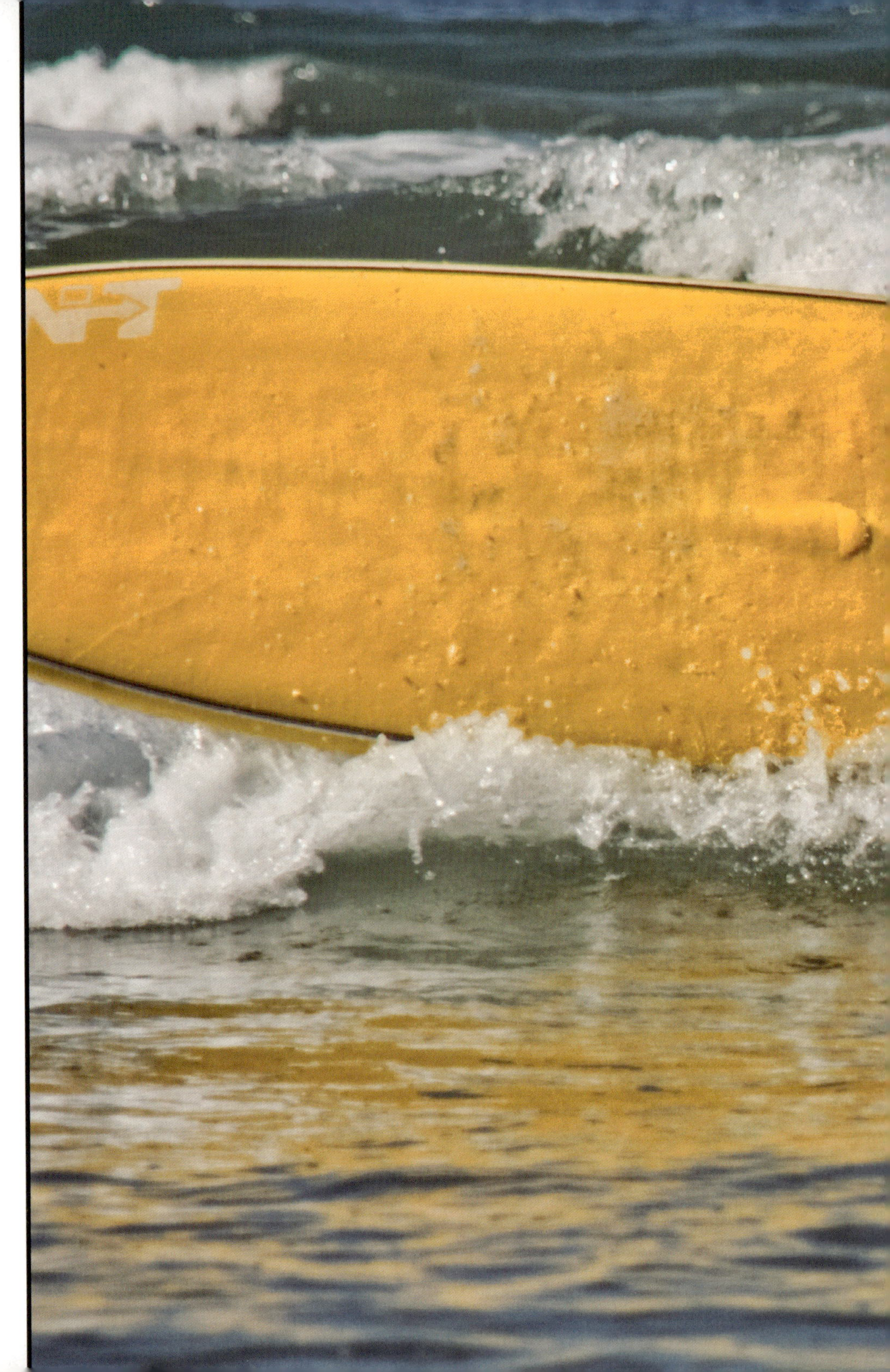

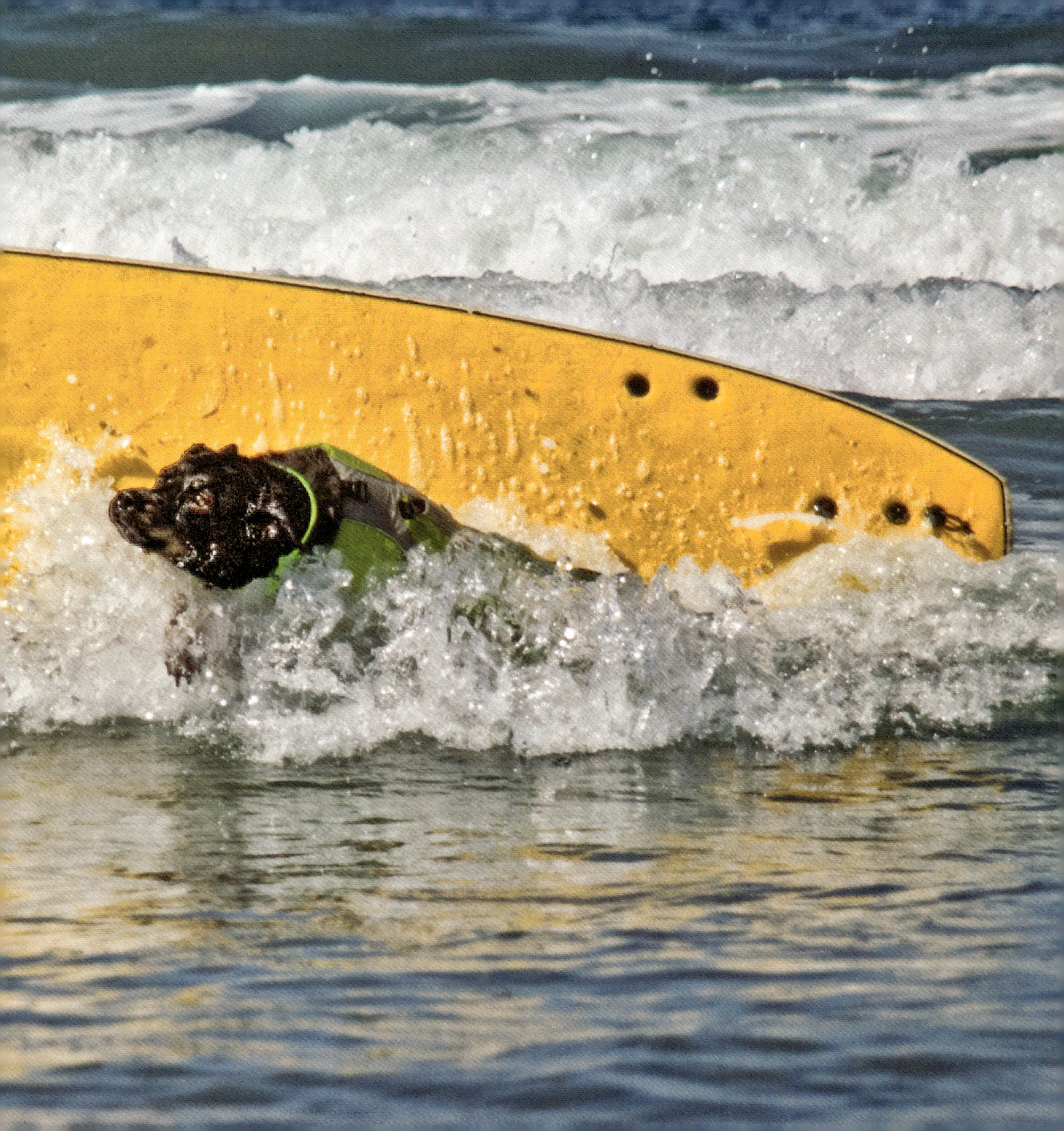

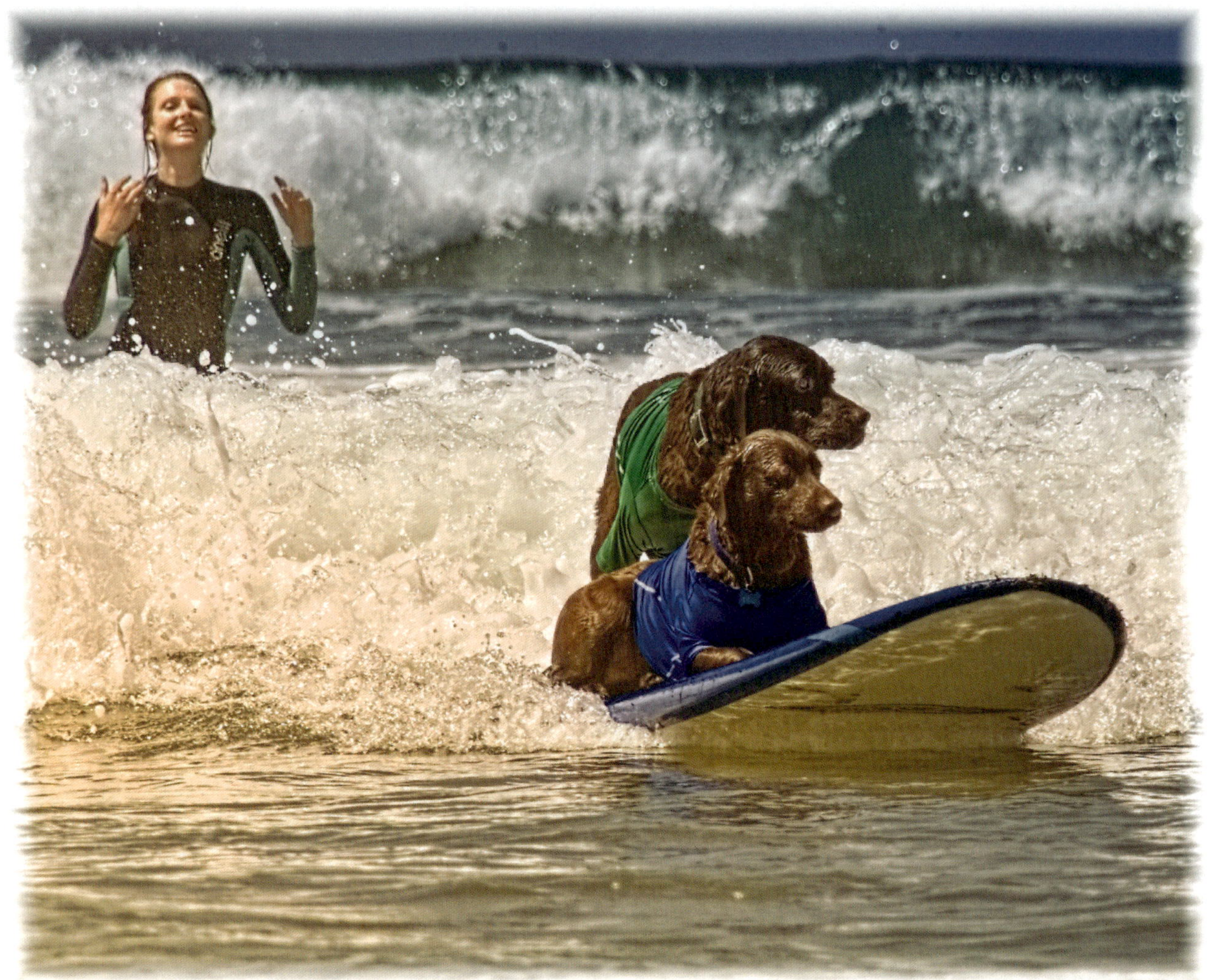

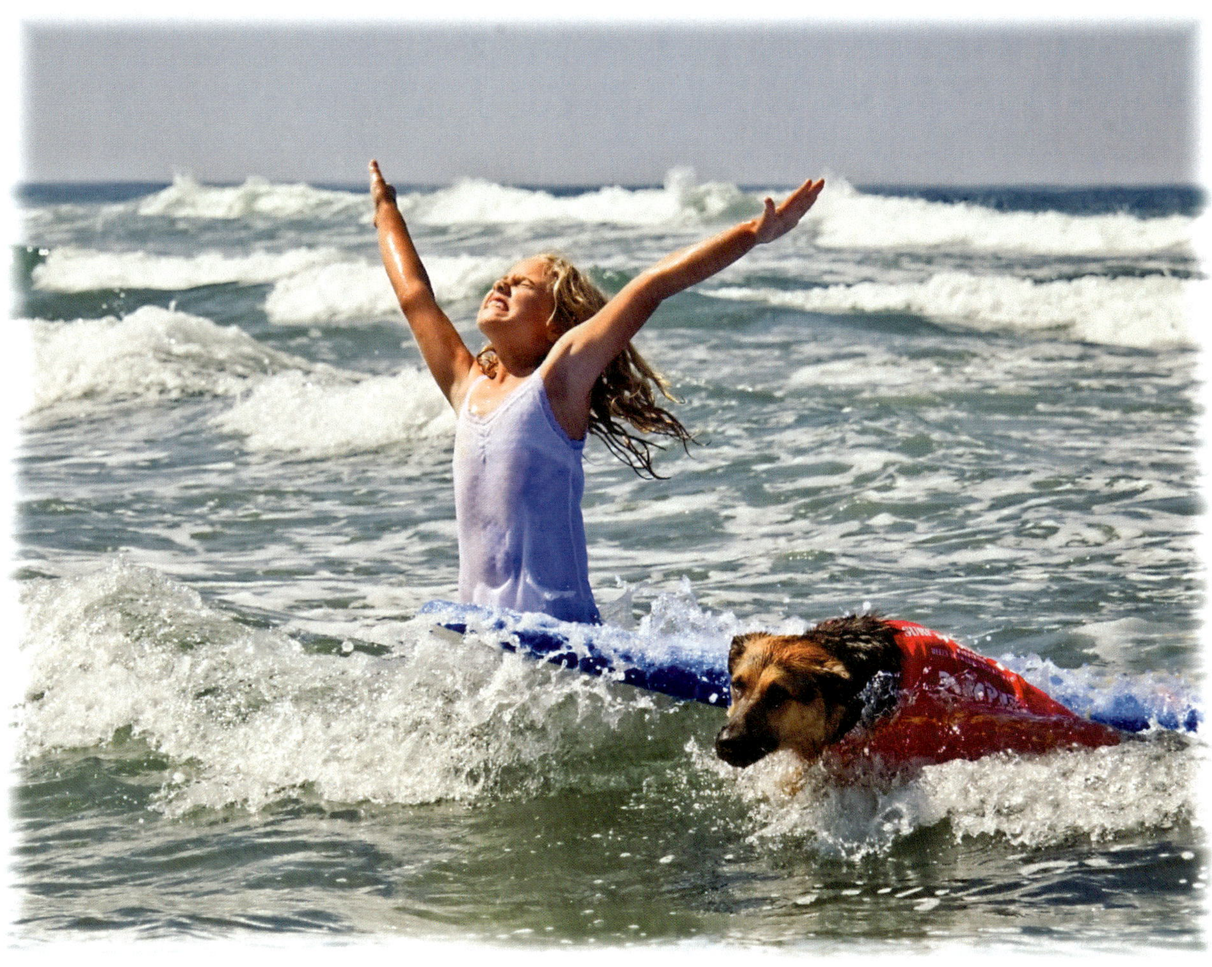

There are no such things as too much joy, too much fun, or too much action. They are what makes the world go around—what makes us inventive, creative, and ready to make the changes necessary to excel in our rapidly changing society.

Motion is emotion. Consider taking your dog  and your family on a long walk every day. You'll enjoy it and recharge your batteries. But wait! There's more. Doing so will add several healthy, active years to both your dog's, your own, and your family's lives.

## See you at Dog Beach

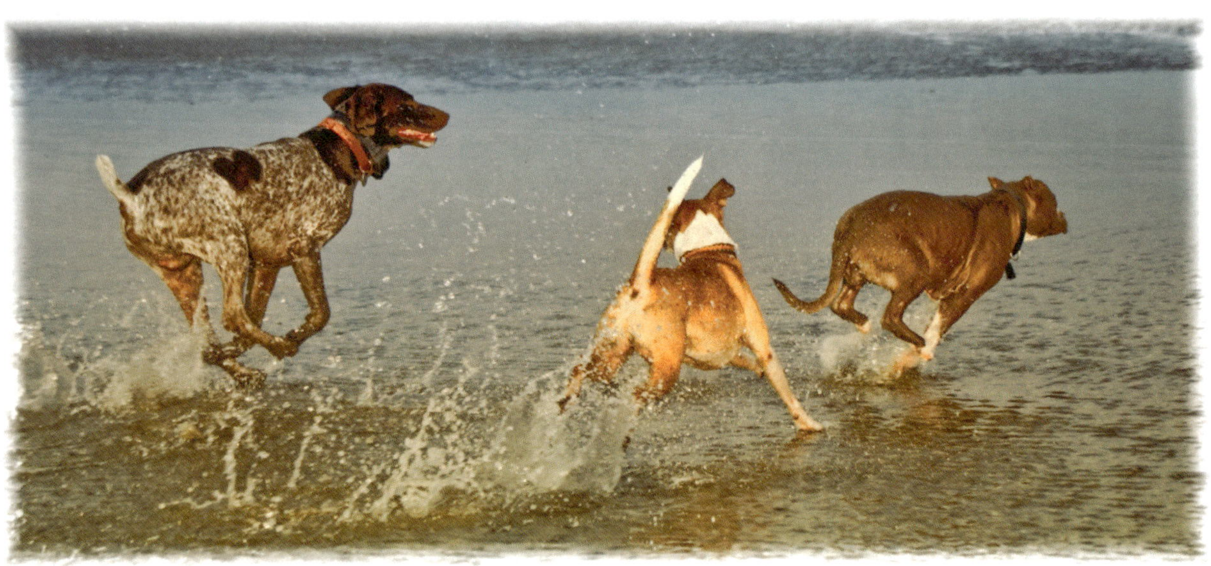

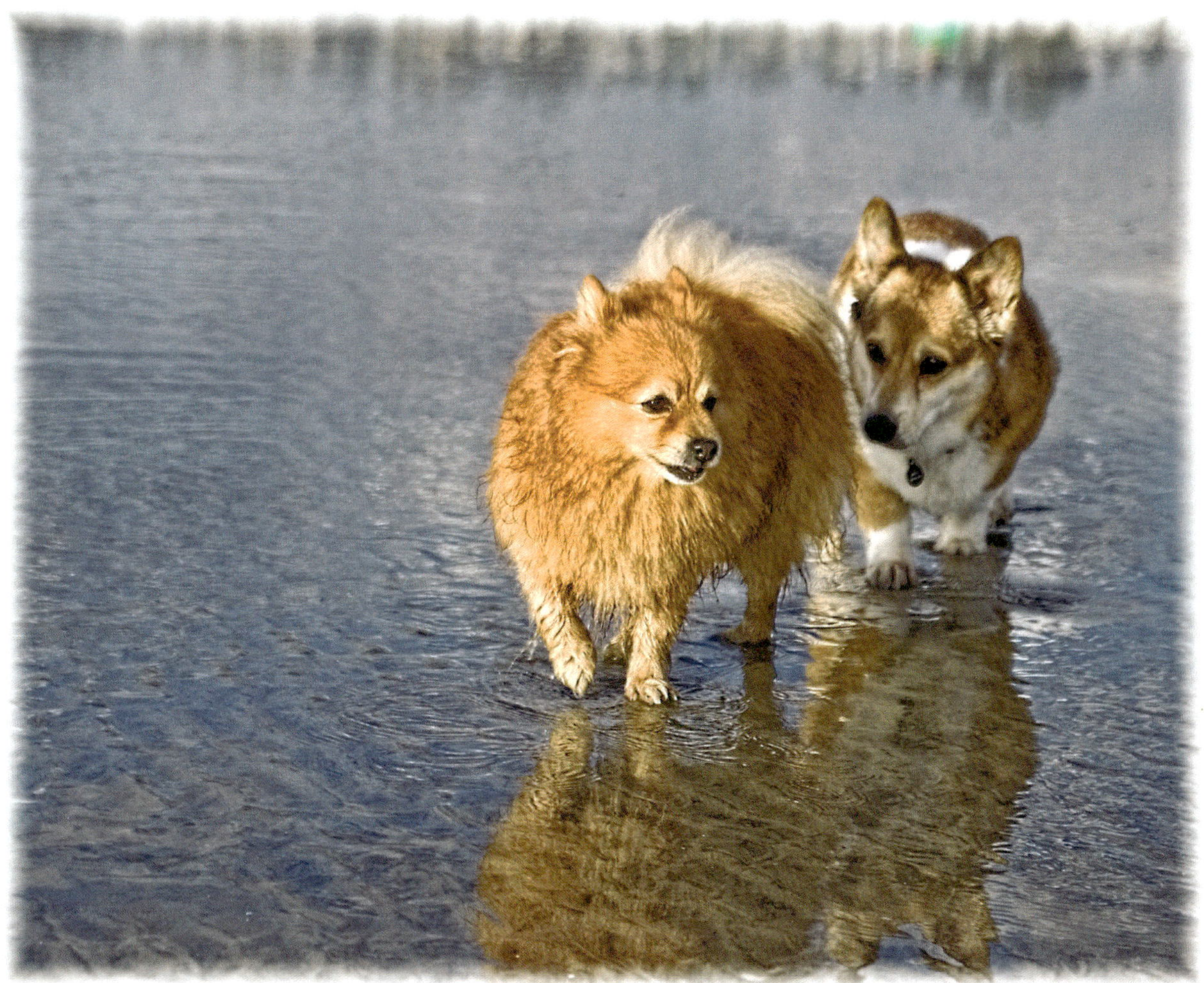